THREE PATHS TO CHRIST

THREE PATHS TO CHRIST

EXPERIENCING THE SUPERSENSIBLE

14 lectures given in various cities between
January and December 1912

TRANSLATED BY CHRISTIANA BRYAN

INTRODUCTION BY MARGARET JONAS

RUDOLF STEINER

RUDOLF STEINER PRESS

CW 143

Rudolf Steiner Press
Hillside House, The Square
Forest Row, RH18 5ES

www.rudolfsteinerpress.com

Published by Rudolf Steiner Press 2023

Originally published in German under the title *Erfahrungen des Übersinnlichen, Die drei Wege der Seele zu Christus* (volume 143 in the *Rudolf Steiner Gesamtausgabe* or Collected Works) by Rudolf Steiner Verlag, Dornach. Based on shorthand notes that were not reviewed or revized by the speaker. This authorized translation is based on the fourth German edition (1994), edited by Robert Friedenthal and Hella Wiesberger

Published by permission of the Rudolf Steiner Nachlassverwaltung, Dornach

A catalogue record for this book is available from the British Library

ISBN 978 1 85584 607 4

Cover by Morgan Creative
Typeset by Symbiosys Technologies, Vishakapatnam, India
Printed and bound by 4Edge Ltd., Essex

CONTENTS

Publisher's Note xii
Introduction, by Margaret Jonas xiii

LECTURE 1
MUNICH, 11 JANUARY 1912
Nervousness and Ego Development

The application of spiritual science in life. Nervousness as a modern problem. Types of nervous anxiety. Haste in soul life, indecisiveness, imitating organic pathologies. The causes of nervousness: weakening the ether body in contemporary culture and carrying out work without interest. Strengthening the ether body with simple exercises, its influence on the physical body. 1: Conscious placing of objects to counteract forgetfulness. 2: Changing handwriting habits. The importance of connecting one's inner core with activities. Effects of exercises on the ether body that prove its existence. 3: Reversing the sequence of events in thinking. 4: Observing one's own gestures, doing things differently on purpose, such as writing with the opposite hand. Controlling astral activity with one's I and the help of will cultivation. 5: Denial and suppression of small wishes. 6: Suspending one's own debate regarding for-or-against an issue and 7: through withholding opinions and judgements, especially when one is involved. Observing how the single actions of another chime together. Self-education and—discipline, controlling the elements of our being in this way.

Pages 1-16

LECTURE 2
WINTERTHUR, 14 JANUARY 1912
Human Soul Activity through the Ages

Application of reason to results of spiritual science. The threefold nature of inner experiences and its relation to the moment of falling asleep: 1: Concepts being tiring, falling asleep easily. 2: Fluctuating feelings, self-interest—difficulty in falling asleep. Clairvoyance as conscious sleep. The transformation of medical forces into clairvoyance in Nostradamus. 3: Impulses of will: feelings of bliss resulting from good motivation, pangs of conscience as a hindrance to sleep. The connection between soul life and higher worlds. The sense for reincarnation.

Training of soul capacities throughout cultures. Today's culture: conceptual life, Graeco-Roman culture: perceptions. In future cultures: educating the fluctuations of feeling and, finally, training in morality. The laming of intellectual capacities resulting from bad impulses of will. The connections of perceptive abilities with the physical, conceptual-imaginative capacities with the astral world, fluctuations of feeling with lower- and morality with higher Devachan. Perception of Christ in different epochs. Present perception of Christ in concepts and Imaginations.

Pages 17-27

LECTURE 3
ZURICH, 15 JANUARY 1912
The Path of Knowledge and its Connection with Human Morality

Soul purity and morality as a basic requirement for inner development. The nature of morality; no outer causes but the emergence of morality through awareness of one's inner core. The emergence of luciferic motivations in the astral body. The axiom of occultists: the inner path of knowledge modelled on moral imperatives. The structure of the Ten Commandments. Three relate positively to spiritual circumstances (Thou shalt...) while seven relating to the physical world are negative (Thou shalt not...). The exception is the fourth Commandment. Suppressing outer impulses in moral action and in pursuit of clairvoyance. The false path to clairvoyance through 'pumping up' hidden forces from the three lowest elements of the human being into the conscious I (weakening truthfulness). Opposed to this, a direct path through the conscious I and moral impetus, aesthetic and mathematical judgement. Four prerequisites for the path of knowledge: awe, reverence, sense of harmony and submission to world processes. Morality as Earth's goal. Three Rosicrucian sayings as the three moods of western esotericism.

Pages 28-43

LECTURE 4
BRESLAU, 3 FEBRUARY 1912
Anthroposophy, Conscience and Wonder—Pointers to Past and Future Spiritual Vision

Two facts of everyday life that indicate the spiritual world and its disconnection during dreaming. 1: wonder and 2: human conscience. Wonder as the origin of all knowledge. Transformations of conscience from clairvoyant (Erinyes, Furies) to inner experience. Precondition to amazement: something known in different guise. Dreams as remnants of earlier clairvoyance. Human descent to Earth to gain knowledge and conscience. Experiencing the spiritual world. The significant moment of falling asleep. Conscience as a premonition of human condition necessary to enter spiritual worlds. Amazement indicating earlier vision, conscience indicating future vision: living signs of a spiritual world. Ability to wonder even at the mundane indicating more advanced souls. 'Reflective' natures know of reincarnation in last life. Future vision of karmic balancing of our lives. Future suffering of robust, material natures.

Pages 44-57

LECTURE 5

MUNICH, 25 FEBRUARY 1912

Reflecting Levels of Consciousness

The reflective quality of sense organs and brain for normal consciousness. Revelation of subconsciousness in artistic creation, dreams and disposition. Possible errors when descending into soul depths. Mistaking projections of one's own inner life with objective spiritual facts e.g. mistaken self-identification as reincarnation of Mary Magdalen. Careful training to avoid error. Exercise to develop feeling for karmic connections: 'construction' of a person conscious of—and contributing to—all unexplained events. Taking karma calmly creates discernment of truth and falsehood in soul's depths. Blavatsky's antipathy towards things Hebrew and Christian. Christ's temptations. Emergence of higher sense organs in astral and their reflection in ether bodies. Similarities of experience in soul depths with Kamaloka: being locked in to one's own desires and passions. Congruence of natural and spiritual laws in Devachan. Life in Devachan is dependent on quality of person e.g. effects of lying, ambition, vanity. Physical plane: spiritual laws are hidden behind natural laws e.g. volcanic eruptions. Relationship of beauty and morality in differing worlds; ugliness destructive, beauty a fructifying element in Devachan. Truthfully worked-through feelings become truth detectors.

Pages 58-78

LECTURE 6

MUNICH, 27 FEBRUARY 1912

Hidden Forces in Soul Life

Conscious soul life: concepts, feelings, will forces. Hidden, unconscious soul levels: Imagination, Inspiration and Intuition, premonitions, visions, 'second face'. Their correspondences in physical organisms. Vision as primitive Imagination, premonitions as primitive Inspiration. The connection between the living and the dead. The helplessness / fainting of normal consciousness in the sense world. The powerful effect of sympathy and antipathy in the subconscious; their connection with breathing and blood circulation. Nurturing and destructive influences in feeling realm e.g. lax attitude to lying. Differentiating subjective from objective in vision and imagination by the power of active watching.

Kamaloka: built of our own inner world. Influence of our experiences on the elemental world after death. Consequences of training nuances of feeling on colours and tones for clairvoyance. Perceiving one's own physical constitution. Effects of forces sent from the dead into the physical world e.g. polter activity, most easily perceived while falling asleep or waking up. The connection of human experience with realities of the subconscious (magic).

Pages 79-91

LECTURE 7

STOCKHOLM, 16 APRIL 1912

Three Soul Paths to Christ (in Two Parts)

First Part: The Path via the Gospels and the Path of Inner Experience

Today's longing for a deeper understanding of Christ. Three paths to Christ: 1: through the Gospels, 2: through inner experience and 3: by initiation. Experiencing the Gospels in previous centuries. Interest through images conjured in feeling, not in historical reality. The Gospels and spiritual science; an understanding of human nature as a requirement for the path of inner experience. The twofold course of inner human development caused by luciferic influence. Elaboration of the I entity at age 20-21. Emergence of I-consciousness around age 2-4. Effects of the sundering of I-consciousness from I-entity; illness, age and death but also opportunity for freedom. Strengthening the I through Christ's impetus. The difference between Christ and Buddha. The feeling for Christ in the first three post-Atlantean cultural epoch: their relation to ancient planetary conditions; seven holy rishis—old Saturn; Zarathustra culture—old Sun; Osiris culture—old Moon. The possibility of inner Christ experience within one life.

Pages 92-106

LECTURE 8

STOCKHOLM, 17 APRIL 1912

Second Part: The Path of Initiation

Initiation as a path transcending religions; anthroposophy's task of disseminating Initiation Mystery wisdom; its possibilities for the honouring and recognizing all other religions such as Buddhism. Origins of religion: personalities of founders. Origin of Christian initiation: the death of Christ, the Mystery of Golgotha. Illness and death as the bastions created by benevolent powers against the influences of Lucifer. The relationship of humans to the animal kingdom: consequences of maltreatment rectified on Jupiter in the embodiment of parasitic entities in humans. 'Bacillii' as forerunners of these parasites. The Mystery of Golgotha. The principle of transformation in supersensible worlds. Christ's entry in the world to counteract the luciferic principle, seen from earthly and spiritual perspectives. Initiation principles revealed. The Osiris-Seth myth in this connection. The valuing of single incarnations in Egypto-Graecian times (Pythagoras and Euphorbos). Christ as the lord of karma. Tending Christian initiation in the brotherhood of the Grail and in the Rosicrucian community; the reason for the hundred-year silence regarding their leaders. No further prophets since the Mystery of Golgotha. Anthroposophy as a synthesis of all religious faiths.

Pages 107-125

LECTURE 9

COLOGNE, 7 MAY 1912 (WITHOUT INTRODUCTION)

Mysteries of the Kingdoms of Heaven in Parables and Real Form

The revelation of mysteries in parables. External nature as a parable. Spring and autumn in relation to waking and sleeping. Elemental beings' ecstasy at St John's tide. The festival of the Spirit of the Earth at Christmas. Withdrawal of spirits into sacred spheres at Easter. The significance of Easter as a moveable festival. The present fifth epoch as a reflection of the third, Egyptian epoch. Re-emergence of Ancient Egyptian wisdom in Tycho Brahe. The spiral growth of plants mirroring the movement of planets. Outer signs of inner processes: renewal of ancient astrology in the *Soul Calendar (Twelve Moods)*. Calculating time in relation to the Mystery of Golgotha, a universal deed for humankind. The weekly verses in the *Soul Calendar*—formula for connecting inner soul life with processes of divine-spiritual experience.

Pages 126-136

LECTURE 10

COLOGNE, 8 MAY 1912

Prophecy and Heralding Christ's Impetus. The Spirit of Christ and its Sheaths:
A Whitsun Message in Memory of H.P. Blavatsky

Thoughts in memory of H.P. Blavatsky on the anniversary of her death day (White Lotus Day). Recitation of Hegel's poem 'Eleusis'. Mention of Blavatsky's *Isis Unveiled*. Reasons for the choice of Blavatsky as an 'instrument' of the Masters. Her antipathy towards Hebrew and Christian elements. *The Secret Doctrine*, 'an assemblage'. The need to complete the theosophical movement by adding the Sinai revelations and the Mystery of Golgotha. The necessity for a pure sense of truth. Juxtaposition of oriental culture's focus on individuals over several incarnations versus occidental focus on the single individual's life. Fourfold heralding of Christ's impulse by the same individuality in the personalities of Elijah, John the Baptist, Raphael and Novalis. The Mystery of Golgotha and the Christ as Spirit of the Earth. Forming Christ's sheaths from humanly-developed forces: 1: Forming an astral body through wonder and amazement, 2: Forming an ether body through compassion, shared joy and love. The conflation of love with sex—worst manifestation of the present age. 3: Forming a physical body through conscience. Future depictions of Christ in art.

Pages 137-156

LECTURE 11

MUNICH, 16 MAY 1912

Synthesizing Worldviews—A Fourfold Herald

Spiritual science as a tool for mutual understanding e.g. Buddhism and Christianity as opposed to today's studies of comparative religion. Max Müller's criticism of H.P. Blavatsky. Metamorphosis not death in spiritual kingdoms. The Mystery of Golgotha as a circumstance of the Gods and to compensate for Lucifer's actions. The fundamental trait of Christianity: not an individual founder but a deed, an event, as its origin. Oriental ways of thinking: focus on an individual over many incarnations, occidental view: focus on individual incarnation. The four personalities of Elijah, John the Baptist, Raphael and Novalis: a fourfold heralding of Christianity by the same individuality. Enlarging the limited view of a personality by including a spiritual-scientific view of the individuality. Waking up and falling asleep of earth spirits in autumn and spring compared with these activities in human beings. The rushing ascent of elemental spirits at St John's. The Earth awakening in winter. The essential mobility of the Easter festival. The significance of the *Soul Calendar* for spiritual life and the particular way time is calculated.

Pages 157-171

LECTURE 12

ZURICH, 17 DECEMBER 1912

Love and its Significance in the World—with a question answered

Does one have to know about Christ's incisive deed into history for his strength to imbue the soul? The non-egotistical love of wisdom with increasing age. Life's wisdom as the seed for the subsequent life; interpreting this seed as a divine spark among Mystics. Karma and love. Deeds of love not initially rewarded in a subsequent life. Love as 'repayment for debts already incurred'. Morality as the Sun of the world. Interest in all existence is a human duty. Love as all that is creative in the world. Love in comparison with wisdom and power: power and wisdom can be graduated, love cannot. God retains love, power and wisdom given to Ahriman and Lucifer respectively. Love as perfect and complete; humans can only gradually absorb it. Christ's deed as counterweight to Lucifer's actions. The connection of love-united-with-wisdom (philosophy) and Christ's impetus. Three Rosicrucian sayings. Self-completion/fulfilment and love. Love—making sense of evil.

A question about necessary lies: These are a complex, egotistical act, binding the perpetrator with the weakness of the other being 'protected'.

Pages 172-182

LECTURE 13
BERLIN, 24 DECEMBER 1912
The Birth of the Light of the Earth out of Christmas Darkness

Christmas, festival of love. Threefold aspect of Christ's impulse and the four Gospels. 1: the spiritual-regal aspect in Matthew's Gospel. Three Wise Men, Magi. 2: the cosmic perspective of Mark and John's Gospels. The clash of old pre-Christian and the Christian worlds in Empress Eudocia's poem about *Cyprian.* 3: the childlike perspective of Luke's Gospel. The greatness of love compared with wisdom and power. Lucifer, opponent of wisdom, Ahriman, opponent of power. Omniscience, almightiness-omnipotence, universal love. The child Jesus in Luke's Gospel as personification of love between the all-wise and the all-powerful. Roman Saturnalia and the Christian Christmas festival. The task of Christmas and the tasks of the new Anthroposophical Society.

Pages 183-197

LECTURE 14
COLOGNE, 29 DECEMBER 1912
Novalis—Proclaimer of a Spiritually Conceived Christ Impetus

Novalis as the prophet of recent times; his irradiated suffusion with Christ's impulse. The reincarnated soul of Elijah, John the Baptist, Raphael in Novalis. Novalis' contemporaries Goethe, Schiller, Fichte. Goethe's relation with Spinoza and Leibniz; the relatedness of Monadism with Sankya philosophy. Fichte's resuscitated Vedanta words. Novalis' spiritually-borne—also Schiller's—ethical individualism. Novalis' praise of Schiller. Goethe's saying: 'Wisdom is only in wisdom' as a motto. Novalis' path of incarnation as a guiding star: his poem 'When numbers and figures...'

Pages 198-203

Notes 204

Rudolf Steiner's Collected Works 217

Significant Events in the Life of Rudolf Steiner 231

Index 247

Publisher's Note

THE first lecture of this volume (11 January 1912, given in Munich), which in terms of content bears a completely different character to the other lectures of this period, is likely to have been the result of the following letter, dated 8 November 1911:

Dear Doctor!

You are unlikely to remember that on 19 July of this year I asked you for your kind advice on how I could learn to control my thoughts when I was nervous. At the time, you recommended that I recite, for a reasonable amount of time every day, German poems, or something similar, backwards. I was to report to you on the success after a few months, and you would then be kind enough to offer further advice. I did these exercises regularly. Since I soon ran out of German poems, I conjugated Greek irregular verbs backwards and said historical charts backwards. The success was obvious, and I am extremely grateful to you, dear Doctor, for your friendly advice. It is true that success is still in its infancy, but I am already dealing with the thoughts that used to dominate and depress me in a completely different way. Would you be so kind as to give my brother-in-law or sister-in-law, who is handing you this letter in person, another new exercise or rule of conduct, which they will then kindly report to me?

With heartfelt thanks again for your advice on this matter, which is so important to me.

Your very devoted Professor Dr K

INTRODUCTION

IT is helpful to approach these lectures if we look at them in their relevant historical context. They were given throughout 1912, which was a critical year for the development of anthroposophy. Until the end of 1912, Rudolf Steiner was still the leader of the German Section within the Theosophical Society but relations had become extremely strained due to the activity of the Society's leaders Annie Besant and Charles Leadbeater's having, since around 1909, set up an order within the Society known as 'The Star of the East'. The pair had perceived a certain spiritual stature around the young Indian boy Jiddu Krishnamurti and proclaimed that he was to be the vessel for a physical reappearance of Christ Jesus. In adulthood, Krishnamurti was to publicly reject this claim, break from the Theosophical Society and establish his own pathway of spiritual development. Rudolf Steiner knew from *his* own esoteric research that Christ had entered the earth in a physical body once and once only, and rejected the claim wholeheartedly. By Christmas 1912 the Anthroposophical Society was formed and was formally expelled from the Theosophical Society in 1913. Therefore, a number of these lectures allude to these events and the term 'theosophy' is used, whereas later it would be replaced by 'anthroposophy'.

The lecture given in May 1912 in memory of the Theosophical Society co-founder Helena Petrovna Blavatsky, shows that Steiner continued to revere her enormous contribution but that she was unable to understand and appreciate Christianity (and Judaism) properly. He indicates here how people can create new 'sheaths' for Christ's continuing work in the earthly sphere by learning to develop the qualities of wonder, amazement, compassion, love and conscience. He was thus anxious to make clear that the newly developing

Society would be following a very different path, one which would be the successor to the Rosicrucian movement of earlier centuries.

The lectures here were given in various cities in Germany, Switzerland and Sweden and therefore a certain amount of repetition inevitably occurs. This need not feel tedious as each lecture often expresses something in a slightly different way and casts additional light on the subject. They cover a variety of themes and only a few have been published in English previously.

The title of the series *Three Paths to Christ* refers in fact to just two lectures of the same name given in April 1912 in Stockholm, but in a sense they are at the heart of the collection, describing the three principal paths to finding Christ: via the Gospels, inner (mystical) experience and initiation. The first two are still significant paths although they present certain difficulties for contemporary people, but the path of initiation as revealed by spiritual science makes clear the understanding that, in order to combat the activities of the adversary powers, the higher Gods sent Christ to earth to experience death in a physical human body, which no God had previously done. This would make human incarnations continue to be possible until no longer needed in the same form. This 'deed' of Christ is what distinguishes Christ Jesus from other spiritual teachers, who have nevertheless given humanity the most profound teachings. Steiner goes on to speak of the protectors of this Christian path as being those who taught the mysteries of the Holy Grail and later the Rose Cross. He makes clear that it is not possible to identify publicly certain personalities as bearers of these Christian mysteries whilst they are still in physical incarnation. Had this lecture been republished in English since it first appeared in 1942 and been made better known, it might have saved considerable strife within the anthroposophical movement.

One significant lecture describes how we can overcome 'nervousness' – a term broader than anxiety, here covering a restless instability of thought, memory and hasty action. This lecture has appeared in print before, and gives helpful exercises such as changing one's handwriting, going through events in our memory backwards, and suppressing any unnecessary and trivial desires and wishes. A number of lectures stress the path of 'moral' development: sympathy for what is good and beautiful, aversion to evil and ugliness; combining other exercises with moral judgement; and being prompted from our innermost core to act without reference to our physical needs. We learn to develop wonder, reverence and harmony—here the latter means being in harmony with cosmic processes, in other words karma—and that *we* ourselves choose and bring about subconsciously those unpleasant things that happen to us, which we think we do not want, as karmic recompense for our past actions. Understandably, this latter is a very difficult and sensitive subject to treat and can't be spoken about glibly but only worked on inwardly over a period of time.

In Lecture Four we learn that development is easier for more 'pensive' types of people, who can experience amazement and awe easily and who have stronger consciences, because they have had direct experiences of incarnating in cultures where reincarnation was taught. More 'robust' types had lives where it was not known about and these people are in the majority nowadays. This may explain many attitudes found in outer life.

In Lectures Five and Six, Rudolf Steiner makes clear how our health and our moods are less affected by outer circumstances than by suppressed painful memories in the subconscious, causing 'waves' in the soul—a tenet of most paths of psychotherapy today. We can reach these memories by developing Imagination—an enhanced power of thought reaching into our life tableau—but there can be a danger of errors: we may be overwhelmed with images and imagine that we lived before as an important historical personality—Steiner recounts the number of Mary Magdalenes, Julius Caesars, etc. that he has encountered! Reflecting on those things that have happened and that we have *not* consciously wished for in our lives as an exercise, helps us to discriminate when faced with 'visions'. The higher spiritual world or 'Devachan' will reject any lying, vanity and ambition in our souls after death. The next lecture continues with this theme of 'visionary' experiences such as 'second-sight', which is basically atavistic though hereditary in certain populations. These two lectures are both helpful in situations where people may be struggling with a surge of visionary images on their path of spiritual development.

Other lectures mention our connection to sleeping and waking and introduce the newly created *Calendar of the Soul*, on which by meditating can lead us into experiencing the seasonal path of the year in harmony with spiritual beings and processes. As a comfort to those who find this difficult to connect with, Steiner points out that it can take years to really make these meditations one's own. Further themes touch on the reappearing of Christ within the earth's etheric; the previous and subsequent incarnations of John the Baptist; that Raphael's *School of Athens* painting depicts St Paul preaching Christianity (not Plato and Aristotle), a little known Christmas lecture and one on Novalis.

Last but not least, we find included that most important lecture on 'love and its meaning for the world' and how giving love does not accrue karmic credit but is really a 'repayment'—we are not rewarded for it. The spiritual significance of love is highlighted with the all too necessary reminder that if spiritual science were to develop without love it would actually be a danger to humanity.

There is much to enhance and enrich our lives, to reflect upon and work with in these fourteen, highly relevant lectures.

Margaret Jonas
February 2023

Lecture 1

MUNICH, 11 JANUARY 1912

Nervousness and Ego Development

In the context of much of what we already know—which may still be useful to some of us—a stimulus will today be given, which could lead to a more focused way of observing the nature of human beings and its connection with the world. Anthroposophists will have ample opportunity—aside from the usual ripostes and objections to spiritual science encountered in recent public lectures[1]—to encounter what those outside anthroposophy often assert. Ever and again we face objections from both learned and untutored people when in spiritual science we speak of a stratification of the whole human being into the four elements we always cite: a physical body, an ether, etheric or life body, an astral body and an I or ego.

Sceptics might object that for someone in whom certain usually concealed soul forces have been developed it might be possible to discern something of this fourfold nature, but for someone not able to see such an organism, there would be scant grounds for surrendering to any such view. Now it must be emphasized that human life—observed attentively—not only confirms what spiritual science has to say but rather that, when what can be learnt from spiritual knowledge is applied in practical life, it turns out to be exceptionally useful. You will discover that these uses—I don't mean uses in their base sense but benefits in a more elevated sense—will eventually confer on us a sort of confidence, even if we do not want to commit to what clairvoyant observation offers.

It is only too well known that nowadays people complain at length about what is implied in those much-feared words *nervousness or anxiety*.

We need not be surprised that some feel compelled to claim that nowadays there is hardly anyone who is not to some extent nervous. Why would we not find such a statement plausible? Regardless of social relations and conditions to which causes of nervousness could be ascribed, conditions described collectively as nervousness simply exist and they manifest in the most diverse ways.

At their simplest and least uncomfortable, we might call such people soul-fidgeters or soul-fretters. They can be described as unable to hold onto a thought properly nor to follow it to its conclusion, who continually jump from thought to thought and, if one tries to anchor them to a single thought, have already leapt on to another. A certain haste in their soul life is often the mildest form of nervousness.

Another type of nervousness is one whereby the person hardly knows how, of themselves, to initiate action or, in relation to things they need to resolve, are unable to make progress and actually never quite know what they should do in a given situation.

This can in turn lead to other, more serious, conditions where nervousness leads increasingly to other forms of illness for which no organic cause can be found, but which speciously mimic organic pathologies such that one might believe a person was suffering from a severe stomach complaint when in fact they have nothing more serious than what can be summed up under the minor heading of nervousness. They are, of course, symptoms under which the person concerned suffers just as much as if the illness originated from an organic source.

Numerous other conditions could be mentioned and who has not experienced examples of this through their own suffering or that of those in their environs? One doesn't need to go far—I am not about to digress onto other subjects—in order to speak of the momentous events of outer life as 'political alcoholism', something recently couched in terms of anxiety-ridden happenings in public life and which manifest as if driven by the sort of conduct usually only seen when an individual is slightly affected by alcoholism. The term is apt for the ways and means by which political affairs have been conducted in recent months in Europe. Here in external life you see not only such manifest nervousness, but also that it is experienced as highly distressing. Such nervous anxiety is perceptible on every hand.

What has just been described will certainly not improve for people in the near future, but will become ever more acute. Auspicious prospects for humanity's future are not warranted if people remain as they are today, because there are many pernicious influences affecting our lives to an exceptional degree and, transferred from person to person in a way I have to call *epidemically*, result in affecting not only those who are predisposed but also those who are fundamentally healthy, if perhaps somewhat weak.

Something incredibly detrimental for our times is that a large number of those attaining leading positions in public life have studied in the way presently favoured. There are whole branches of scholarship nowadays, of which it can be said that one's year-round university life is spent following pursuits other than those demanding thorough deliberation and perusal of what college professors have to say. One goes in now and then but whatever needs to be known for passing exams can be acquired in a couple of weeks. In other words, one crams the bare necessities. The worst aspect of this is the cramming itself. Because to some extent this attitude to study reaches back into lower schools, the damaging results are not inconsiderable. The main trouble with cramming is that any real connection between soul-interest—that innermost core of a person's being—and the matter being swotted is not present. Even among pupils in schools the prevalent opinion is: Oh well, no matter if what I learn is soon forgotten; so that the passionate longing to retain what one has learnt is absent. A lean band of interest links the core of the human soul with whatever it is embracing.

As a direct consequence of this fact, human beings cannot develop themselves sufficiently to engage in public life with much effectiveness. This outcome of cramming what they should have embraced results in finding no connection with the tasks of their profession; in soul they remain remote from what they have been pursuing with their heads. There is hardly anything worse for the essential being of humankind than remaining remote in heart and soul from what one has to carry out with one's head. This is not only inconsistent for more sensitive souls but is something that greatly undermines the strength and energy of ether bodies, specifically the human ether body. Ether or life bodies become ever weaker under such driven conditions due to the meagre bond existing between the core of the human soul and what it carries out. The more a person has to perform actions in which they have no interest, the more do they weaken their ether or life body.

Anthroposophy is intended to work upon those who assimilate anthroposophy healthily in such a way that they not only learn about a human being consisting of physical body, ether body and so on, but that these four elements in human nature can evolve strongly and vigorously.

If a person carries out a simple experiment but repeats it diligently, this trifle can work wonders. Forgive me if I talk about isolated observations, about details that are and can become meaningful for human life. The occasional slight forgetfulness shown by some people relates closely to what I have just characterized. Slight forgetfulness disturbs us. Yet anthroposophy can show how this forgetfulness is most extremely harmful to health. However odd this may sound, it is true. Many outbreaks within the human constitution bordering on the further reaches of pathology could be avoided were human beings less forgetful. Now you could object that people just *are* forgetful. Who can—and we can easily clarify this with an overview of life—who can totally *absolve themselves* of forgetfulness?

Let us take a frequent yet trivial example: people catch themselves being forgetful, never remembering where they have put objects they need. Isn't this what often happens in life? One person can never find his pencil, another always misplaces his cufflinks in the evening, and so on. It may seem banal and trifling to talk about such things, yet they happen in life. Observing what can be learnt from anthroposophy, there is a good exercise relating to the matter in hand, namely that the kind of forgetfulness just characterized can be remedied very easily. Let us assume a lady puts her brooch—or a gentleman his cufflinks—somewhere and they find next morning that they cannot locate them.

Now you could certainly maintain that they could get used to putting them in the same place every day. One couldn't do this for every single item, but let's not talk about this right now, but rather about a more effective method of curing oneself. Let's assume a person who had noticed their absentmindedness might say: I am going to put that item I need to find in various places. I will never put that object in places other than the one about which I have generated the thought: I place this item in this specific place. I note pictorially the environs in terms of shape, colour and so on and I try to allow all this to imprint itself upon me. Let's say we place a safety pin on the corner of a table, just at an angle, accompanied by the thought: I am putting this on the edge and I imprint on my mind in pictorial form the right-angled corner and the way the safety pin is near two intersecting edges and so on. Relieved, I now leave the item. I will see—maybe not if I find the item once, but if I make a rule of linking such thoughts with the item over time—that my forgetfulness will gradually diminish.

This is based on the fact that a quite specific thought has been grasped, namely: I am putting the safety pin here. My I is brought into connection with the action, with what I am carrying out, to which is added a pictorial image. Clear imagery in thinking, visually imagining what I am doing in addition to associating my action with my soul-spiritual essence—with the core of my being, with my I—this is what can sharpen our memory quite significantly. This is how becoming less forgetful can benefit our lives. You need not worry that you are achieving only this aim because far more is gained through it.

Let's assume that it had become a sort of customary habit for people to foster such thoughts when putting certain items down. This simple habit would generate a strengthening of human ether bodies. Through doing this, the human ether body is ever more consolidated, becomes ever stronger and stronger.

We have learnt from anthroposophy that the ether- or life-body serves in a certain way as the bearer of memory. If we do something that fortifies our forces of memory, we can immediately understand that strengthening our memory is going to be of benefit to our ether- or life-body. As anthroposophists we need not be surprised by this. Imagine that you would not only recommend this method to a forgetful person, but to someone exhibiting symptoms of a nervous condition. Imagine you would advise a fidgety or nervous person to carry out the exercise of placing articles and accompanying this action with thoughts in the way described. You would notice that not only do they become less forgetful through intently practising this exercise but, by strengthening their ether body, they gradually become capable of overcoming their nervous or anxious condition.

Here everyday life provides us with proof that what anthroposophy says about the ether body is true. When we relate appropriately to the ether body, it becomes apparent that it gains forces, gains strength. In achieving such successes, we are provided with proof that accepting the ether body as characterized is justified.

Let us move on to another subject, which again appears minor but which is extraordinarily important. You know that the elements with which we are familiar as the physical and ether bodies exist in immediate proximity to each other in the human being. The ether body is intimately embedded in the physical body, that is, these two bodies interpenetrate one another. Nowadays you can observe an idiosyncrasy, which is far from rare and about whose existence those in whom it is observed can do nothing. In observing this—while having a healthily compassionate soul in our breast—we will feel sorry for those observed to have this condition.

Have you ever noticed in officials at a post office counter—or others who write a great deal with pens—how they make peculiar movements before setting pen to paper? They create a sort of run-up in the air with their pens before starting to write. Though it may not actually transpire, it indicates a tendency to a worse condition when people do things like this in their profession. It might stay at this stage—you can observe it yourself—that when people write they first have to give themselves a certain shove for each stroke, or they may write in jerky bursts instead of flowing evenly up and down. You can see it in handwriting written like this.

A condition such as this can be understood in terms of spiritual-scientific knowledge as follows. In completely healthy human beings—healthy as far as their physical and etheric bodies are concerned—the ether body, which is directed by the astral body, needs to be totally capable of acting on the physical body. The physical body in turn has, in every one of its movements, to be capable of serving as the tool of the ether body. If the physical body produces movements of its own accord that go beyond what the soul can intend—what the astral and ether bodies intend—this is an unhealthy state and a predominance of physical body over ether body is evident.

In all those having the condition described, we are dealing with a weakness of the ether body, which manifests in its inability to fully direct its physical body. A relationship between the etheric and physical bodies of this kind underlies—from an occult perspective—all cramp-like, convulsive conditions. This is the fundamental connection between an ether body exercising less command over its physical body than it should, allowing the latter to dominate and make all sorts of involuntary movements, whereas the movements of a healthy person are subservient to the intentions of their ether and astral bodies.

There is an opportunity to help such a person if their condition is not too entrenched. However, the spiritual facts have to be taken into account, and this includes strengthening the ether body itself. This involves to some extent believing that the ether body exists and that it is capable of being strengthened. Imagine the poor person who is in such a bad way that his fingers incessantly fidget before writing a single letter. It will always be beneficent to advise they go on holiday, have a break from writing so much and their nervous tics will vanish. But this is only half the story.

Much more could be achieved by adding another, second element to this advice, such as: Make the effort—without over-exerting yourself (fifteen to thirty minutes suffice)—to adopt a different script. Change your handwriting so that you are obliged to abandon your mechanical way of writing and instead pay attention to how you shape each letter. Let's say you write an F like this, now try to make it different, more sharply slanting, so that you have to take more notice. Get used to carefully drawing each letter.

Were spiritual knowledge to be more widespread, managers would not—when someone afflicted returned from leave—say: You crazy individual, you've changed your handwriting; it's completely different! An anthroposophist employer would understand that this is a significant remedy. By changing their handwriting, a person is forced to direct their attention to what they are doing. Deploying attentive focus onto what we are doing always involves bringing our innermost core into close congruence with our actions.

Everything that unites the inner core of our being with our deeds reinforces our ether- or life body and we become healthier as human beings. It would not be in the least foolish to work towards strengthening ether bodies throughout education and in schools while pupils are still young. This is where anthroposophy should be putting forward proposals—which will not be taken up in practice because anthroposophy has long been regarded by those at the forefront of controlling education as something hare-brained—but no matter.

Imagine, when teaching children to write, that they would initially be taught a certain style; one would wait a couple of years and see to it that they changed their writing without inducement. A change in writing of this kind and its attendant increase in attentiveness would have an enormously strengthening effect on their developing ether bodies. In later life these young people will suffer from fewer nervous conditions.

So you see that, throughout life, we are always capable of doing something to fortify our etheric or life body, and this is exceptionally important because it is precisely such weaknesses in the etheric or life body that attract countless harmful conditions today. It can even be said—and it is actually not said often enough—that certain forms of illness, which may be based on things against which seemingly not much can be done would, with a strong ether body, take quite a different turn from that taken by the weakened ether bodies so characteristic of present human beings.

Here we have indicated something we can call *conditioning* the etheric or life body. We implement certain exercises to strengthen the ether body. No such exercises can be brought to bear on something we deny or claim is not there. By showing that it benefits our ether body when we carry out certain exercises and can demonstrate their effectiveness, we prove that an ether body exists and is present. Everywhere, life provides the corresponding evidence for what anthroposophy has to offer.

Our ether bodies can grow stronger if we do something else to improve our memory, something referred to in another context, but which will be repeated here because, for all illnesses in which nervousness plays a part, one ought to be able to resort to such advice. One can strengthen one's ether or life body enormously by mentally running through things one knows, not just in the way one usually thinks of them, but by running through them *in reverse order.*

Let us say, for example, that at school one is required to memorize a sequence of dates—of battles, of rulers—with their corresponding years. It is extremely good not just to learn them in their conventional, neat sequence but to assimilate them in the opposite order by going through everything from end to beginning. This is exceptionally important. Because when we do this comprehensively we are contributing enormously to increasing the vitality of our ether body. Thinking through whole dramas from end to beginning or recalling in reverse stories we have read, these activities are of the highest importance for consolidating the ether body.

Today you can experience how almost everything known to be effective in strengthening our ether bodies is not in fact carried out, either with requisite regularity or indeed at all. There is little opportunity in today's restless daily busy-ness to create the inner quietude needed to tend such practices. Most working people are usually too tired by evening, too harassed to think about where they are placing their things, or with which deliberation they are doing so. If, however, spiritual science were to really permeate hearts and souls, it would become evident that much of what goes on in today's world could be avoided and that the time spent on these strengthening exercises would be abundantly rewarding for each person. Remarkably beneficial results would soon become apparent, especially when care is taken of this advice in education.

Let me mention another detail, one which may be of slightly less benefit in later life, but which is nevertheless worthwhile, especially if it has not been tended in their youth. That is: that we immediately review what we have done or accomplished—regardless of whether it does or does not leave a trace. This is relatively easy with handwriting. I am sure that many would drop their ugly writing habits were they to try and review—letter for letter as their glance swept over it once again—the manner in which it had been written. Reviewing one's handwriting contemporaneously—evaluating what one has done—in this way is relatively easy.

Yet there is another sound practice—albeit one that ought not to be practised for long—that involves watching yourself while walking; how your hands move, how you tilt your head, the way you laugh, taking conscious pictorial account of your gestures. You will see from observing life how few people are aware of their gait, how few can visualize what they look like when walking.

But it is useful to gain an impression of the results of one's deeds, though, as I said, it must be a short-lived exercise if it is not to contribute too greatly to vanity. Apart from the fact that we will certainly correct several aspects of ourselves in life, this task is of enormous positive value in consolidating the ether or life body and also in enhancing the astral body's control of it. In observing their movements, in watching what they do while making imaginative images of this, people can succeed in increasing the benefit they gain from their astral body being in ever stronger control of their ether body. In this way, they can be in a position deliberately to suppress, change or eliminate, when necessary, some trait or modus operandi that lies within their habits.

It is among the greatest achievements of human beings, in some circumstances, to vary the way they do things. It is certainly not the aim here to found some sort of school of handwriting conversion. People usually only contort the strokes of their writing in aid of some wrongdoing. Yet it is helpful—with honest intent—in fortifying one's ether body to consciously vary the way one forms one's script. It is entirely healthy to be able to bring variety to the way in which one carries out something one intends to do, instead of being compelled to do it only in one way.

Similarly, while nobody needs to become fanatically ambidextrous—using left and right hands with identical facility—it is nevertheless valuable to try to do at least certain jobs with a measure of fluency in both hands, perhaps using your left hand instead of the usual right hand, and again not being reliant on one single method. This need not be continued beyond a basic ability, yet it will have a most positive effect on the astral body being able to take charge of the ether body as it should. Fortifying human beings in the sense described through spiritual science is something that needs to be brought into our culture through the dissemination of anthroposophy.

What one can call a culture of will is of great concern. It has already been pointed out that nervous anxiety may often manifest precisely in modern people not knowing how to start doing what they really intend to do. They are frightened of carrying out their intentions; they simply do not manage to do things. What can be summarized as a certain weakness of will is caused by the diminished ability of their I to take proper control of its astral body.

Insufficient control of an astral body by an ego is always symptomatic of people wanting something—or perhaps not wanting something—or at least not getting round to carrying out their intention. Some cannot even muster a serious enough will to will what they should be willing. Now, there is a simple means of strengthening your will for your daily life. This remedy is: to suppress wishes you harbour, precisely not to carry out their fulfilment—and obviously not to do this were such non-action to cause harm. If you check yourself all day long in daily life, you will notice countless things for which you wish and whose fulfilment would be very nice. Yet you will find just as many wishes whose fulfilment you can afford to relinquish without detriment to yourself or anyone else, without reneging on a duty, wishes which might have brought you joy but which can just as well remain unimplemented. If you proceed systematically in suppressing—among other wishes—those of which you can say: No, that wish can remain unsatisfied—this means avoiding those wishes that could cause harm, and only those that give delight, joy and contentment—then each denial of some small desire will contribute to an influx of willpower, to an empowering of your I over your astral body.

We would to some extent be able to catch up with such a process of self-education in later years, a practice which is largely neglected in the education of children nowadays.

It is basically difficult to work therapeutically in education in the area just characterized. One has to take into account that if, in a teaching situation, one is in a position to grant a child or young person's wish and one then denies it, one not only denies the wish but a certain antipathy can be elicited. Educationally, this can be upsetting.

Some might say there is a dubious aspect to wish-denial if antipathy is the result. Here you are on something of a cliff edge. If a father wants to educate his son by saying: No, Charles, you are not having this, the result may well be that the antipathy this calls forth towards his father is worse than the desired effect of being denied a wish. You may ask: What should one do here? There is a very simple remedy: you do not deny the child their wishes but instead deny yourself, so that the child becomes aware that you are foregoing something.

In the first seven years—and also later in life, as an after-effect—children have a strong urge to imitate, and we will see that when we firmly deny ourselves this or that in the presence of children we are to educate, that they will imitate it and, however unconsciously, perceive it as an aim worth pursuing. In this way we will have achieved something of enormous significance.

Here we see how our thoughts just need to be directed and guided in the right way through all that spiritual science can offer. Then spiritual science will not just remain a theory but will become life's wisdom, something that can really support and guide us throughout life.

The two public lectures[2] I have held here present a means by which much can be learnt about the I controlling the astral body. A unique feature of these lectures was that arguments both for and against were postulated. If you now examine, on a soul level, how people relate to life you will notice that their thoughts and actions usually settle upon what can be said either for or against any matter. This is the norm. But in life there is no single subject about which there can be an absolute for or against, not one. In every case there is both a pro *and* a con. We will do well—in every case—to become accustomed to taking account not only of one but of both sides, weighing up not only arguments for nor indeed against, but considering both the pros and the cons.

In whatever we do it is valuable to establish for ourselves why—and under which circumstances—we would do better to refrain from a particular action or at least be aware that there are also good reasons against such a course. Vanity and egotism often tend to speak against laying out counter-arguments that go against doing what one wants to do because far too often people just want to be good people. One can find proof of being a good person if one only does what is applauded yet refrains from doing what contradicts this. It is slightly uncomfortable that one can find objections to almost everything one does in life. I say this because it is extremely important for life: we are not nearly as good as we believe ourselves to be.

In every single thing we do—even when we do it because life demands it of us—this general truth only becomes useful to the extent that we also rehearse what would lead to us refraining from doing it. What can be achieved through this becomes evident when bringing before our souls the following simple example. You will certainly have met people who are so weak in will that they can barely resolve to do anything, preferring others to make decisions for them, which they only need to carry out. They shrug off responsibility, preferring to ask what they should do rather than weighing up reasons for this or that course of action. I am not just bringing this example for its own sake, but to achieve something else.

Whilst much can be said in support of what I have just said, objections can also be raised against it—in fact one can barely say anything in life against which, in certain senses, no objection can be brought—so let us take the person who is fond of asking others for instructions. Standing opposite each other are two people, both offering advice on the same subject. One says 'Yes, do it', the other says 'No, don't do it'. You will see that in life one of these advisors decisively gains the upper hand over the other. The opinion of the one with the strongest will is victorious in influencing the questioner. What phenomenon have we here? However inconsequential it looks, it is a very significant phenomenon. If I face two people and one says yes, the other no, and I carry out the yes, the willpower of that advisor works on in me, gaining such predominance that it empowers my deed. Their power of will has triumphed over that of the other advisor; the will of another person has won within me.

Assume for a moment that I do not now face two other people, each of whom advises yes and no respectively, but that I am quite alone and in my own heart lay out the yes and no, complete with their reasons so that nobody helps me. I do this alone; no other person approaches me as I weigh up the rationale for and against, then I carry out the yes, in that I have said to myself: this has unfurled a strong force, but this time within myself. What another person previously enacted through me I now carry out myself, thereby nurturing a force in my soul. So that, when inwardly faced with a choice, a strength has prevailed over a weakness. This is immensely valuable because it restores the sovereignty of your I over your astral body, re-empowering it enormously. Checking the reasons for and against in all possible detail is not something one should view as an inconvenience. You will discover just how much this does to strengthen your will if you try to carry out what has been typified here.

However, this can also have its shadow aspect, namely that, instead of strengthening will, a weakening could occur. If, after having examined the rationale of for-or-against and resolved upon the one or the other course, one fails—out of sheer slackness—to do anything at all, taking neither choice; this looks as if a choice of against has been taken, yet one is actually plain lazy. It is therefore preferable—if taking spiritual science into account to any extent—that you do not attempt any such reasoning when you are tired, leaving decisions to a time when you are not exhausted but feel strong enough and know that you are no longer worn out and can really act upon the choice you have put to your soul. You have to pay attention to the time at which you pose such soul questions.

Among further things that contribute powerfully to strengthening one's I over the astral body is this: that we put aside everything that creates a polarity between us and the rest of the world, between us and our surroundings. This ought to belong to the basic obligations we place upon ourselves as anthroposophists. Justified criticism is unavoidable for—if it is factually objective—it would be a weakness to substitute bad for good, something one can never do. But we have to learn to differentiate between what we ourselves criticize and things whose influence on our personality is just uncomfortable and annoying. The more we can make a habit of ensuring that our judgement of others is independent of their behaviour towards us—the more we can do this—the better it is with regard to fortifying our I's sway over our astral body. Not by way of self-congratulation saying: You are a good person because you don't criticize your fellow human beings, but in order to reinforce your I.

To this end, it is constructive not only to refrain from judging as bad such things as you dislike because they make you feel uncomfortable, but rather—especially where appraisal of people is concerned—only to voice opinion when you yourself are not under consideration. As a theory this is easy to embrace, but exceptionally difficult to practise in real life. It is good when, for example, someone has lied to you, to suspend your antipathy towards them. This is no case for recounting to others that the person has lied to you, but rather that your feeling of antipathy is withheld. Whatever we notice about a person, how consistently they conduct their affairs on any given day, can all help to form an impression of the person in question.

Whether someone speaks sometimes like this, sometimes differently, we need only compare what they themselves say to arrive at quite a different basis for our opinion of them than just one that emphasizes their attitude towards us. It is vital to let things speak for themselves, not judging a person on each single deed but rather on how their actions chime together as a whole. You will soon find, even in those you held to be hard-bitten detractors, who cause nothing but ill, that there is much that contradicts their usual behaviour. We do not need to focus on their conduct towards us at all. We can ignore ourselves, placing the person within their own behaviour in our mind's eye and—where necessary—coming to a view about them. In aid of strengthening the ego it is also good to ponder that the majority—nine-tenths—of the opinions we form can readily be abandoned. Experiencing—within one's own soul—just one tenth of the opinions we form about the world is more than enough for one lifetime. Our life of soul will in no way be disadvantaged by relinquishing the remaining nine-tenths of our opinions.

Today I have brought what may seem like trifles, but now and again it must be our responsibility to look at things such as these. Precisely in this way can we demonstrate how small things can have mighty effects; how we need to grasp life from the completely opposite end, as it were, if we wish to structure the sheaths of our bodies strongly and healthily, differently from the way life is habitually grasped.

It is not invariably right to send someone to the chemist for the right medicine when they are ill. The right thing will be to organize one's life in such a way that one is less susceptible to illness or that those illnesses are less severe. It will be less onerous if a person carries out such exercises as strengthen the influence of their I over their astral body, their astral body over their ether body and the influence of this in turn on their physical body. Self-discipline and its impact on development are themes that can proceed from the fundamental ethos of anthroposophy.

Lecture 2

WINTERTHUR, 14 JANUARY 1912

Human Soul Activity Through the Ages

T ODAY it would be good to pursue some spiritual-scientific questions that might, one way or another, be useful in cases where anthroposophy is to be defended. It is just when we meet for the first time in places where anthroposophy is beginning—or its initial stages are in prospect—that it is worthwhile drawing soul-attention to some of the moral questions with which we are often faced in our branches when people not acquainted with spiritual science have questions that could possibly lead to their increasing confidence in spiritual science, or at least to having some relationship with it.

Spiritual science relies on supersensible, on spiritual, experience. In that news of spiritual science reaches us as a narrative, an account of that which the spiritual researcher can reveal—having made their soul an instrument able to investigate the spiritual world—it contains as much certainty for them as facts such as roses, tables and chairs have for observers of external phenomena. In other words: it has immediate visual certitude.

What does this mean for us? What are the implications for those who do not have such immediate visual certitude, some might ask. For us it can only lead to believing what the spiritual researcher says. I have always emphasized that this is not the case. Admittedly, matters of the higher worlds can only be known by probing them searchingly. Yet when they are portrayed logically, it is equally true that everyone can grasp them if they deploy their reason sensibly. They can say to themselves: Everything said here concurs to a greater extent with reality than do other philosophies. We can use our reason with assurance and we will find—based on the logic underlying phenomena—that they can be understood. Though it may not be altogether easy, the non-seer can also come to a soundly based understanding.

As actual proof for strangers this will not suffice. Yet by taking widely accepted examples that anyone can know and comparing them with what the spiritual researcher tells us, we can make quite some progress. Let us take just one fundamental spiritual-scientific given: that the human being consists of four elements. These are a physical body, an etheric, an astral body and what we call an I or ego. The outer world only recognizes a physical body and anyone is at liberty to deny the existence of an ether, an astral and an I.

One could say: Everyone speaks from out of an ego or I,[3] but this is nevertheless denied. The I is like a sort of flame, whose fuel is our physical-bodily nature, which is consumed like a wick. This is how they wanted to refute Bergson,[4] the philosopher whose view was based on the continued persistence of the I.

However, we can see how the I outlives particular conceptions. Each day proves this to us, in that every night our I is extinguished and is not experienced as continuous.

You might assume that these supersensible elements can be denied. Yet one aspect is undeniable, namely, that human beings perceive three sorts of inner experience. One is that they experience concepts in their soul, because everyone knows that when they see something and then turn away, they retain the impression they experienced and this is an image or concept in their soul. Secondly, human beings experience—and this has to be separated from their concepts—the fluctuations in their feelings: delight and suffering, happiness and pain, sympathy and antipathy. People can also not deny a third element: that they have impulses of will.

Let us take the realm of concepts. Human beings can imagine in that they allow the impressions of the world to act upon them. They can also imagine when reading a novel because reading is also a route to imagining. You all know that imagining can be either difficult or less difficult. Those images, to which people are instinctively glad to give themselves up, influence them differently from those to which they are reluctant to submit or which cause them difficulties. You all know that a thorny calculation has a different effect on your imaginative powers than does a novel. We notice that imagining tires us if it is demanding. This is all the less debatable because picturing is a means of helping us to fall asleep, albeit images cannot be irritating nor worry-inducing but rather those we merely find strenuous to create. In any case, one thing we can experience is that we can easily fall asleep if—before going to sleep—we can permeate ourselves with such a world of concepts, one to which a sense of obligation is linked.

Let us now look at the flow of feelings. Delight and misery, joy and pain, worries, grief and suchlike are states that can, at the time, cause us outer hardship. Someone heavily in thrall to their feelings does not fall asleep easily. Even happy experiences may hinder a peaceful slip into slumber.

If you observe such occurrences you will soon notice that erratic fluctuations in feeling are an even greater hindrance than concepts when passing over into a state of sleep, especially mood swings connected with the most intense ego involvement. Some people do not sleep for weeks before an anticipated event. Try it yourself: an event that is largely expected, such as the appearance of a comet, will allow you to sleep well if, that is, you happen not to be an astronomer with their own troubling ego-interest in seeing their calculations confirmed.

We can now look at mood swings from another angle. In a certain sense sleep can be connected with what is clairvoyant in human beings. The condition of sleep is one in which the human being is unconscious. Clairvoyance is only sleep suffused with spiritual light, conscious sleeping, if we can define it thus. It must therefore be favourable for clairvoyance if one is free from oscillating feelings and unfavourable if filled with them.

This can be confirmed by external knowledge, among much else by Nostradamus,[5] who was a significant visionary in the sixteenth century of the kind who could prophesy in such a way that purist historians could not doubt that the events he put into verse did indeed come about, and which demonstrate, after all, that he gave wonderful indications. Even the historian Kemmerich[6] recognizes this because it cannot be denied. Kemmerich himself recounts how he had set himself quite different aims,[7] only wishing to provide proof that health conditions had improved since the sixteenth century. This is how he came to be occupied with Nostradamus.

Following up on Nostradamus, it will be interesting to focus on his life situation. He was a man who possessed the clairvoyant faculties that were present in his whole family. They arose in him in such a special way, however, because he was a wonderfully devoted doctor. He gave particularly excellent service during an outbreak of plague in Provence. It then happened that people put it about that he was a secret Calvinist.[8] This was so harmful to him that he was obliged to give up his medical practice. You must understand what this means! Those forces remain in a personality! Physics maintains that whenever forces in nature are dispersed, they are deployed and utilized elsewhere. It is only in spiritual matters that people do not wish to know about things such as this.

If someone evolves forces such as these in their profession, unfolding them with as much rich blessing as he did as a doctor, the forces thus freed must manifest themselves elsewhere. In Nostradamus they were all transformed into clairvoyant powers because he possessed a certain original, latent psychic gift, in just the same way as did Paracelsus.[9]

So you see: Nostradamus illustrates for us how he became able to foresee future events.[10] He had a laboratory. This was no laboratory of the sort chemists have. It was a space, a room, next to his house, which had a glass roof. From here he would observe the course of the stars and would let the changing constellations work upon his soul. It was from such sources that he was able to speak of the future. Springing from his feeling-imbued mind, they would appear to him in the form of an intuition. But in order that such intuition could arise, he had to be free of any worries, cares or excitable feelings. Here we have an example of the fact that clairvoyance—just as healthy sleep—requires an absence of emotional turbulence.

Let us move on to inquire into the human being's relation with their will, inasmuch as will is connected with all that is moral. Let us return to the moment of falling asleep. This is an important moment for human beings because, as spiritual science tells us, this is when they pass over into the astral world.

Let us observe moral impulses at the moment of falling asleep. To observe this process requires great exactitude and those who muster such attention report the following experience: the moment of falling asleep approaches. Where their eyes had previously seen clearly, outlines now become less distinct; something akin to fog is laid over everything, causing the person to feel as though they are cut off from their surroundings. Changes also take place in their physical body, specifically that they can no longer move their limbs. They cannot access a force to which they previously had entry. Further, certain things, which must be described as impulses of will, become noticeable, arising almost of their own accord and being drawn before their souls.

Things they have done appear to them as a unity, things with which they need not reproach themselves. They feel a wondrous sense of bliss about all that they did well. Benign spirits see to it that human beings are protected from ill appearing likewise to their souls.

Experiencing such blessedness about what is good can naturally not occur if nothing good has been done. Yet human beings are not generally so base that they have done no good at all.

Those who are alert can experience something that arises like a thought that is dim yet which remains vivid to the soul: Oh, if only this moment could be held fast, if only it could remain like this forever! Then there is a jolt and that consciousness vanishes.

Whilst impulses to do good call forth blessedness and help one to fall asleep, the impetus to do ill hinders this even more than does emotional turbulence. Pangs of conscience are most unconducive to good sleep. Impulses of will can sometimes hinder us—even more than churning emotions—from entering the spiritual world into which we must enter. Conceptual life makes crossing into spiritual regions relatively easy, agitated feelings more difficult and the most hindrance originates in pangs of conscience over our reproachable behaviour.

Concepts—that is, our concepts—tend to keep watch. If we allow images of the day to pass before us, we generally go to sleep quite well. If, however, feelings are added, they are less of a good sentinel; we fall asleep less easily with stimuli of this kind. Most assiduously of all do our impulses of will keep watch—those spurs of will which have led us to benevolent deeds—giving us best access to the realm of Devachan. If, during our review of the day, we arrive at a point where we are satisfied—at which we are filled with a sense of moral sufficiency over a good deed done, a deed in which our will has been expressed—that moment of grace may arrive, which will carry us over into Devachan.

If you take note of what spiritual science says, you will find that there is agreement between these observations and what clairvoyance reveals. For spiritual science tells us: it is with their ether bodies that human beings belong to the astral world. In that they live etherically in the astral world, they live in their concepts as in an element that is foreign to the physical world. This physical world gives us perceptions, from which we need to turn away. This leaves us with one thing: concepts, which are already something supra-sensible. Human beings have concepts because the forces of the astral realm extend into their ether bodies, so that a certain bond with the astral world pertains.

Secondly, spiritual science tells us: waves of emotion are not only connected with the astral world but also with a higher realm, because fluctuating feelings in human beings are associated with lower Devachan. Thirdly, spiritual science and all occultism teaches us that, through the moral working of will, human beings find their connection within the higher Devachan region, amid the world of the so-called formless Devachan.

Thus do these three forms of human soul life indicate three means of connecting with the higher worlds. Just compare what you experience in ordinary life with what spiritual science can tell you. It is all in agreement. Imaginings do not hinder sleep because we need to go through them to gain entry into the astral world. By contrast, in order to succeed in entering into the Devachanic world, our emotions must be such that they allow us to do so. Emotional turbulence that makes us toss and turn in our beds prevents us from falling asleep.

The realm of moral will-impetus signifies our relationship with the higher Devachanic world. Even less will we gain admission to this realm if we have carried out no deeds for which we need not reproach ourselves. We cannot enter into proper sleep if we suffer from pangs of conscience. We are locked out. And the blessedness described, which we experience over a good deed, is an outer token of the message: You may enter into the world of Devachan. It is no wonder that human beings experience this as grace and long to remain within it. Here they feel interrelated with the higher realms of Devachan and they long to stay there. The non-clairvoyant can only picture this highest state as a sense of falling asleep arising as blessedness and moral sentience.

In this way we can show how you contain your soul life within you. What you imagine manifests by bringing you into contact with a higher entity, one that eases your way into higher worlds and is related to the astral. What human beings undergo is like a shadow of higher worlds. Emotional sensations further separate us because through them humans relate to the lower Devachanic world. Impulses of will, however, separate us even more than the previous, because they are interrelated with the higher realms of Devachan.

All this forms part of further realities: what is most potent after death in Kamaloka are currents of feeling and moral impulses. Images of the physical world die away and only those of a spiritual nature can human beings take with them. By contrast, emotional turbulence follows us powerfully after death and it persists. It is this that detains us for a certain time in Kamaloka. For example, someone who had done ill during his life would—due to their pangs of conscience between death and a new birth—be completely unable to rise up into Devachan and would have to reincarnate without experiencing it. Without moral prompting they would not be able to ascend into Devachan and would soon return and be obliged to make up for their failing. Having no positive emotional life, the lower Devachan realm is also closed to them.

This is how we can evaluate and show how we can gain a perspective on the facts of daily life—of normal soul life—through explaining them in terms of what spiritual science tells us. I would like to add to what has been said by mentioning another fact, which will be important to you if you turn your spiritual gaze towards the fact and teaching of reincarnation, of repeated earthly lives. If we incarnate repeatedly on earth, there must be a certain reason for this. Evolution would have no purpose were we not to experience something! What sense is contained in the fact that we reincarnate?

Through the truths of a spiritual perspective we come to see how very varied human life is in different ages. Just think back to ancient times, when we spoke Greek or Latin and did what was generally done then! What is expected nowadays, such as sending children to school, only emerged later. Whereas now we view someone who cannot read as an illiterate, uneducated person, this was not the case then; otherwise our statisticians would have to count Wolfram von Eschenbach,[11] for instance, amongst the uneducated.

Something else not seen as education today existed in Ancient Rome: every Roman citizen—even those ploughing their fields—knew precisely the content of their Law of Twelve Tables (*Leges Duodecim Tabularum*) and much else besides to do with the legal constitution of a citizens' state. No Roman needed to run to their solicitor over every detail—this is just an example. If these great differences were taken into account, people would not need to ask why we always have to reincarnate as children! No, it's not like that! Each time we return, culture has changed to such an extent that we have to learn things anew. So: we were born into quite different circumstances and it is entirely necessary to keep on returning until Earth has arrived at its goals.

Now we can best of all discern what human beings can become in subsequent cultures if we know how those characteristics—which were today among those we called an inner soul life—evolve gradually in external culture. It is a characteristic of our times that among the incentives mentioned, the greatest value is placed upon concepts. We live in a culture of conceptual life. Intellect is developed.

In Greek and Roman culture thinking was not so prevalent; perception, however, was all the more vivid compared with modern people. Hebbel,[12] the dramatist, wrote something comical in a notebook:

Imagine that Plato is reincarnated. He would go to a classical grammar school and would have to read Plato in ancient Greek. His teacher finds it most unsatisfactory that he doesn't understand Plato and gives him the cane. Hebbel wanted to dramatize this. On the one hand it is quite funny, yet on the other quite understandable. Because it is true that a classics teacher of today conceptualizes far more than even the great Plato in his day.

In a certain sense we look at the world short-sightedly. Farmers today think more than Greek philosophers did. By contrast, in those days their perceptive abilities were cultivated to a far higher degree. Human beings were interwoven with nature. Perception then was like image-forming is for us. Today perception is no longer schooled at all other than by those who are undergoing such a training. It is perfectly possible that someone may be an expert and go far within their laboratory setting yet be naïve in nature and not know the difference between wheat and rye. We can therefore say that today human beings have great cognitive capacities but in olden times they were trained in perception. We can say that two epochs can be distinguished: one of perception and one of concept-forming. A third will in future follow, in which the undulations of feeling—which nowadays merely exist alongside the two mentioned—will be trained.

Someone who today begins to undergo a certain training does indeed pre-empt what the general culture of tomorrow will undergo. They must tend to their feelings. It can easily happen that someone who has made a beginning in cultivating their life of feeling towards higher worlds comes into contact with another who has primarily cultivated concepts. They will be able to observe that here a feeling of rightness can be felt, there one of wrongness, of falseness. A solely intellectual person will accept what is right on purely logical grounds, rejecting what is false.

A higher stage of culture will be a long time in coming, one in which people will feel a sense of wellbeing in face of what is right and true and a sense of dissatisfaction when faced with wrong or falsehood. This will provide certainty when faced with the nature of truth and lies, because more than just a concept of truth and falsehood will be required. We will not need long to prove something because we will grasp it in a trice. Nowadays we have to prove things, to develop them. There will then be no need for proof; it will just be a matter of liking it. Following on from the Greek culture of perception and the concept culture of our times, a soul-culture will obtain by the time we reincarnate. Thereafter a culture concerned with impetus, with motivation—with will—is to follow, in which impulses of will are to undergo a great transformation. Those incarnated at this future point will undertake to pursue something of a Socratic ideal. Without this, regardless of how clever a person is, yet they will remain the epitome of a scoundrel. In vain would Hamlet[13] have written on his tablet the words: 'One may smile, and smile and be a villain.'

Following after the age of fluctuating emotions or sensations, there will be one of incisive morality. Occult research shows a particular phenomenon. Let us assume that people become ever cleverer and cleverer. This can happen under present modes of ideation. This cleverness can also be used to orchestrate evil deeds. Yet, remarkably, in the next but one future epoch, it will be the case that evil in will-motivation will have a laming effect on intellectuality! The extraordinary feature of that moralistically inspired cultural epoch will be that immorality will have the power to deaden intellectuality. The person of this era will therefore need to have developed themselves to the extent that their morality will be congruent with their intellectual capacities. We can therefore say: In Greek and Roman cultures we have an age of perception culture; our own times are intellectual. Then follows an age of emotional education, thereafter a culture of actual morality.

Now it is interesting to observe how important stimuli take effect on human beings in these subsequent cultures. We need to refer to what was said earlier: perceptive faculties bind us to the physical, conceptual powers with our astral bodies, emotions with the lower regions of Devachan and morality with higher Devachan.

Whenever any stimulus of this kind was to approach human beings in Graeco-Roman times, they would be trained to become especially alert to what approached them externally. It was for this reason that Christ's impetus manifested as an external percept in the world. We now live in a culture of concepts, of ideation. For this reason our cultural epoch will achieve its goal in that we know Christ as something emanating from the astral world, perceptible in the form of an inner idea or conception. He will reveal himself from out of the astral world in the form of an etheric figure. In the next epoch, during the age of feeling-transformation, human beings will, to an especial extent have to lay bare their feeling life in order to perceive Christ in the astral. Later, in the age of morality, Christ will be revealed as the very highest paragon of which humanity is capable of experiencing: as an I radiating into humanity from the highest Devachan.

So even the perception of Christ will evolve. Human beings will now naturally perceive Christ in their concepts, in their imaginations.

We see from these descriptions that human beings can find a certain concurrence between what spiritual science relates and what takes place in the world—assuming that the individual can make their own contribution towards it.

These are issues that could be mentioned in consolidation of our common understanding and in answer to some of the numerous questions as to how human beings can draw nearer to the spiritual world.

Lecture 3

The Path of Knowledge and its Connection with Human Morality

The sequence of lectures we are holding today and tomorrow could perhaps serve to cover topics which are similar. They will first be discussed in a manner suitable for those members and friends whose groups have for some time been engaged in aligning the perspectives from which we are proceeding with those underlying their own worldviews. Tomorrow in the public lecture[14] similar subjects and starting points will be introduced, but in a manner more suited to those less acquainted with spiritual science who are approaching this movement directly from the mundane world.

Today we will begin from a challenge well known to all those who wish to make progress, perhaps not only in spiritual science, but in developing their inner human nature. It has ever and again been emphasized that for inner development—which could lead to people having their own experiences in the spiritual world—it is of enormous importance for human beings to achieve purity and love in their aims and intentions.

We could possibly say from one point of view—though everything said is bound to be one-sided—that a spiritual researcher, or indeed anyone striving to enter and discover something in the spiritual world, must above all have a particular soul characteristic. This quality of soul must be such that they sympathize—that they in fact sympathize heartily—with all that is good, noble and beautiful and that to some extent they experience an aversion to evil, towards what is ugly. In relation to the path into the spiritual world, purity of soul is always essential and we can say: For a genuine ascent into spiritual realms in a contemporary sense it is absolutely essential for one's soul to be thoroughly permeated with sincere moral intentions and goals. We will hear later how it is possible to acquire clairvoyant faculties without any such founding conditions, though this always entails a dubious element.

In order to understand this, we need to make clear what exactly we mean by human beings' moral nature. We are initially inclined to speak about people's moral character when focusing on those drives prompting someone to act; to desires or wishes that come from the external world. When a person is conditioned by their natural needs, be it thirst or hunger, to undertake—or even to want or wish for—this or that, we do not generally call such wanting or wishing a moral act. Neither need it necessarily be immoral. When a stone falls to the ground we do not feel this to be a moral act and we are unlikely to apply morality as a yardstick. No more are we inclined to call moral those actions that fulfil the natural demands of our organism, such as eating or drinking. We do not speak of morality when a person sees a beautiful flower or some other lovely thing, because it makes a pleasing, satisfying impression, even if they covet or desire it. We do not call this morality either.

When, in fact, do we speak of morality in human nature? Only really when no external demands such as hunger or thirst or the satisfaction elicited by some object are present, prompting us to act; only when an action originates from the innermost core of our being like an order, like a command from within, which is independent of any outer compulsion. We become particularly aware of the difference between what is moral and—let me not call it immoral—what is morally indifferent when we take into account how we might possibly do this or the other in response to outer prompting, yet which we then fail to carry out because the inner command—which we are calling a moral impulse—gainsays it.

Let us take an immediate if trivial case of someone who has an overwhelming urge to drink too much. They would, given the opportunity, simply drink. Or they could follow their inner voice, which has nothing to do with their urge but is opposed to the outer compulsion and which says: What you are externally compelled to do should not happen! Here we see that something can speak within us that contradicts outer instigation. So we see that everything of this contradictory ilk, that judges our actions, can be called moral. We can only speak of acting morally if we ignore all external effects, are free of everything that exerts pressure on us, and only focus on what issues from within. The fact that human beings can hear this from within raises them above animality; that they can hear it and are able to go beyond outer susceptibility, able even to reject the susceptibility itself.

We must experience that in morality we have something that is, by its very nature, true. That is the fundamental trait of all moral impulses: that, by existing, they are inherently true. Outer conditions can contribute nothing to whether an action is to be called moral or immoral. If we judge something to be moral in relation to apparent external criteria, such a verdict will often cause us to fall prey to illusion. Were one to say, for instance, that human beings organize life such that they not only respond to hunger and thirst but to the axiom that it is essential to tend their organism in order to maintain themselves in the outer world; in other words, that the necessities of life are the decisive factors, this would be an illusion. Only when we can add to such outer necessities the inner spur that tells us it is right and good for humans to maintain their existence on earth, not only for practical undertakings but for the sake of the inner tasks that can follow from them, only then is morality a reality; otherwise it is mere semblance. The hallmark of morality, therefore, is that it does not emanate from the external world but springs purely from the forces of our souls.

Someone could of course say: There are also evil voices within; we often follow the dictates of what we clearly recognize as inner stimuli and which are entirely not such as can be called moral. Though this subject cannot be gone into today in any detail because we have set ourselves a different task, one could say: If a human being follows one of these apparent inner promptings, which are false and evil, they are in truth not following themselves but are instead following motivations of whose origins they are ignorant and which they are confusing with those emanating from within.

We all know from our spiritual-scientific studies about luciferic forces. They do not originate from within but, in a certain sense, from without in that luciferic beings have attached themselves to our astral body and not to our ego, so that, in defining what is moral, we encounter countless contradictions. Going into this more fully, we will find that what is characteristic of every moral impetus is that it must arise from the innermost core of our being. We can equate what, as it were, pleases us, what calls forth our moral wellbeing, what can fill us with enthusiasm and delight with the ideal of all that human beings can—quite of themselves—*be* in their inner self.

Even though it is extremely useful and necessary in normal life for us to grasp—only in terms of moral judgement or judgements that arise in similar manner—that we are entirely alone and by ourselves, for practical occultism this is a fundamental requirement. This must be recognized as a basic requirement of occultism. It is vital that events occur in line with moral motivation, that nothing takes place in the soul on treading the inner path of knowledge that does not align with the archetype of genuine moral motivation.

It is significant that anyone who wishes to tread the path of the practical spiritual seeker should undertake not to carry out anything of which they cannot say: If I compare this action with what exists within the human being—with what I call morality—both must be similar. The path of knowledge may at no stage stray from all that is proven to be akin to human moral conduct. The similarity of the path of knowledge with moral motivation applies in every detail. This will be illustrated by a particular example.

There is something specific about morality and the way people are today. Basically, the Ten Commandments[15] are still the most significant aspect among our laws. The Ten Commandments are, on closer examination, constructed in a most extraordinary way. Of the ten, only three are phrased: Thou shalt, you shall do something. The other seven are formed such that they forbid: Thou shalt *not,* you may not. From this it follows that world powers envisaged a far greater necessity to give humankind moral laws that said: Thou shalt not do something than those requiring something to be done. So the proportion of those forbidding actions to those requiring actions are seven to three. We can therefore say that, in general, morality must affect human nature such that its decrees issue especially from the standpoint of 'Thou shalt not'.

We can further compare the proportion of seven to three in the Ten Commandments. Looking at the seven that command you *not* to do something, they all relate to matters of the external world, to what is forbidden in the physical world. By contrast, the three Commandments containing the exhortations to do something—Thou shalt—actually refer to actions that go beyond the physical world. We are told to believe in a single God, not to take the Lord's name in vain and so on. From this we see that the Commandments are positive in relation to the spiritual concerns of the soul.

Contrasting this, all the Commandments concerned with moral behaviour in the outer, physical world contain a prohibition: Thou shalt not. If we also suppose that the fourth Commandment: 'Honour thy father and thy mother ... that thy days be prolonged, and that it may go well with thee in the land which thy Lord giveth thee' to be positive, we nevertheless sense that, basically, it is strongly negative in character, much like the remaining six Commandments. It is something of a transitional commandment, referring as it does to the physical world while already ascending, as it were, into spiritual realms.

This can also be corroborated in its detail, I would say, in that all ancient religions were founded upon ancestor-honouring, and among the ancestors and forefathers was entailed a divine element. In this respect, veneration of ancestors—of whom immediate parentage formed only a specific case—represented a sort of transition from the sense world to higher realms.

However, this fourth Commandment referred especially to the physical world, to the relationship between children and parents. As far as parents are concerned, we can satisfy this Commandment; we can feel that this fourth Commandment is given in a positive manner, that it transcends human beings so as to prevent something. In the first Commandments the objectives towards which they are directed do not exist in the physical world.

Through the structure of this Ten-Commandment-entity we are directed towards that which forms the fundamental moral features of the sense world: that moral motives may contradict all that humans would do, were they to follow solely the inducements of the physical world. What this means for the path of knowledge—which has to be grounded in the paradigm of morality—is that we are clearly told: On an occult path, we must make moral our entire cognition or knowing, and what is otherwise mere theory of knowledge must become inner moral law.

In other words, whatever relates primarily to the physical plane—once a human being faces the things in their immediate vicinity, that are laid out before him or her—must be extinguished, such that they say to themselves: I have extinguished them, just as I rid myself of lower tendencies when 'Thou shalt not' is calling out. In fact, this is the reason why—in every true description of the path of knowledge—one is instructed that the safest ascent into higher worlds is by ennobling the power of cognition through moral impetus. This is expressed in every detail.

Let us assume we have some plant. What can we identify as an external impulse emanating from it? Take the plant's foliage. We can identify as an external effect that the green of the leaves affects us. In the physical sense world, for instance, rose leaves are green. Let us now assume that it was expected of a practising occultist genuinely striving towards higher knowledge that they should emulate the ideal of moral cognition. Most of the images arising when faced with the green leaf would call forth with their greenness an inner response: you should not be green. It should be possible to look at the rose leaf with such power of vision that its outer effect does not affect us and, just as with moral judgement, the baser conclusion is extinguished, so the greenness of the leaf is extinguished, let's say, by another force, a clairvoyant force. Indeed, if people develop their clairvoyant forces rightly and as described in *Knowledge of the Higher Worlds*, they will learn to observe the green leaf and, just as moral judgement extinguishes baser tendencies, so the greenness of the leaf—as it pertains only in the physical world—is likewise extinguished. And where greenness would otherwise appear, here in the light of clairvoyant capacities it will appear as light rose pink or a colour resembling peach blossom. This appears when, through clairvoyant forces, we are able to get rid of what manifests as illusory maya, of what exists on the physical plane.

In this way, by clairvoyant means, we rid ourselves of what exists at a physical level and release the supra-sensible that underlies the sense world. We can therefore say: Treading the path of knowledge really does proceed in like manner to human moral experience. Contrasting the supra-sensible with the sense-perceptible world is akin to the way in which moral motivation acts upon immoral tendencies. Were we, on the other hand, to look at the rose itself—a rose such as this one with its luscious red colour on the physical level—we would perceive a radiant, transparent green, whereas for a lighter rose we would sense a sort of rich green with slightly blueish tones.

We have seen in this one example that occult findings consistent with clairvoyant vision are established at a soul level in the same way that moral judgements eclipse what is immoral. From this we can conclude that what we said at the outset is consolidated here. In order to attain to higher knowledge we must learn to banish all immediate physical impressions, to make the illusions of maya disappear, so that they are replaced by something different. It is well known that we learn best when we can approximate what has to be internalized with similar subjects. Nobody would practise on subjects unrelated to the study matter in hand. I have never heard of anyone becoming a mathematician merely by going for a walk because this is nothing similar. So we are only able to acquire soul capacities that are similar to moral motives if we are able to practise on what people already know in everyday life.

We do not yet have clairvoyance, as it is something that has to be acquired slowly and by strenuous effort. But we all have opportunities to contemplate and ask ourselves: What do I think of as morally good and what do I consider morally reprehensible? Most people do not act immorally because they are unaware of what is moral but because their propensities, their urges, craving or passions are in opposition to their moral insight. Only when we have examined ourselves in relation to this can we return to what we discover within, such as endorsing what we know to be moral. If we now practise this meditation, asking ourselves: How are we to judge this or that in the world in accordance with our moral thinking? We can create images and immerse ourselves in them so that they become habits of feeling, which will truly ripen in our souls and which are akin to clairvoyant forces.

Another thing that individuals can do to awaken clairvoyant forces is for their morality and actions to unite as one. This is the best training for clairvoyance. That is why it is always emphasized that the optimum route to super-sensory vision entails nothing but raising and improving one's moral character.

If we focus on this, we will also have to ask the question: Are there not other routes to clairvoyant vision? We often see that people can attain a high level of clairvoyance without making an impression of exceptional morality on us, so that we cannot assume that they have, first and foremost, subjected their morals, their good fortune, their misfortunes, their enthusiasms to any great moral scrutiny.

We see that people who have developed all manner of clairvoyant forces by other means display certain dire qualities, which they previously barely had—or had not at all. They may begin to lie through their teeth when they start to have clairvoyant sight. It can sometimes be a really dangerous thing for the character of an individual to start developing visions of this kind or clairaudience.

Clairvoyance is not as dangerous as clairaudience. How does this chime with what was said earlier? As you perhaps recall its being mentioned at crucial points in my book *Knowledge of the Higher Worlds*, the path to higher worlds, as it is described for today, has to be adhered to. It is equally doubtless that other paths exist. You only have to study this path in the right way for you to soon understand that traits of the sort just described can arise. We must be clear that we contain that soul-spiritual core within us, the centre of which we encapsulate at its core when we say 'I' or 'I am'. This soul-spiritual core of our being is embedded in astral, etheric and physical bodies. As human beings today, we live inwardly in the world as an actual I. Because all soul activity in the waking human being is in some way connected with their I, they all manifest with the I as their background.

I have often cited the real-life example of one of my school friends[16] who as a boy was already a confirmed materialist thinker. He used to say: Whenever we think or feel, we are only dealing with processes in our brains. It is thanks to the brain's workings that we think and feel. Even then he had contrived quite a few theories. How can we speak of an I, of the core of one's being, when it is the brain that thinks and feels? I would counter him by asking: Why do you tell lies so persistently? How can you maintain that your brain thinks and feels when you say 'I think' and 'I feel' or 'I will' while believing that your brain does all this? You could say that this is a cheap and trivial example, but the fact remains that it is ultimately correct—substantively, instantly and actually valid.

Between waking up and falling asleep we remain connected with our I and cannot disengage it from all that we think, feel and will. All that we experience inwardly that is enmeshed with our I is, as it were, embedded in our astral, etheric and physical bodies. We are not directly aware of these bodies during normal life. All manner of obscure and inexplicable phenomena surface from the astral body, but most people don't know what takes place within it; just as when you look at the surface ripples on the sea you cannot know what is happening in the depths. You only need to observe life to realize how much remains unknown, how little we know of life's secret processes.

Let's, for instance, take a seven-year-old child who experiences being unjustly treated by its mother or father. As a result, a distressing commotion ensues, which goes unnoticed because, to all outward appearances, it has soon vanished. However, it has only sunk down into the astral body, where it continues to churn and heave. The child continues to grow up, is at school and reaches the age of sixteen or seventeen. Something happens: a teacher does this or that. Another child would only have had a fleeting upset but this young person commits suicide! Anyone observing life superficially will come up with all sorts of reasons as to what caused them to commit suicide. Only someone who observes life in all its profundity—including all the astral churning and heaving—will recognize that injustice experienced at age seven is one of the most dangerous root causes lurking in the depths, which is only wrenched forth by the school incident. Had this injustice not been festering, suicide would not have followed.

We know scarcely anything about what takes place just below the threshold of consciousness when the astral body undergoes experiences in the present, let alone how the astral is structured as regards its forming; how its elements are combined, how its being is actually constituted. In this respect we are embedded within what the soul-spiritual beings we call the hierarchies have implanted into us. Below in the astral, as in the depths of the ocean, countless forces exist that remain invisible as long as the surface ripples are all we notice. In the same way as surface ripples relate to the depths does the conscious I relate to all that goes on in the astral body below. The only diver you need to plumb these astral depths is the seer.

This is the case to an even greater degree in relation to the ether body, where the depths are even more concealed—let alone with those of the physical body! While human beings can observe the physical externally, they have the least power over it and can merely do what their stomach dictates. Given a choice of combatting stomach pain or immoral propensities, most will put aside their moral exertions in favour of a healthy stomach. Our physical bodies are subject to laws not present in the human I, laws which we annex from the external world through maya. Astral, ether and physical bodies are permeated with forces from the beings of the higher hierarchies. Yet this does not prevent them from acting upwards into the conscious I—preventing these forces from welling up from the hidden depths of human existence into the conscious ego—in the way we saw in the real-life case of the child.

As a result of the injustice inhabiting the astral body since the age of seven, a force was provoked in the now sixteen-year-old that erupted into consciousness from their astral body when struck in the face with a blackboard cloth by a teacher. Leaving the classroom, he finds the chemistry lab unexpectedly unlocked, goes in and takes poison. All the resources available to modern psychology were unable to deduce how forces residing in the astral body would emerge and play out.

However, what exists below in the human subconscious can rise into the conscious I through certain behaviour. Via the conscious I, forces from the astral body can potentially be pumped up into consciousness and thus become a chattel of clairvoyance, that is, of super-sensory powers. In this, we are siphoning powers given to us by the Gods. This is, in fact, something recommended in many of the books giving indications for treading the path of knowledge. Often even those writing such books have no idea of the true process because they lack the requisite conscientiousness essential for such an undertaking.

Now, it is understandable that those forces, which have streamed into our astral, ether and physical bodies from higher hierarchies, do belong there. When we siphon them up, we extract something from our constitution; we remove something of what the Gods have given us and weaken ourselves in doing so. This weakening can manifest such that the integral truthfulness, which was streamed into us by the Gods, sustains damage. Forces which previously prevented human beings from lying become depleted to such an extent that they start lying. Herein lies the great difference between attaining clairvoyant powers by the means just described and the consistent method which you will find set forth in my book *Knowledge of the Higher Worlds*.[17]

What is the basis of this method? Simply this: that on the path of knowledge nothing is developed that is not carried out in accordance with the paradigm of pure moral judgement. This will never flow from the astral body but must be won in the form of something that rises up like an inner voice into the self-aware I. For whatever is not in possession of a self-aware I cannot be addressed as a moral being. We can speak of morality only in relation to an entity in a position to allow only those impulses to arise that are connected—within their innermost being—with the very core of that being.

Forces other than those of a moral nature are now to arise, forces that help the soul ascend into spiritual worlds. If these are not to issue from our astral body, they cannot issue from us at all. It is impossible that they should issue from ourselves because what originates in us would have to have its origins in our conscious I. Yet, apart from moral impulses, at most aesthetic judgements discerning matters of beauty—and in a certain sense mathematical verdicts—arise out of the conscious I. And they are not to be pumped up from the astral body. Where, then, can they originate? From the spiritual world in which we have been placed and which, after all, has generated our three bodies.

These forces are not to originate in our three bodies themselves. In other words, the path chosen must not be a diversion via our three bodies, but be a path that brings us into direct contact with spiritual realms, with the beings of the hierarchies, such that the forces of these higher worlds can flow directly into us.

We must have an entrance to these worlds, through which higher forces can flow into our souls. For this it is essential that all higher knowledge is connected with something other than commonplace knowledge. Everyday knowledge will not grant entry into higher realms. For access into higher worlds a very particular and fundamental mood of soul is necessary. That is the first requirement, emphasized even by the time of the ancient Greek philosophers: anyone merely capable of thinking well, who just wants to intellectualize, to synthesize everything by mere philosophizing and cogitating, will never gain entry into the spiritual world. One has to start from somewhere else. Before one can knowingly face a subject, one has to approach it differently.

All knowledge begins with wonder[18] and only those who make wonder their starting point are on their way to truly rightful knowledge. Anything in the presence of which we have not been awed or amazed will never lead us to the correct path of knowledge. However much education proclaims that one must start from looking, from observing, if there is no prior awe and amazement, everything will remain mere intellectual recognition. Wonder is the first prerequisite.

A second element that allows us entry into the spiritual world is that we learn to revere—a reverence for what manifests as effect through an object. Knowledge that is not inter-connected with the soul in such a way that a soul is initially filled with awe and wonder for what is heralded *through* an object will not progress beyond intellectual comprehension.

Thirdly, to feel in harmony with world affairs. Spiritual science offers many means to this end, especially the concept of karma, which we bear within us with all possible earnestness in life. It is a long stretch between accepting the concept of karma in human life and it becoming a truly serious element pervading life.

Were we truly convinced of karma, we would not say, on being slapped round the ear: 'I don't appreciate being slapped round the ear', we would need to say: Who has actually slapped my ear? I myself have done so because, in an earlier life, I did something at some time that gave rise to another person slapping me. I have not the slightest cause to tell them that they are doing me a disservice but rather that I have, in a certain sense, installed an automatic mechanism, not one where I find myself at variance with world affairs but in harmony with them. This is the third precondition.

The Bible itself offers a similar teaching: should someone strike your right cheek, offer them your left cheek.[19] If one is aware that to seek a cause through karma is to seek it within oneself, if one acknowledges—however it may manifest—that whatever one has elicited through one's own wilfulness or guilt, then one arrives at a point of knowing oneself to be in harmony with world- or cosmic processes. That is the third aspect.

A fourth is: complete surrender to these world- or cosmic processes; seeing oneself as just one element among them. We can thus enumerate four qualities through which we can relate to the outer world, towards life's externals. Firstly, with wonder and awe, secondly with reverence, with veneration, thirdly by knowing oneself to be consonant with world- and cosmic processes and, fourthly, by utterly surrendering to those world processes.

By developing these qualities we open our souls, we unfasten them so that forces can infuse us in vestal purity from out of the spiritual world—forces we can breathe in like fresh mountain air after having breathed stale air expended by other organisms. In this way we see the difference between what can be bequeathed by the grace of the higher hierarchies themselves and whatever can be pumped up from forces laid into our organism by them. By observing all this we learn really to distinguish two paths, both of which lead to actual clairvoyance. Yet one of these pathways leads to a clairvoyance by which human beings place themselves in direct opposition to beings of the higher hierarchies.

Human beings have not always been moral beings. While humans were initially elaborating their astral, ether and physical bodies, one could not speak of moral momenta or stimuli. We are speaking here about the human of ancient Sun who was acquiring their ether body and about the human of ancient Moon evolution to whom was added an astral body. However, during these evolutionary periods, nowhere was a moral realm to be found. It belongs to the evolutionary task of Earth to add morality to what human beings can otherwise experience. The task of acquiring such forces as can lead us into the spiritual world consists in this: that human beings must *themselves* evolve beyond what has been acquired over the course of Saturn-, Sun- and Moon evolution.

From all this it can be inferred—because reason proves it—but it cannot be claimed that human beings can trust the paths of knowledge open to them indiscriminately as to whether it be black magic or moral conduct. You simply have to allow reason to test matters. Just undertake to go into today's descriptions thoroughly and what has been said will turn out to be true, so that, by taking these accounts of paths to knowledge as a benchmark, you will be able without much ado to distinguish between them. It is important that we learn to say to ourselves: For me, any depiction of a path to knowledge that is not in every detail congruent with the paradigm of morality is suspect from the outset. Anyone not viewing as suspect a pathway opposing all that can be sensed as moral, anyone unable to feel the necessity for moral motivation, would have to hold themselves responsible for the danger in which they would find themselves.

It was therefore by no means superfluous—among descriptions we could have focused upon—to select this example, because it is quite right and proper that someone interested today in spiritual science not only absorbs the fruits of research but, equally, familiarizes themselves with the means by which it has been discovered. Let us take the case of someone who wants to embrace spiritual science but does not wish to embark on a path of initiation in this incarnation. It is valuable for them, too, to imagine how such knowledge is gained. They can acquire a view of it—just as a chemist can arrive at an axiom by hearing an account of the experiment by which it was achieved—even if they themselves have not carried out that particular experiment.

At this point, it is important for those wishing to follow the path to higher knowledge to take note of what has been described because we live in times when human beings are called upon to become ever more independent. In times gone by, right back to the Mystery of Golgotha, it was the case that into human beings—to some extent without their active participation—clairvoyant forces used to flow, much like an inheritance from primeval human ages. But since the Mystery of Golgotha human beings are to live consciously in relation to everything. For this reason it is essential that people acquire such a mood of soul as is reached through the four virtues, the four forces mentioned: through wonder and awe, through reverence, through harmony with world processes and by submitting to these world- or cosmic processes. It is precisely in developing these virtues that we open ourselves freely to the influences that can approach us from the higher hierarchies.

On the basis of the most fundamental soul motivation, the potential exists to transport ourselves into a soul mood similar to that achieved through the four virtues in their relationship with the world. If we repeatedly, over and over again, give ourselves up to the thought that—though we stand in the world and while we are inter-woven into the web of maya, that great illusion whose origins remain in the spiritual world—we have our own origins in divine powers. Living in the illusory realm of maya does not prevent us from sub-mitting—notwithstanding that we live in a world full of illusion and maya—from surrendering to those spiritual powers from which the maya originates.

Maya resembles life, is like the play of wavelets, which exists on the surface yet is thrown up by the sea and remains one with the sub-stance of the sea. Just as truly as ripples emerge from the realm of the sea, as spume is formed from the substance of the sea, just so does the realm of maya arise from its spiritual substratum. We can there-fore say: Even though we are enmeshed in this world of illusion, we nevertheless stem from the divine. Western esotericism expresses this as 'Of God we are born', we stem from the divine: *Ex deo nascimur.*

A second fundamental perception is that we may not pump upwards those forces which divine powers have laid in our astral, etheric and physical bodies but that we must surrender directly to the spiritual world—that we must die into that world. We do this through the four virtues: wonder and awe, reverence, harmony and experiencing surrender to world-processes. These are moods which bring us ever closer to what western esotericism expresses as 'In Christ we die': *In Christo morimur.*

This in turn raises hope that we will approach an awakening in the spiritual world, that forces will arise in us, will be newly bestowed on us, as they were once bestowed on the astral body. Through the Holy Spirit we will be newly reawakened, will again be transported to spiritual worlds so that human beings can again ascend to higher realms: *Per spiritum sanctum reviviscimus.*

We should be aware that the esotericism suitable for modern times must shun all methods which pump upwards—from lower bodies up into the I—forces intended to lead to higher knowledge. We are healthy only when those forces are kept down, below. It is a false esoteric path if we cloud our consciousness in one way or another and then deem certain things to be right merely by having pumped upwards forces which—had they remained in their rightful places— would not have allowed us to consider them correct.

These are serious matters, which can lead to understanding, properly, why in the book *Knowledge of the Higher Worlds* the forces for developing clairvoyant faculties are located by the larynx. These are in the highest possible sense moral capacities, qualities also portrayed in the teachings of Buddha as the Eightfold Path. To a certain level, these are moral capacities; further on, they also lead to a thorough moralization of our knowledge, to its saturation with what otherwise remains among our morals.

LECTURE 4

BRESLAU, 3 FEBRUARY 1912

Anthroposophy, Conscience and Wonder

IT might be beneficial—as we can meet so rarely—to touch on questions relating to the way in which anthroposophy directly affects life. The question often arises among anthroposophists: How does anthroposophy relate to those not yet in a position to see into the spiritual world clairvoyantly? Basically, such spiritual-scientific content is received from communication obtained, shared and based on research by clairvoyant consciousness.

At this point it must be emphasized yet again that all the facts and correlations stemming from clairvoyant knowledge, which are researched and communicated, must be understood with healthy common sense. For when matters that have been located through clairvoyance are present, they can be grasped and understood with the logic naturally embedded in human beings, but only if judgement remains sufficiently free of preconceptions for the duration. It can further be asked: Is there nothing, are there not certain facts in normal human life, certain experiences of this normal human life that from the outset point to the claim by spiritual research that, underlying our physical world and all its manifest phenomena, there is a spiritual world? Now, there are many such specifics in everyday life, of which it can be said that human beings will never comprehend them—though they are obliged to accept them—if they have heard nothing about the existence of a spiritual world.

Today we would like to begin our observations by pointing to two facts relating to mundane, normal human consciousness in everyday life, which must be inexplicable where people do not take the presence of a spiritual world into account. Two specifics, known to us from everyday life, will be used, as they are not generally put under the right spotlight. Were we to do this now and then, the need for a materialistic world outlook would not be necessitated. Let's bring one of the two facts before our souls, as follows, and it will connect with well-known events of normal life.

If someone is faced with a statement or situation they cannot explain using concepts they had hitherto acquired, they will be plunged into bemusement. In fact, taking the concrete example of someone seeing a car or a train for the first time—something no longer the case even in, say, deepest Africa—they will be extremely amazed, their thoughts might go like this: After all I have so far encountered, it seems impossible for something to tear across the Earth without being pulled. And yet I see it and it is not being pulled. That's astounding! What someone doesn't yet know elicits amazement; what they do know no longer causes astonishment. Only things with which no connection can be made with prior experience causes bemusement. Let us keep this everyday example in mind.

Now we can connect this with another fact, which is quite remarkable. In everyday life, humans are faced with all sorts of things with which they are unfamiliar but which they accept without bafflement. There are numerous examples of this. What is happening here? It would certainly be highly astonishing if, for example, someone sitting quietly in the normal run of things in their armchair were to be whisked up the chimney and find themselves flying through the air. That would indeed be bewildering, yet if that happened in a dream, they would be participating without a qualm. We experience even more bizarre things in dreams which fail to baffle us despite being incapable of connection with daily events. In waking life we are indeed surprised if someone jumps inordinately high yet, when dreaming, we can fly and are not shocked. The fact is that in waking life we can be shocked by things as yet unexperienced whilst dreaming causes no such astonishment.

This second fact, towards which we are turning our attention by way of introduction, is a question about conscience. In the course of doing human deeds—and in sensitive individuals this may include thoughts—something stirs in us that we call conscience. Conscience is actually independent of what those outer deeds may signify. We could, for instance, have done something that might have been very useful to us and yet our conscience judges that deed. When conscience stirs, everyone feels that into the judgement of a deed something else flows, an element that has nothing to do with its usefulness. It is like a voice speaking within us: You should have done this, or: You shouldn't have done that. We are confronted with the fact of a conscience and we know how strong this cautionary power of conscience can be, how it can follow us through life. We know also that the presence of a conscience cannot be denied.

Let us return to the fact of dreams, how we do the most extraordinary things there which, were we awake, would cause us the most frightful pangs of conscience. Everyone will be able to confirm from their own experience that they do things in their dreams without the slightest stirring of conscience, things which would make their conscience shout out were they awake. So these two facts— that of astonishment or bewilderment and that of conscience—are, strangely enough, switched off in dreaming. Things such as this generally go unnoticed in normal life and yet they illuminate deep into the substrata of our existence.

In order to shed some light on these aspects I would like to point to another fact, one that relates less to conscience than to astonishment. In Ancient Greece a saying was current that all philosophy stemmed from wonder, from awe. The feeling contained in this sentence—and by this I mean the feeling those Ancient Greeks felt about it—is not to be found further back in Greek evolution and only appears from a certain point onwards in the history of philosophy. This is because those in greater antiquity did not yet feel in the same way. Where does the idea come from—precisely in Ancient Greece from a certain time onwards—to state that we are amazed?

Well, we have just seen that we are astonished by things that do not fit into what we have hitherto known. If we are bemused by the surprises in everyday life, this contains nothing special, nothing much more than an amazement at something 'extra-ordinary'. Those surprised by cars or trains are merely in awe of something not yet witnessed and their amazement is no more than wonder at something extra-ordinary. Far more astonishing than surprise at seeing cars or trains or the wonder at what is non-usual is the fact that human beings can also start to wonder at what is usual.

For example, to be astounded by the fact that the Sun rises each morning. People with everyday consciousness accustomed to this fact are not amazed by such phenomena. But when amazement is elicited over the everyday occurrences one is accustomed to seeing, this is the genesis of philosophy and knowledge. Those richer in knowledge are the ones who can experience awe and wonder at the ordinary things conventional people take for granted. Only at this stage does one become a person striving after knowledge, and it is for this reason that the Ancient Greeks coined the phrase: Philosophy begins in wonder (*thaumazein*).[20]

How do things stand with conscience? Again, it is interesting that the word *conscience*—obviously the concept, because the word only crops up once a concept has arisen—can be found in Ancient Greece, but only after a certain point in time. There is no likelihood that you will find a word that could be translated as conscience in even older literature from roughly around the time of Aeschylus. By contrast, one such word is present in the literature of the younger Greek playwrights and poets, such as Euripides.[21] With this one can almost pinpoint that—just as with wonder at what is familiar—conscience is also something of which human beings were only aware from a certain point in Ancient Greece onwards. From that point onwards, what became the stirrings of conscience was, for the Greeks of ancient times, something quite different.

In times of more remote antiquity pangs of conscience were unknown to those doing something wrong. Then, people had a primal, elementary clairvoyance and were we to go back to shortly before the Christian era we would find that everyone still had this primal clairvoyance. If a person did something wrong, they would not suffer pangs of conscience. Instead, their primal vision would see a demonic figure, which would torment them, and such figures they called Erinyes or Furies. Only once humans had lost their faculty of primal vision to see these Furies did they gain the capacity, when doing wrong, to feel conscience as an inner experience.

We should ask ourselves what such facts show us and what is actually going on with everyday givens such as wonder; for instance, were an individual from a remote indigenous setting to experience being transposed into a city full of speeding cars and trains. Their initial astonishment assumes that something enters their life that was not previously present or which they had previously pictured differently.

If more widely experienced people feel the urge to clarify many things for themselves, to delve into everyday phenomena because they are able to feel wonder, this also assumes that they previously saw things differently. Nobody would come to a different conclusion about a sunrise from one based on visual appearances—of the Sun rising—did their soul not contain a sense that they had previously viewed it differently. Some might contend that we have been seeing sunrises since earliest childhood, so is it not idiotic when we educe wonder at it?

There is no other explanation for this than to say: If we nevertheless feel wonder at a sunrise, we have experienced it differently, in conditions other than today's, in this life. For if spiritual science tells us that—between birth and a previous life—we existed in a different state, we have, in the fact of wonder at such an everyday occurrence as the usualness of a sunrise, nothing other than an indication of that previous condition in which we perceived a sunrise, although in that state it was without physical sense organs. We perceived all this with spiritual eyes and with spiritual ears.[22] At that moment people felt dimly: You are standing in the light of the rising Sun, by the roaring sea, by burgeoning plants and you are astounded! At this very moment, within the wonder, lies the knowledge that you once perceived this differently than you do with physical eyes. It was with spiritual organs that we perceived this, before we descended into the physical world. Dimly we feel that it looked different when we saw it before. This was—and can only be—before birth.

A fact such as this requires us to recognize that knowledge would not be at all possible had human beings not stepped down from a previous supra-sensory existence into this life. There would otherwise be no explanation for wonder and the knowledge contingent upon it. Of course, people do not remember in clear concepts what

they experienced differently in their prebirth life but even if this is
not clear in thought it nevertheless arises in feeling. Only through
initiation can it be brought with one in the form of a clear memory.

Let us go into the fact that we are not amazed in dreams. The first
question to answer is: What exactly is a dream? A dream is an ancient
fragment inherited from previous incarnations, from a time when
human beings in earlier lives experienced different states of consciousness of a clairvoyant nature. In the further course of evolution, however, this ability to look into soul-spiritual worlds was lost.

It was a twilight clairvoyance and its evolution began earlier with
a dim vision that led gradually to the clear waking consciousness of
today. This in turn could develop in the physical world to the point
that—once fully unfolded—it could again ascend into soul-spiritual
realms, but now with capacities which the I could gain through wakeful consciousness. What had human beings won long ago through
ancient clairvoyance? Something of that gain persists as dreams. A
dream is distinguishable from archaic clairvoyance in that it is experienced by a modern person, one who has developed a consciousness
containing the drive towards knowledge. Dreams, being remnants of
an earlier clairvoyance, do not contain this urge for knowledge and
it is for this reason that people experience the difference between
wakeful consciousness and dream consciousness.

However, what was not contained in the old dim clairvoyance—
wonder, awe—can similarly not enter dream consciousness nowadays. Wonder and amazement cannot find entry into dreams, yet
they are present in waking consciousness when we turn towards the
external world. When dreaming, humans are not in the outer world;
dreaming is a translocation into the spiritual world, where things of
the outer world do not pertain and are not experienced. It is precisely
in their connection with the outer world that human beings have
learnt wonderment. While dreaming, they just accept everything that
approaches them, as they did when they still had their dim clairvoyance. In those days they could simply accept everything because
spiritual figures would come and show them what they had done in
terms of good or evil. For this reason humans had no need of wonder. In this way dreams show us—purely through being constituted

as they are—that they are an inherited remnant of ancient times, times when there was no amazement at commonplace things and conscience did not as yet exist.

We are now at the point when we ask ourselves why it was necessary for humans, who were at that time clairvoyant, not to remain so. For what reason did humans descend? Did the Gods senselessly banish them down here? Actually, it is the case that human beings would never have achieved what is inherent in wonder, nor what is inherent in conscience, had they not descended as described. This descent was in order to gain knowledge and conscience, because they can only be acquired by being separated from spirit worlds for a while. Human beings have been acquiring knowledge and conscience down here to enable them to re-ascend, but now together with them.

Spiritual science shows us how, between death and a new birth, human beings spend a certain timespan in a purely spiritual world. Immediately after death we undergo a time of Kamaloka, the condition in which we tarry in a soul region for the cleansing of cravings, in a place, as it were, half in the spiritual world where human beings look back upon their instincts and sympathies, still attracted through them to what bound them to the physical world. Only when this time of Kamaloka has been expunged can they experience a purely spiritual life or Devachan.

What does the human being experience when they step into this purely spiritual world? How does each person experience this? Even normal, everyday intellectual consideration shows that the regions between death and another birth must look quite different from our physical environs here. Here we see colours because we have eyes; we hear sounds because we have ears. But when—in the life beyond death, in spiritual existence—we have no eyes and ears, we can no longer perceive these colours and sounds. Even down here we see and hear less well or not at all if we do not possess good eyes and ears. To anyone who thinks about this a little that will be obvious. Evidently, we need to imagine the spiritual world differently from this world in which we live between birth and death. How the world has to change when we step through the gate of death can be imagined if we make a small comparison.

Let us imagine that someone sees a lamb and a wolf.[23] That person can perceive the lamb and the wolf with all the organs of perception available to them in physical life. They see the lamb as a material lamb and the wolf as a material wolf. They can also recognize other lambs and wolves and call them respectively lambs and wolves. They have a conceptual image both of lamb and wolf. One could say— and indeed one does say—that this conceptual image of animals is not visible, it exists within the animal; one does not materially see the nature of lamb nor wolf. One forms concepts of the being of lamb and wolf, yet the being of the animal is invisible.

There are theoreticians of the view that the concepts we form of wolf and lamb only exist within ourselves and have nothing to do with wolves or lambs per se. Anyone who maintains this should be required to feed a wolf with lambs for as long as it takes until it has been scientifically proven that the wolf, in every particle of its body, now consists entirely of lamb substance. Then they would see whether a wolf has been transformed into a lamb! If it should transpire that the wolf has not become a lamb, then it will have been proved that the concept 'wolf' can be distinguished from a material wolf and that the conceptual wolf transcends its material counterpart.

This invisible element, only created as a concept in normal life, is visible after death. Neither the white colour of the lamb nor the sound it emits are audible there, but what is perceptible is the invisible principle governing the lamb, which is just as real and is present for those living in the spiritual world. Coexisting within the same space occupied by the lamb is a genuine spirit element, which is visible after death. It is the same with all phenomena of the physical environment. The Sun is seen differently, the Moon differently, everything is seen differently. We bring something of this with us when we enter a new existence at birth. When we are seized by the experience that we have seen this quite differently before, then— amid the wonder and amazement—knowledge descends.

It is something different when one observes the actions of a person. Conscience is then added. If we want to know what that is we need to turn our attention to a fact that is verifiable even without having developed clairvoyance. We need to focus on the moment of falling asleep. One can learn to do this without any exceptional vision and anyone can experience it for themselves. When you are just on the point of falling asleep, things lose their sharp contours, colours fade, sounds not only become fainter but it is as if they recede, moving far off. As if from great distances do they seem to sound, growing ever fainter, receding and appearing as if a mist were being drawn across them. Limbs become heavier, they feel unlike their condition when awake; they seem to have a weight of their own.

Were one to take account of this during waking hours, one ought really to sense that, when walking or lifting one's hand, they are weightless. Why does my hand seem weightless? Because it belongs to my body. Now imagine that you were carrying a hundredweight in each hand. Why do we feel this as a heavy weight? My hand belongs to me so that I do not feel its weight. But the hundredweights are external to me and, because they are not part of me, I feel their weight.

Imagine a Martian landing on Earth without prior knowledge of conditions here and the first thing they would see was a person holding a weight in each hand. That Martian would initially be of the view that the weights were an integral part of the human hand and overall form. If they later had to accept the concept that humans distinguish between weight and hand, they would be astounded. It really is the case that we only experience as heavy what is external to us. When people falling asleep experience their limbs as heavy, it is a sign that the person is leaving their body, is exiting their corporeal body.

We now take into account a delicate observation relating to the moment when feeling the heaviness of falling asleep. It consists of a strange feeling that speaks to us: You did this, you neglected to do that. The deeds of the past day flow past like a living conscience. And where they contain something we cannot endorse, then we toss and turn in our beds and cannot fall asleep. If, on the other hand, we can be content with what we have done, a blessed moment occurs when falling asleep, causing us to say to ourselves: Oh, would that this moment could continue for ever! Then follows a jolt and this is the moment we step out of our physical and etheric bodies and are in the spiritual world.

Let's focus on the moment when we experience a living conscience arising. Not having the strength to do anything sensible, a person tosses and turns in their bed. This unhealthy state prevents them from falling asleep. This happens at the very moment when they are about to leave the physical plane behind to enter another world which, however, does not want to receive what we call a bad conscience. We cannot fall asleep because the world into which we ought to enter during sleep rejects us. This is why the exhortation to do deeds in harmony with your conscience is nothing less than having a premonition of the sort of human being we ought to be in future: a person capable of entering the spiritual world.

If in wonder we encounter an expression of something we have seen earlier, so conscience is a manifestation of our future ability to see in the spiritual world. Conscience is an indicator as to whether we will shrink in horror or whether we will feel blessed when we are eventually able to evaluate our deeds in Devachan. Conscience is a prophetic preview of the way in which we will view our deeds after death.

Amazement and the desire for knowledge on the one hand and conscience on the other are living signs of the spiritual world. These phenomena cannot be explained unless the spiritual world is included in the explanation. The person who can experience world realities in reverence will be more inclined to become an anthroposophist showing reverence and awe in face of world phenomena. It is precisely the more developed souls who will be able to experience ever greater wonder. The less one is able to wonder, the less advanced is the soul in question. It is the case that people express far less wonder at daylight events—towards the everyday phenomena of life—than, for instance, in face of the wondrous starry firmament in all its majesty.

Yet higher soul development actually only begins when one is able to wonder as much at the smallest flower, the tiniest leaf, the most unassuming beetle or worm as the mightiest cosmic processes. It is basically quite strange. People are generally keen to ask for explanations of the things that move them sensationally. People living near volcanoes, for instance, will ask about the causes of volcanic eruptions because they need to pay more attention to such facts than to other everyday events. Even people living far from any volcano seek information because this is both exciting and sensational for them. But when someone has a soul configured such that they enter life being amazed at everything because they sense that their entire surroundings contain a spiritual element, they are no more astounded by a volcano than by the minute bubbles and craters in their milk or their breakfast coffee. They are equally amazed by what is small as by what is large.

Approaching everything with wonder is a memory of how we could see before we were born. By approaching all our deeds with our conscience means having the vivid anticipation that every deed we do will appear to us in a different guise in future. People who feel this are predestined—to a greater extent than others—to be drawn to spiritual science.

We live at a time when certain things emerge that can only be explained by spiritual science—things which defy other explanation. People behave very differently when confronted with such things. Nowadays we can doubtlessly observe all sorts of human characteristics, yet within the most varied of character nuances, two main types of nature stand out.

One of these natures can be seen as pensive, tending towards reflection, able to feel astonishment at everything and who always feels the stirring of their conscience. All sorts of distress, of gloomy, melancholic moods can settle in such souls under the aegis of an unsatisfied longing for explanation. A sensitive conscience can make life more difficult.

Another sort of person is also prevalent today, however. They do not long for any such clarification of the world. For them every explanation of the world based on spiritual research is frightfully boring. They prefer to launch into things robustly rather than seek explanations and, if one starts to give an account of anything, they will start yawning. It is certainly true that conscience stirs far less in people constituted in this way than it does for those others described earlier. Why is it that such opposites in character manifest? Spiritual science is motivated to explore the causes as to why some can be distinguished by their contemplative nature and their thirst for knowledge while others set out only to enjoy life without seeking for elucidation.

If one investigates the scope of the human soul through spiritual science—and I can only give isolated indications here, as it would take many hours to explore this thoroughly—one finds that many of those endowed with a thoughtful nature, who cannot live without making sense of life, had direct soul knowledge in previous lives of the reality of reincarnation. Today there are countless people on Earth who know about this and for whom reincarnation is an absolute fact. Just think of Asia and all those people who connect—if not necessarily directly—a contemplation of their present life to another, previous existence when they knew about reincarnation.

However, the other, more robust human natures hail from lives when nothing was known about earlier lives on Earth. They feel no urge to burden themselves with a conscience in relation to their deeds nor to bother much about the reasons behind anything. Many people in the western world are constituted in this way and it is simply a characteristic of western culture that people have, as it were, forgotten their previous lives. Yes, they have forgotten them; but we are now at a turning point where memory of past lives will again be revived. This is why people living today face a future which can be outlined as one in which a connection with the spiritual world will be reinstated.

Today this only applies to a few people, but during the course of the twentieth century it will be a widespread feature among populations. It will be like this: let's imagine that someone has done this or that and afterwards their conscience is plaguing them. It is like that now. Later, however, once a spiritual connection has been restored, human beings will feel compelled—after having done something or other—to retreat slightly from their deed as if with eyes bound shut. A picture similar to a dream image—but quite a vivid dream picture—will arise of the necessary future consequences of their deed. And, when they experience this, will think something like this: Yes, though *I* am the one experiencing this, I have not yet experienced what I am now seeing.

For all those who have heard nothing of spiritual science this will be something terrible. On the other hand, those who have prepared themselves for what will face all future humanity will say to themselves:

Though I have not yet undergone it, in future I will nevertheless know it to be the karmic adjustment for what I have just done.

Today we stand as if in the forecourt of times in which karmic compensation will appear prophetically to people, as if in a dream image. Now imagine this experience becoming ever stronger and more compelling over the course of time and you will see the humanity of the future who will be able to see how their deeds are karmically rebalanced.

By what means will it come about that human beings become capable of seeing this karmic compensation? This is connected with the fact that the human beings of old had no conscience but instead, following wrongdoing, they were plagued by the Furies. That was ancient clairvoyance and it has passed. Then there followed a time when the Furies could not be seen: the Middle Ages when what the Furies used to exact arose inwardly as conscience.

Now we are gradually approaching times when we will again perceive karmic recompense. Having won a conscience, humans will henceforth be enabled to gaze into spiritual worlds. If certain people of an inward nature presently become aware that they had in former lives gained forces which manifest—through wonder—as a memory of those former lives, people of today will also take with them into future incarnations such forces if they today acquire knowledge of spiritual worlds. But those who have baulked at absorbing an elaboration of the laws of reincarnation will, by contrast, have an awful time of it in the future world. For such souls, this will be a terrible fact.

Today we live in an age where people just about manage to get by in life, even if they have no concept of life as regards spiritual worlds. But this age—condoned, as it were, by cosmic forces—ends such that people who have no connection with the spiritual world will in their next lives grow up not understanding the world into which they are born. And when they leave what has become an incomprehensible physical existence at death, they will continue to have no understanding for the spiritual world in which they are to mature. Obviously, they will enter the spiritual world but they will not be able to grasp it. They will find themselves in a bewildering environment that makes them feel as though they do not belong in it and which plagues them as only a bad conscience can. When they enter their subsequent incarnation, it will be just as dreadful; they will suffer all manner of urges and passions and will appear to be living in illusions and hallucinations because they can evince no wonder or amazement. Today's materialists face a future in which they will be horribly beset by torturous illusions and hallucinations; because what that person thinks in this life will later be experienced as delusions and hallucinations.

We can imagine this most intensely. By way of example, let us take two people walking along the road together. One is a material-ist, the other a non-materialist. The latter says something about the spiritual world. The other says or thinks: Oh, that's all nonsense! It's just a load of illusions! Indeed, for this person it *is* illusion, but for the one mentioning the spiritual world it is not illusory. After death, the consequences for the materialist will set in, let alone when they reincarnate. Then it will be the case that they experience spiritual worlds as an excruciating reproach. During their time in Kamaloka between death and rebirth, they will experience no dif-ference between Kamaloka and Devachan. Once reborn and faced with a spiritual world, as described, it will seem unreal, illusory and hallucinatory.

Spiritual science is not merely something with which to satisfy our curiosity. We are not gathered here because we are simply more curi-ous than others about the spiritual world. We are here because—to a greater or lesser degree—we sense that the people of tomorrow will not be able to live without spiritual science. All other aspirations that fail to take this into account are heading towards decadence. Now, matters are such that those who today resist being open to spiritual science will in future have the opportunity to approach it during their future embodiments. However, there need to be out-posts. People who today, through their karma, have a longing for spiritual science thus have the opportunity to be such outposts. This opportunity comes towards them because they are forerunners and need to be outposts. Other human beings will see the longing for spiritual science emerging among humanity as a whole as part of universal human karma.

LECTURE 5

MUNICH, 25 FEBRUARY 1912

Reflecting Levels of Consciousness

TODAY and the day after tomorrow it will be my task to discuss some of the more important aspects of consciousness and karmic connections.

Essentially, I would like to follow on from the topics of yesterday's public lecture.[24] Our situation is such that, in public lectures for a wider audience, certain matters have to be presented differently from the way in which it is possible to consider them in branch meetings because branch members, having worked together and concerned themselves over longer periods with such material, have been prepared to receive and understand things in a way that cannot apply to larger public settings. We saw yesterday[25] that we could speak about hidden aspects of human soul life and we need to contrast these unseen soul aspects with the specifics of normal, everyday consciousness.

If you cast a superficial glance at the concepts, moods, impulses of will in addition to all the perceptions with which we are faced from the external world from waking in the morning to falling asleep at night, you have a collection of what can be called the sum of everyday consciousness. Everything contained in our conscious daily life, all this depends on the instrument of a physical body. You find the most immediate and obvious proof of what has just been said in the fact that human beings have to wake up in order to participate in the actualities of normal conscious life. For us this means that they have to dive down into their bodies with the elements that remained outside their physical bodies during sleep. Their physical bodies, as tools or instruments, need to be at their disposal for the facts of daily living to take place. The question immediately arises: How does a human being—as a spiritual entity—make use of the physical instrument of their body, of their senses and their nervous system in order to live their daily life?

In the material world the belief persists that human beings experience the reality of their consciousness as a product of their physical instrument. I have often drawn attention to the fact that this is not so and that we should not imagine that, say, our brain or sense organs might produce our state of consciousness, just as little as a candle would produce a flame. It is the case that the relationship to our physical instrument of what we call consciousness is quite different. We can compare it to the relationship between a person who sees themselves in a mirror and that mirror itself. When we are asleep we live in our consciousness as if we were to go straight into a room. If we go straight into a room we do not see ourselves; we do not see what our noses or our foreheads look like. Only at the moment when someone steps forwards holding a mirror do we see ourselves. Then what had existed throughout approaches us; it is then visible to us. It is similar with the realities of our everyday consciousness: they exist continuously within us. Of themselves, they have as little to do with our physical bodies as our individualities have to do with a mirror.

Materialistic theories in this field are nothing but nonsense. They are not even a plausible hypothesis; because what the materialist asserts can only be compared with the claim that, because people can see themselves in a mirror, it is the mirror that produces them. If you want to submit to the illusion that the mirror produces you because you only see yourself when a mirror is held up to you, then you are also capable of believing that parts of your brain or your sense organs can bring forth the contents of your soul life. Both would be equally 'spiritually rich' and equally 'true'. Claiming that mirrors produce people is just as true as stating that brains create thoughts. The realities of consciousness exist. We only need our organism to be able to perceive those realities of consciousness. For this we need our physical body, which we see mirroring factual consciousness. Thus we have in our physical body something which we can call a mechanism for mirroring or reflecting the occurrences of our daily consciousness.

This is how the facts of our normal consciousness live in our soul-spiritual being. We perceive them in that what exists in us—which our souls, however, cannot perceive, just as we cannot see ourselves until a mirror is placed in front of us—has the mirror of physicality placed in front of it. That is the factual state of affairs. Only in our bodies we do not have a passive instrument of reflection but something in which processes take place. You can therefore imagine that, instead of the mirror being coated so as to produce a reflected image, all sorts of processes have to go on behind it.

This comparison is sufficiently extensive to really characterize the relationship of our soul-spiritual being to our physical bodies. We would like to posit that, for everything we experience in everyday consciousness, the physical body is the corresponding reflective device. Behind—or, if you like, below—these events of normal consciousness are also those components which well up into normal soul life and which we know to be realities living in the hidden depths of our souls.

Poets and artists experience something of this—if they are a true poet or artist—when they are aware that they are not inspired by logical considerations nor by what they perceive in the normal course of events but by what emerges from unknown depths and does really exist, without having been constructed by the forces of normal consciousness. Yet other elements emerge from the veiled depths of our soul life. Here we have influences which, without us normally being aware of their origins, play into our daily consciousness.

We saw yesterday that we can delve much deeper, into the realm of semi-consciousness, the realm of dreams, and we know that dreams rise upwards from the hidden recesses of soul life and that we cannot simply or conventionally dredge them up through the exertions of our consciousness. When a dream picture, long buried in memory, emerges in the soul—as so often happens—it is the case that by far the majority of people would never, through sheer contemplation, be in a position to retrieve such pictures from the subterranean repositories of their souls because their normal consciousness does not reach deep enough.

However, what lies beyond the reach of normal consciousness is readily accessible to the subconscious. In that semi-conscious state of dreaming, what has been relegated to storage in oblivion can be hauled up; it is dislodged and it breaks out. Only such things surface as have not found expression, have not had their effect in the usual way that forgotten, submerged things of the soul's depths find their outlet in experience. We become healthy or sickly, ill-humoured or cheerful, not due to factors that usually affect the course of our lives, but as a physical state which—as a result of our life experience having been suppressed and no longer remembered—works on in our soul, shaping the person we become in life.

Many lives would be quite explicable if we knew what had become submerged over the course of that life. We would understand individuals much better in their thirties, forties or fifties if we could trace their lives back to childhood. We would then know why they were in a particular state, why they felt so deeply dissatisfied with this or that relationship without being able to say what has caused their distress. Were we able to do this, we would arrive at a view as to why parents and other individuals in the child's surroundings had affected that child; what joy and sorrow, what enthusiasm or pain had been caused—all of which may have been completely forgotten but which has had its effects on the entire disposition of that person. Because what has rolled downwards out of our consciousness works on, causing waves in the buried depths of the soul.

The strange thing is that what is continuing to work affects us ourselves first and foremost, remaining within the sphere of our personalities. When clairvoyant consciousness descends to those levels—and this is achieved through Imagination, through what we call imaginative knowledge—where the subconscious elements mentioned hold sway, it is here that the human individuality finds itself. It finds in itself what lives and undulates. And that is good because human beings need to find themselves, must get to know themselves in true self-knowledge, must really look at all the instinctive forces working within them and truly recognize them.

If human beings press onward with clairvoyant consciousness into their subconscious, having practised exercises in imaginative knowledge yet without being mindful that they will initially encounter only themselves—complete with everything that they are and they contain—they will be subject to the widest array of errors. This is because—in parallel with normal modes of consciousness—one is not in the slightest aware that one is only dealing with oneself.

At a certain point it can happen that one has visions or, let's say, sees figures, which are completely new in the context of what one has hitherto garnered through life experience. That can happen. Were one to imagine, however, that these must already be manifestations of higher worlds, one would be in the grip of serious delusion. Such things do not manifest in the same way as aspects of inner life appear to normal perception.

If you have a headache, this is a fact of ordinary consciousness. You know that the pain is located in your own head. If you have a stomach ache, you perceive this to be in yourself. If you descend into those depths we called the hidden recesses of soul, you can only be within yourself, and yet you can construe what confronts you there as if it were external to yourself.

As an example, let's take a striking case of someone who had the dearest wish to be the reincarnation of Mary Magdalen. I once related that I had encountered twenty-four Mary Magdalen cases in my lifetime.[26]

Let's assume that someone admits to no such wish; we don't need to admit our wishes to ourselves with our upper consciousness—that is not necessary. So, someone reads the story of Mary Magdalen in the Bible and is extremely taken with it. Simultaneously, in their subconscious, the desire can grow to be Mary Magdalen. In their upper consciousness they have nothing more than an admiration of this figure. In their subconscious, such that they know nothing of it, a certain greedy ambition to be this figure is engendered. This person now makes their way through the world. For as long as nothing else crops up, their daily consciousness—in other words, what they are aware of—simply approves of Mary Magdalen. Their subconscious, however, harbours a burning desire to actually be Mary Magdalen, though they are unaware of this. They are therefore unembarrassed by it. They proceed in accordance with the paradigm of their normal consciousness; they can go about the world without their upper consciousness being troubled by any desire to be Mary Magdalen.

But let's imagine that, by applying some occult means or other, such a person is able to access their subconscious. They descend into their subconscious. They do not need to notice the fact that 'in me is a voracious wish to be Mary Magdalen' in the same way as one would notice a headache. Were they to notice this mania to be Mary Magdalen, they would have a chance to be sensible. They would behave in relation to this desire in the same way as they would towards a headache: they would try to get rid of it. But when such an abnormal intrusion happens, it does not proceed like that but instead situates the lust outside the personality as an external fact, as a vision: You are Mary Magdalen. It confronts the person; it projects itself as fact.

A person of today—as presently constituted in terms of their development—is then not in a condition capable of controlling such a fact with their I, with their ego. Under conditions of good, proper and absolutely meticulous schooling, this cannot happen because our I accompanies us into every sphere. However, as soon as something happens without our I accompanying us, it will appear to us as an objective, external verity. Observers then believe themselves to remember back to the events in and around Mary Magdalen and feel themselves to be identical with that Mary Magdalen. This is quite possible.

I emphasize this risk today because from it you should see that it is only through careful training—the care with which you find your way into occult matters—that can save you from falling victim to such errors, if you know this: that you must first see an entire world in front of you, you must perceive facts, verities, but not as something that you apply to yourself, not as something which is within you, yet which appears as a world tableau. If you know that, you will do well to regard what you first see as a projection of your own inner life. Then you will have a robust means of counteracting the errors along this path. That is the very best course: initially to regard everything as facts or events arising out of yourself. These usually stem from our desires, vanities, ambitions, in short from those qualities connected with our own egotism.

These things are primarily projected outwards and you may ask: How can we avoid such errors of illusion? How can we protect ourselves from them? In the normal state of consciousness you will not avoid them. Error comes about precisely when you place such a world tableau in front of yourself in reality but cannot extricate yourself *from yourself*; you remain enmeshed within yourself. From this you will gather that it actually depends on us somehow getting out of ourselves, somehow learning to distinguish: here is one vision and here is a different vision, both of them external to us. One vision may only be the projection of a desire, the other a factual reality. Yet these visions are not as different from each other as—in normal life—someone else saying they have a headache and you yourself having one. One's own interior is equally projected into space as is someone else's. How can we become capable of differentiating?

Within the occult field we must learn to differentiate; we need to distinguish true impressions from false ones, even though they all intermingle and all arise claiming a similar right to authenticity. It is as if we were to look out into physical nature and, among real trees, see imaginary trees, between which we could not differentiate. As if, cheek by jowl with real and phantasmal trees, there were real factual realities which were external to us and only arose in our inner life. How can we learn to discriminate between these two realms, which are interleaved with each other?

One does not initially learn to discriminate through consciousness. If you remain only within the sphere of your imagination, you actually have no means of distinguishing, whereas any potential for discernment lies solely in the slow occult education of your soul. As we progress ever further, we do eventually learn to discriminate, and this means doing in the inner, occult realm what we ought to have been capable of doing when those real and fantasy trees appeared side by side in front of us. We can pass through the fantasy trees but we collide with the real trees.

Something similar—but now obviously among spiritual facts— also has to come towards us in spiritual fields. If one proceeds correctly, it is relatively easy to discern the true from the false in this realm: not through concepts but by a resolve of will. A willed resolve of this kind can come about in the following manner: when we review our lives, we find two clearly delineated and distinguishable groups of phenomena. We often find that some event is either successful or unsuccessful and that we regularly link this with our own competence. Because we may not be very clever in a particular area, we can equally understand why things do not succeed there. On the other hand, where we can ascribe certain abilities to ourselves, we understand why outcomes are successful.

Maybe we do not always need to make so explicit the correlation between our capabilities and what is carried out through our agency. There is a less clear-cut way of understanding this link. For instance, when someone in later life is affected by a stroke of destiny, they may think back and say to themselves: I was someone who did not sufficiently bestir myself, or: I have always been a reckless chap. On the other hand, they may be able to reflect: It is not immediately clear to me how my downfall is connected with what I did, but it does occur to me that a reckless, lazy person cannot succeed in the same way as one who is conscientious and hardworking. In short, we understand that there are instances when success or failure is the result it turns out to be, while others fail to see any connection, reflecting: Despite having this quality or that ability, which should have ensured success, it simply failed.

There is, however, another sort of success or failure, in which we are at first unable to see how it is associated with our capacities. That is one thing. The other is that, in the face of what we otherwise consider to be blows of destiny in the objective outer world, we can ponder: Yes, it actually seems fair because we provided all the preconditions for this to happen. Yet other things happen which may cause us to think that they just happen without us being able to find their cause. So we have two types of experience: those that stem from us and are connected with the capabilities we know we possess and the other sort just characterized. And again: events for which we cannot admit to having provided the preconditions as opposed to those to which we know that we have contributed.

Let us review our lives a little. There is an experiment, useful to everyone, consisting of the following. We can all muster events in our lives whose causes we cannot fathom, successes on which we must conclude that 'the blind chicken just found the grain' in cases that ascribe no credit to ourselves. We also summarize remembered instances of failure in the same terms. Then we can focus on external events which have struck us as coincidental and for which we know of no motivation nor cause.

Now let's try the following experiment: we'll construct a somewhat artificial human made up precisely of those qualities which, unbeknown to us, contributed to our successes. If something has succeeded due to the essential wisdom we were too foolish to provide at the time, we construct for ourselves someone who is particularly wise in that area and for whom the undertaking ought to have succeeded. Or for an external event we do this: let's say a tile falls onto our head. Initially we cannot fathom what caused this but we imagine a person who has provoked this tile-onto-head event: they run up onto the roof and partially pull loose a tile such that they only need to wait a short while before it falls down; then they run downstairs and the tile hits them. This is what we do with certain events, towards which we know perfectly well—in terms of our normal consciousness—that we have not ourselves contributed, events which in fact strongly counter our will.

Say that someone hit us during our life. To soften this, we'll place it in our childhood. Imagine we had somehow engaged someone to beat us; we did everything to provoke this beating. We are constructing someone who takes upon themselves something, the context of which we cannot grasp. You see, if you wish to progress in occult matters you have to accept certain things that contradict everyday facts. If you confine yourself to doing only what seems sensible in mundane terms, you will not make headway in occultism because what pertains in higher worlds can at first seem irrational to the everyday mentality. So there is no harm if even the methods seem irrational to hard-headed prosaics. Hence we are building up this imaginary person. It may seem grotesque to be constructing such an entity while still unaware of its purpose, but anyone trying this will make an extraordinary discovery, namely that they do not want to rid themselves of the being they have so carefully fashioned, that it starts to interest them. If you try this out you will see that you cannot rid yourself of this synthetic being; it just lives in you.

Strangely, it not only lives in you but it metamorphoses within you, so strongly in fact that it becomes something it was not previously. It becomes something we can only call a fixture in us; anyone can try this out for themselves. From what has been described, from the being that is no longer the fantasy-built entity it was at the outset, it can be said that it is something existing within us. It is a product of the seemingly causeless events in our life. Thus you find in yourself an entity called into being by the otherwise inexplicable. In other words, what I have described is a path by which you can avoid gawping [sic] into your own soul's life in search of phenomena but which is, instead, a way out of your soul life and into the surroundings. Because the things in which we do not succeed do not remain with us but belong to our surroundings. In this way we have extracted from the environment something which does not correspond with our factual consciousness but yet presents itself as if it were within us. You then have the feeling that you do in fact have some connection with whatever appears so inexplicable in your life.

In this way you can gain a sense of your connection with your destiny, with what we call karma. This soul-experiment provides a genuine path for you to experience some degree of your karma in a more concrete manner.

You might object: I don't rightly understand what you are saying. But if you say that, you are not understanding what you believe you don't understand—yet which is childishly easy to understand. It is merely something about which you do not think. It is impossible for someone who hasn't tried this experiment to understand it, and only those who have actually carried it out will understand it. This description is no more than something anyone can attempt and experience. Everyone can arrive at the understanding that something exists in their inner life that is related to their karma. If they knew this from the outset, they would not need to be given guidance by which to find it; as a rule, it is entirely to be expected that someone who has not tried this will not grasp it. It is not a matter of understanding a report of something your souls can undertake. If your soul undertakes this route, it not only becomes accustomed to living inwardly—in its desires and appetites—but to relate outer occurrences to itself, to really focus on outer events. It is to this that our souls become habituated.

Precisely those things we have not ourselves wished for are the very things we have constructed into the true meaning of the matter in hand. And if we can arrive at a point where we relate to our destiny by accepting it with composure and not railing against it in the usual outraged way, we may think: We accept it gladly because we have imposed it on ourselves. Then a frame of mind may ensue which—in any given situation and by entering into those hidden depths of soul—is able to distinguish truth from falsehood, which can with wonderful clarity and absolute certainty differentiate between what is true and what is false.

When looking at some visions with spiritual eyes, while putting aside all the forces perceptible to one's innermost being—having come to know them and then, as it were, putting them aside, conjuring them away and using only that inner gaze—they turn out to be mere phantasm. If, however, one cannot put all this aside as described and can only get rid of what reminds one of the outer world—that is the visionary part—and the spiritual element remains as a firm fact, then it is true. This distinction cannot be made before having carried out what was described. There can be no certainty in distinguishing truth from falsehood at the spiritual level if the training described has not been carried out.

The essential element of this soul experiment is this: with our normal consciousness we are always accompanied by what we desire. Through this soul experiment we become accustomed to seeing what our normal consciousness does not in the least want—something it would normally avoid—as something we have ourselves willed. In this sense, you can have attained a significant level in inner development; but if you have not—via this experiment and through your connection with all that you have *not* willed—taken a stand against the desires, the longings, the sympathies and antipathies inherent in your souls, you will make mistake after mistake.

The biggest mistake in the present Theosophical Society has been made by H.P. Blavatsky,[27] by directing her spiritual gaze towards the realm where Christ is to be found. But because in her desires, passions and, in short, in everything existing in her upper consciousness, she also harboured an antipathy for—and an enduring and even passionate rejection of—everything Christian and Hebrew, she would show her preference for every spiritual culture spanning the Earth: that is, every culture except Christian and Hebraic. And because she never undertook what has been described today, a totally false concept of Christ appeared to her, something naturally to be expected.

This notion was transmitted from her to her closer pupils and continues to be touted around today, just coarsened into a grotesque form. These matters reach into the highest realms. One can see many things on an occult level but the ability to discern is something quite different from mere vision, from mere perception. This needs to be starkly emphasized.

Now the question is this: Basically, when we dive into the hidden depths of our souls—and every seer has to do this—we are initially submerged in ourselves. Through this we need to become acquainted with ourselves so that we can really make the transition into the domain spread out before us, in which Lucifer and Ahriman constantly promise to grant us all the riches of the world. This means that our inner being is arrayed before us and the devil states: This is the objective world. Such precisely is the temptation, which even Christ himself could not avoid. The illusions of our own inner being are laid out. Yet Christ's energy was so strong that he instantly recognized that this was no real world but that it existed within.

It is only through this inner realm—in which we must discern two elements, one of which we can banish, that is: all that constitutes our own inner world, whilst the other remains—that we navigate through our soul's internal life and out into the objective supra-sensible world itself. Just as our spiritual core—to outer perception, in terms of the facts of normal consciousness—has to make use of the reflective capacity of our physical bodies, by the same token—in respect of their soul-spiritual core and of the spiritual, supersensible facts initially confronting them—must human beings use their ether bodies as a mirror, as a reflective mechanism.

Those higher sense organs, if we may call them that, arise in the astral body; but what inhabits the astral has to be reflected in the ether body, just as the soul-spiritual element of which we are aware in our everyday lives is mirrored by our physical bodies. Now we need to learn to handle our ether bodies. This is quite natural, because though we are not usually aware of our ether bodies, it represents what enlivens us. So we must first get to know our ether body ourselves before we learn to recognize what comes towards us out of supra-sensible worlds and which can be reflected *in* this ether body.

What we experience by delving into the unseen depths of our souls—where we primarily encounter ourselves and the projection of our desires—is very similar to the state of being generally called Kamaloka. It is only distinguishable from actual Kamaloka by the fact that whilst one proceeds in normal life to a state of being locked within oneself—we have to call it that—our physical bodies are still present and we can always return to them, whereas in Kamaloka our bodies have departed together with even that portion of our ether bodies capable of reflecting us.

Now it is the all-embracing world ether surrounding us that serves as a reflective device and which reflects all that we contain. The period of Kamaloka is such that our inner life—consisting of all our desires and lusts, encompassing every aspect of our feelings and our disposition—assembles itself around us as our objective surroundings. It is important for us to understand that our life in Kamaloka is initially characterized as revolving around us, being locked into ourselves; and that this imprisonment within ourselves is all the more constrictive because we have no physical life to which we can return and to which our entire existence can relate. Only when we have undergone this life in Kamaloka in such a way that we eventually— and it is a very gradual process—arrive at the understanding that everything there cannot be got rid of from the world in any other way than that we can now feel in a manner quite differently than through desires and so on. Only then can we break out of the prison that is Kamaloka.

What does this mean? Let's assume someone dies harbouring a particular desire. This desire forms part of what is projected out into the domain of Kamaloka and is built into the fabric surrounding them. As long as a desire persists in them, it is impossible for them to unbolt their life in Kamaloka. Only when they become aware that this desire can only be satisfied when it has been disengaged, given up, no longer wished for, in other words, when it is torn from their soul and when they themselves oppose it, only then will the desire and with it all that confines them to Kamaloka be severed from their soul. Only then do we reach the realm between death and a new birth which we have called Devachan, a realm which can also be penetrated by clairvoyance once one has recognized all that belongs only to oneself. In clairvoyance, this point is arrived at through a certain level of maturity, of readiness; in Kamaloka it is over time, simply because time plagues us with our own desires, which are only conquered through duration, through endurance. This is how all that masquerades before us, fooling us into thinking it to be the world and all its glories, is shattered.

The world of truly supra-sensory realities is called Devachan. How do we encounter this approaching world? Here on the earthly plane we can only speak of Devachan because, in clairvoyant vision, when the self has been fully surmounted, we enter into a world of spiritual facts, verities which are objectively present and which are congruent with what exists in Devachan.

Now the most important characteristic of this Devachanic realm is that moral facts are no longer distinguishable from physical facts and laws, but that physical and moral laws are congruent. What does this mean? Isn't it so that in the ordinary physical world the Sun shines alike on the just and the unjust? Those who have committed a crime can be sent to prison but the physical Sun is not eclipsed. This means that in the world of physicality, moral lawfulness and physical legitimacy diverge, each going its separate way. It is not like this in Devachan, not in the slightest.

There it is the case that everything originating in what is moral, wisely intellectual, aesthetically beautiful and suchlike, leads to emergence and development, while all that proceeds from what is immoral, intellectually untrue, aesthetically repulsive leads to destruction and downfall. In fact, there the laws of nature are such that the Sun does not shine on righteous and wicked alike but—if we may put this pictorially—that it really does darken in face of evil.

The righteous individual going through Devachan also has spiritual sunshine there; in other words the fructifying forces that help them progress in their lives. Spiritual forces withdraw from a deceitful or hateful person passing through. Processes are possible there that are not possible here. If two people walk along next to each other, one righteous and the other sinful, the Sun cannot shine on the one and not the other. However, over in the spiritual world, it is absolutely the case that it depends on the quality of human being as to how spiritual forces work upon them. This means that, over there, laws of nature and spiritual laws do not diverge into two separate paths but are one and the same path. Fundamentally, everything depends on this: in the Devachanic world, laws of nature totally coincide—are completely congruent—with moral and intellectual laws.

For this reason the following takes place: once the human being has stepped into the world of Devachan and is living through this, they retain from their last life everything by way of righteousness and unjustness, of good and evil, of aesthetically beautiful or ugly, of truth and falsehood. But all this works in such a way that it is immediately subject to the laws of nature there. There the law—as we call it in the physical world—pertains that someone who has lied or stolen might turn towards the Sun yet not be shone upon; they would eventually contract an illness through lack of sunlight. Or let us imagine someone who had lied could run out of breath in the physical world. This would be comparable with what takes place in the Devachanic world.

Something like this happens to a person who has brought upon themselves some encumbrance or other in relation to their soul-spiritual nature: natural laws are simultaneously and absolutely congruent with spiritual laws. As this person progresses onwards and ever further onwards through Devachan, such qualities gradually settle into the individual so that what they now are corresponds with the qualities they brought with them from their previous life. Let us say that someone lingers for two hundred years in Devachan, having consistently lied during their former life. They live out their time in Devachan but the Spirits of Truth withdraw from them. What would be revived in a different soul—one used to speaking the truth—now dies in them.

Let us now imagine someone of pronounced vanity who has failed to rid themselves of this trait and is going through Devachan. Here vanity is an extraordinarily evil-smelling vapour and certain spiritual beings avoid a foul-smelling individual so pungently redolent of ambition and vanity. This is no pictorial figure of speech. Vanity and ambition really are exceptionally disgusting fumes in Devachan and for this reason the benevolent influence of certain spiritual beings, who then retreat, cannot take effect. This is just like a plant that is expected to grow in a cellar, whereas it can only flourish in sunlight. The vain person cannot thrive. So they develop onwards under the repercussions of this trait. Once they have reincarnated, they do not have the strength to accrue beneficial influences to themselves. Instead of fashioning their organs in a healthy manner, they elaborate a sickly organic system.

How we therefore develop as human beings through life—what we become—is not only evinced by our physical condition but also by our moral and intellectual states. Only when we are no longer on the spiritual plane do natural- and spiritual laws work in parallel. Between death and a new birth they are one and the same: natural laws and spiritual laws together forming a single unity. Forces of nature are implanted into our souls where they work destructively if they are the consequence of immoral deeds in preceding lives, but which work fruitfully if they are the consequence of moral deeds. This applies not only to our inner configuration but also to what approaches us externally in the form of our karma.

The fundamental feature of Devachan is that, there, no discrepancy exists between natural and spiritual laws. This is also the case for the seer who has genuinely penetrated into supersensible realms. These supra-sensory realms are quite different from such kingdoms as apply on the physical plane. It is simply not possible for the seer to make the distinctions that materialists make by maintaining that it is merely an objective law of nature. In truth, standing behind any such objective law of nature there is a spiritual law.

The seer cannot, for instance, walk across an arid field or a flooded area, cannot be aware of a volcanic eruption without thinking that behind all natural phenomena are spiritual powers, spiritual beings. For the seer, a volcanic eruption is simultaneously a moral deed, even if the moral is perhaps on quite a different level from what you might at first allow yourself to imagine.

People who constantly confuse the physical world with higher worlds will say: Well, if innocent people are annihilated, how can one think of this as being a moral act? Appraising it in these terms would be grossly parochial—as would the opposing appraisal be—that is, if one were to view it as an avenging punishment from God, especially for those people living directly by the volcano. Both these opinions can only originate from a philistine point of view on a physical level. Such views are not the crux of the matter; it can be a matter of far wider, more universal implications. People who live on the slopes of a volcano and whose possessions are destroyed by eruptions may be completely innocent within the terms of this life and will be compensated later.

This does not mean that we should harden our hearts and fail to help them, something which would again be a barbarous interpretation of the facts. And yet it is the case with volcanic eruptions that, during the course of Earth evolution, certain things have taken place through human agency which have hindered humankind's overall advance. It is those beneficial Gods who have to work at offsetting and balancing this so that, in fact, compensation for such natural events is generated.

The connection between all these phenomena is sometimes only visible in the depths of the occult. In this way recompense can be made for events that run counter to the course of spiritual advancement—the genuine progress of humanity—and which are perpetrated by human beings themselves. Every incident—to its very foundations and even when it is an act of nature—is simultaneously a moral event. Spiritual beings in higher worlds are the bearers of this morality and it is they who stand behind physical events. If you just imagine a world in which it is impossible to speak of a divergent separation of natural and spiritual laws, a world where, expressed differently, righteousness reigns as a law of nature, then you have imagined the Devachanic world. There is therefore no need for punishment, even of punishable deeds, to be meted out arbitrarily but, through the same inevitability that causes fire to set light to combustible material, immorality destroys itself and morality nurtures itself.

So we see that the innermost characteristic—as it were, that deepest, most vital nerve of existence—is utterly dissimilar for differing realms. We can form no image of these distinctive worlds if we cannot focus on their radically divergent idiosyncrasies, which can well be summarized as: physical realm, Kamaloka, Devachan. The physical world, in which natural and spiritual worlds run in a parallel series of factual data; the realm of Kamaloka, in which human beings are enclosed within themselves as in the prison of their own existence; the realm of Devachan, which is the pure converse of the physical world, where natural and spiritual laws coincide, being one and the same. These are the three categories, and if you focus on them closely and try to feel how radically different from our own a world can be in which what is moral and intellectual—as well as the law of aesthetics—are simultaneously natural laws, then you will sense the nature of existence in the Devachanic realm.

When we encounter a lovely or an unsightly face in the physical world, we have as little justification to behave towards the less attractive-looking person as though they were to be rejected at a soul-spiritual level as we have to treat an attractive-appearing person as though we ought to elevate them as regards their soul-spiritual disposition. This is quite different in Devachan. There we encounter no unsightliness that is not encumbered with indebtedness, nor someone who—as a result of their previous incarnation—is placed under the necessary obligation of bearing in a present incarnation an unsightly countenance, yet who is presently engaged in being truthful and honest, in which case we cannot possibly encounter them in an ugly form because they will certainly have transformed their ugliness into beauty. It is equally true that those who are vain, mendacious and ruthless are transformed into ugly deformity in Devachan.

However, something else is also true: in normal everyday life we do not see ugly faces who continuously self-detract, nor lovely faces who continuously self-enhance. But in Devachan this is the case. What is ugly is the manifestation of continuous destruction and we can perceive nothing beautiful of which we cannot presuppose that it is a work in continuous process of furtherance, of fruitful advancement. We must relate totally differently towards the psychic realm of Devachan from the way in which we relate to the physical world.

You need to differentiate these sensations, appreciating the essentials upon which they all depend, so that you internalize not only external portrayals but that you take with you the feelings and perceptions associated with what spiritual science describes. If you try to bestir yourself to sense a world in which what is moral, beautiful, intellectually true equates with the inevitability of a law of nature, you will have a sense of Devachan. This is why we have to do so much work at compiling and synthesizing: so that what we work on can, as it were, be melded together into a feeling.

It is impossible, at the flick of a wrist, to reach real knowledge of what spiritual science gradually needs to make clear to the world. There are certainly many well-intentioned people who query: Why does so much have to be learnt in spiritual science? Do we have to go back to being students? After all, it depends on *feeling*. Yes, it does depend on feeling, but on the *right feelings*, and these first need to be elaborated! That is the case with everything. After all, it would be much pleasanter for painters if they didn't need to learn all those techniques and if paint wasn't so tardy in covering the canvas, rather than just being *breathed* onto it for a finished work! The peculiar thing in our world is that, the more things tend towards the spiritual, the harder it is for people to grasp that it is not just a matter of breathing! In music, you would hardly expect someone untutored to be a composer—quite obviously. The same could be said of painting, though to a slightly lesser extent. For poetry, even less, otherwise there would be far more poets. Indeed, there has hardly ever been a less poetic age, yet there are plenty of poets. One doesn't have to have learnt this skill; one only needs—and this has nothing to do with poetry—to have learnt to write by hand and to express one's thoughts. Philosophizing requires even less.

This is thought to be obvious, as anyone can have an opinion on world events and perspectives on life because they can take a position. You encounter again and again that it means nothing that someone has researched and understood a subject, using all available inner means. Today it is deemed obvious that the perspective of one who has worked long and hard to understand and to share even a small segment of world mysteries enjoys equal validity in the opinion of someone who only intends to have an opinion at all. Nowadays, basically everyone is considered to be a person of worldwide perspective. And then a theosophist to boot! Some think even less is needed for this; it ought to suffice that you know not even the three founding principles[28] of the Theosophical Society but only acknowledge the first of them, just as you wish. All you really need is to acknowledge, with a degree of truthfulness, that you are a loving human being—whether you are or not is not at issue here—then you are a theosophist and will have the right feelings.

Thus we continually slide downhill when it comes to valuing findings from a given standpoint and the ability to discriminate, starting with music and moving via areas that demand less and less until we end up with theosophy! Because here it suffices—unlike what would be expected of painting—that you just breathe: We are founding the core of a human brotherhood; we are theosophists, no studying required!

However, it depends on us working with all our strength so that whatever insight we gain for ourselves is ultimately gathered into feelings or sensing which only then, through their colouration, give rise to the loftiest, most truthful knowledge. Start by wrestling your way through to a feeling for the world bearing the imprint of natural and spiritual laws coinciding. If you work seriously at this task—however hard you may have worked on this or that theory before—you will be making an impression on the realm of Devachan. If you have really worked at such sentience—not just fantasized about doing so—but have devoted years to the thorough pursuit of it, then these perceived feelings—these nuanced percepts—will have a power to help you advance further than the nuances themselves can reach: you will have become *true* through seriously concerted study.

You will then not be far from the nuances of feeling springing up and actually laying out before you the nature of Devachan. Because when these nuanced feelings are truly honed, they become a capacity for vision. So, when local branch work is patiently pursued, is practised solely on the basis of honesty, free of all sensationalism, then these centres of work will be as they should: schools where individuals are nurtured towards the spheres of clairvoyance. Only those who have no expectation of this or who do not wish to cooperate with others can falsely speculate around today's themes.

Lecture 6

MUNICH, 27 FEBRUARY 1912

Hidden Forces in Soul Life

In recent days we have been talking about the presence of hidden depths in the soul and it is always good if we can take up this theme and engage in issues useful to students of spiritual science. In general, it has to be said that fuller elucidation and elaboration is only possible on a foundation of what has so far been shared of spiritual science.

We have explored from the most varied perspectives what we might call the stratified structure of the human being. It should therefore be fairly straightforward to imagine what now emanates from a different angle in pursuit of hidden depths of the soul, so that we relate correctly to the constituent parts of the human being as we know them from the somewhat elementary depictions of a spiritual worldview so far given.

It has been repeatedly said over the last days that what encompasses our concepts, our percepts, our impulses of will, our feelings and sentience, in short, everything that takes place in our souls under normal circumstances between waking and falling asleep, can be called the activities, idiosyncrasies and forces of normal consciousness. Now we want to describe what comes under the aegis of normal consciousness—that is, everything that a person knows, feels and wills between waking up and falling asleep—in terms of two parallel lines, A and B [see diagram below].

Isn't it so that not only our concepts but also every kind of perception belongs within this area of the parallel lines? If we transpose ourselves via our senses so as to correspond with the outer world,

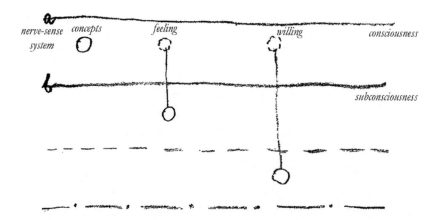

thereby creating a picture of that outer world via all manner of sense impressions, while remaining connected with—in touch with—the outer world, this will also belong to our normal, everyday consciousness. Also belonging to this area are all our feelings and impulses of will, in short, everything encompassed by our normal consciousness. We could say that everything transmitted to us every day through normal soul life also belongs within this area between parallel lines A & B.

Now it is a matter of clearly recognizing that our so-called normal soul life is dependent on the instrument of a physical body, that is to say, on everything contained within the instruments of the nervous- and sensory systems. If we now draw two further parallel lines, we can say: Corresponding with the sense organs and the nervous system in our physical organism are what we might call the tools or instruments supporting this consciousness—especially the sense organs and to a certain extent the nervous system.

Below the threshold of this everyday consciousness lies everything which we designate as the concealed aspect of our soul's life or the subconscious. We will gain a clear concept of all that is, as it were, embedded within this subconscious when we remember that human beings can—through spiritual training—acquire Imagination, Inspiration and Intuition. So, just as we placed concepts, feelings and will impulses in the area of our usual consciousness, we have to place Imagination, Inspiration and Intuition in the area of the subconscious [dotted lines]. Yet we also know that the workings of the subconscious are not only engaged under conditions of spiritual training but can also manifest as a legacy of an original, primitive state of human consciousness in the form of atavism. Then what we call visions arise. These visions in what might be thought of as a more naïve or primitive consciousness correspond with regular, methodically-achieved Imaginations. Inklings or premonitions would have arisen as a form of primitive Inspirations. We can lead straight into an example of what the difference is between an Inspiration and a premonition.

We have often referred to the fact that—during the course of the twentieth century and integral to human evolution—a kind of spiritual return of Christ will occur and that a certain number of people will experience in etheric form how Christ works into the world from out of the astral realm. Knowledge of this phenomenon can be confirmed by means of thorough schooling, training that acknowledges the nature of evolution and—again through regular training—accepts that this must take place in the twentieth century.

Yet it can happen—as is often the case nowadays—that here or there are individuals gifted with that natural, primitive clairvoyance who possess the sort of darkened Inspiration we called premonitions and who will have an inkling of the approaching Christ. It is possible that those individuals will not know exactly what they are encountering; yet Inspiration, even of such essential magnitude, can occur in the form of inklings or premonitions. For primitive or naïve consciousness, something can occur that does not remain within the features of an inkling or vision. Vision replaces a spiritual process with an image.

If, for example, a person has lost someone whose I has gone through the gate of death and is tarrying in the spiritual world, and the latter individual has created some link between themselves and the person still among the living, then the person in this world is likely not to know what their late acquaintance wants of them; they can then form a false concept of what the late person is experiencing in their soul. But the fact that any such connection exists elicits in the living a vision, which is intrinsically false but which may nevertheless be founded on the correct fact that the dead person is seeking a connection with them. This manifests as an inkling or presentiment.

In this way the person who has premonitions somehow knows things either about the past, or about the future, which are inaccessible to normal consciousness. However, if something presents itself to the human soul as a clear perception—not just as a vision, which can at any rate be false—but in the form of a clear perception (be it a process in the sense world or in a region inaccessible to ordinary senses, or be it a process in higher worlds) such manifestations are in occult usage termed specifically: deuteroscopy or the second face, countenance or visage. With this I have only illustrated for you— whether this be achieved by rigorous inner schooling or by naturally occurring clairvoyance—what takes place within consciousness, certainly in the subconscious, but specifically in the human soul itself.

As far as processes going on in the human soul itself are concerned, everything changes markedly once we broach the subject of the subconscious, as opposed to the processes taking place in everyday consciousness. In contrast to all that is our actual subject matter and—to use the mildest possible terms and suggestions that can be used in a public lecture—it can be said that the processes involved in everyday consciousness really amount to a state of unconsciousness. The eye sees a rose. This eye itself behaves such that in us a concept of a rose arises. But this eye is quite powerless in terms of normal consciousness, with all its perceptions in face of concepts of the emergence, growth and withering of the rose. The rose grows and withers according to natural forces. But for as long as normal consciousness pertains, the eye is capable of nothing other than grasping the immediate present; only this is accessible to its perception. It is now not among the realities of the subconscious.

This is what we need to hold onto, as it is extremely important. When we perceive something normally with our eyes—be it colourful pictures or anything else—not only can we change nothing through the very perceiving of objective items, but something else occurs if the seeing is normal: if nothing other than seeing alone confronts the eye, the eye also remains unchanged by seeing. Only when we cross the frontier between normal light and blinding light do we damage our eyes. Thus we can say: Amongst the facts of normal consciousness we do not, if we persistently remain among them, even affect ourselves. Our organisms

are constructed such that, through the verities of normal consciousness, even within ourselves no changes are normally generated.

What takes place in the subconscious is quite different. Supposing
we create an Imagination or we have a vision. Let us now imagine this Imagination or vision to correspond with some benevolent being. This good entity is not in the physically-sensed world
but in the supra-sensory world. Now we wish to mentally move this
world—in which the beings mentioned exist and where we are seeing
this Imagination or vision—into the area [see diagram] between the
two parallel lines. In the world we have mentally moved there, we
wish to seek everything which can constitute an item, a perception
or become an object for the subconscious. We won't write anything
in this space as yet.

But if we represent anything in this world—whether in imaginary
image or in vision—that is an evil or demonic being, it is then not the
case that we ourselves are as powerless, in relation to this presence,
as the eye is powerless in relation to the rose. If, when imagining or
envisioning an evil being, we cultivate the feeling that it should yield
to us, and we do this in concert with a totally clear and imaginatively
visionary concept, then the being existing in that realm would in fact
feel as though it were being thrust aside by a force emanating from
us. It is just like this when we have a similar vision or Imagination of
a benevolent being. It is also the case then that, if we develop a feeling of sympathy, the being can indeed sense the power within themselves to approach us and make a connection with us. All the beings
existing in this realm can sense our forces—whether attracting or
repelling them—when we create visionary Imaginations of them.

As regards our subconscious, we are then in a similar position to
an eye which, simply by looking, were to see not just a rose but also
produce the desire for the rose to come nearer to it and the belief
that it could actually carry this out. Or, indeed, as if the eye were to
see something repugnant, it would not only conclude that it is ugly
but that it could banish this ugliness through antipathy alone. The
subconscious is, therefore, in contact with a world upon which sympathy and antipathy—which claim space in the soul—can have an
influence. We need to lay this out for our souls.

These sympathies and antipathies—in fact all the impulses and motivations—working in our subconscious are not active in this realm only in the way indicated, but affect primarily all that is contained within us as a part of our ether body (not just as part of the human ether body but even including certain forces of the physical body) and which we can now think of as enclosed between those two parallel lines. Into these parallels we must mentally place those forces pulsating through our blood—that is, the powers of warmth within our blood—and also those forces which are alive within our breathing; they in turn being conditioned by the overall health or sickliness of our entire organism. This more or less healthy force of breath we can summarize as its condition or fettle. Also belonging to—and affected within us by—the subconscious is the human ether body.

Our subconscious affects us, as do those hidden forces of our soul life; they influence us through the warmth of our blood and—as this latter is dependent on its overall beat, the liveliness or sluggishness of our blood circulation—you can understand that our blood circulation must to a certain extent be connected with our subconscious. Whether someone has a brisker or slacker circulatory system depends largely on the forces in their subconscious.

If the effect on all the demonic or divine beings in the outer world only occurs when human beings have visions, Imaginations or similar perceptions with a degree of clarity in their subconscious, if *then*—solely through sympathy or antipathy—certain forces become

Creative, physical world	Sense organs	Consciousness
	Nervous system	*Imagining, Perceiving* Feelings, Will impulses
Elemental world ⟵	Forces of warmth in the blood	Hidden aspects of soul life
		-*Subconsciousness*
		Imagination, Inspiration, Intuition
		Visions, Premonitions Deuteroscopy

active in this world as if by magic, then this distinct soul-manifesta-
tion in the subconscious is not necessary to affect the inner aspect
of our organism, which itself consists of what has been described
here. Whether or not someone is aware of which Imaginations might
correspond with a particular sympathy or another within themselves,
this sympathy has an effect on their blood circulation, their breathing
and their ether body.

Assume that a person has for some time had the tendency to
have mainly repulsion-inducing experiences. If they were capable of
having visions or Imaginations, as described the day before yesterday, they would experience as perceptions their own being laid out
before them. This would project into space but would apply only to
their own domain; these visions or imaginations would represent the
forces of repulsion within them. But if someone in this situation
cannot practise self-knowledge—yet may only have the feelings of
disgust because they exist within—they will affect him personally.
They do in fact influence the forces of warmth in their blood and
their powers of breathing.

So it is actually the case—to change the subject—that a person
has a respiratory system that is more or less healthy depending on the
feelings they experience in their subconscious, that their circulation
is more or less vigorous depending again on what they experience
subconsciously. Ultimately, every process and activity in a person's
ether body is dependent on their realm of feeling.

What manifests when the events of the subconscious are really
experienced by the soul is that not only are the two connected but
that they exercise a continuous effect upon the constitution of the
person. Feelings, perceptions or sensations play into the subconscious, instigating particular forms of warmth in the blood, particular
conditions in the respiratory system and the ether body, which either
support that organism or thwart its entire life. What plays out in the
human subconscious always causes either thriving or decay. Human
beings either diminish or replenish their life forces through what is
sent down into their subconscious by their state of consciousness.

If someone feels pleasantly complacent or indulgent towards a
lie they have told and feels no repugnance—the healthy response to

lies—and if they are unconcerned or even pleased with themselves, these feelings will be added to their subconscious. What goes on in the subconscious taints blood circulation, respiratory health and the forces of the ether body.

The consequences of what has been described are that everything remaining in the person when they go through the gate of death causes atrophy, diminishes their strength and that something in them dies which would have been revived had the person experienced revulsion and disgust at the lies told—this being the healthy reaction. This healthy feeling of repugnance against lies would have descended, translating into the forces mentioned, and the person would have sent promising, burgeoning forces into their organism.

We see how forces and issues are continually sent from our ordinary, upper consciousness to our subconscious and how we work at building growth or decay into ourselves. We are not powerful enough in our present state to corrupt other members of our being—issuing downwards from our souls—other than our blood circulation, our respiratory system and our ether bodies; we cannot degrade the coarser, more solid parts of our physical organisms and are only capable of debasing parts of our overall constitution. What manifests as particularly degradable when the remaining parts of the ether body most closely linked with warmth of circulation and respiratory condition are influenced in this way, is that this ether body degenerates through negative feelings.

However, it receives regenerative, nurturing and strengthening forces from normal, genuinely affirmative feelings. We can say that human beings work directly upon the actual thriving or destruction of their own organism through what takes place in their subconscious; put differently, settling into their unconscious from everyday awareness, processes of regeneration or decay take place within their souls, affecting their entire constitutional health.

We have seen how, to varying degrees, our souls can experience and know something which also has an effect on the world which—to use the words current throughout medieval times—we can call the elemental world. Humans cannot relate directly to this world, but only via the detour of first experiencing within themselves the effects of the subconscious as it impacts upon our organism. Anyone who has over time gained some self-knowledge knows that to have an emotion and transmit your behaviour to your subconscious results either in destroying something, which then atrophies or, if experienced differently, corollaries of that feeling settle into your subconscious and nurture you. If you sense this alternating rise and fall between health-giving and destructive forces over time, you will grow ever more mature in self-knowledge.

This is what constitutes true self-knowledge and it can be compared with the following image: self-knowledge arrived at in the way described—when our instincts rise up in face of a lie or some wrongful reaction to a lie—would attract a sensation akin to a scorpion biting off our toe. You can be sure that, were people to be aware of this very real effect, they would tell fewer lies than they do. If our physical body were to be mutilated in the physical world, this would be comparable with what happens—though we do not normally notice it—when daily experiences are transmitted into the subconscious.

When a lax disregard of lying is endemic in the subconscious, something is removed, bitten off our organism, whereby we are impoverished and which we will only be able to retrieve over the further course of our karma. If we transmit a principled feeling into our subconscious—and we need to think of this in terms of a *thousandfold* scale of sensations sinking downwards—then we grow in ourselves, building new life forces into our organism. Observing this growth and decay is what causes genuine self-knowledge to arise within us.

I was told yesterday that some people did not fully understand what I said about distinguishing between a real vision or Imagination—which belongs among what is *objective*—from something that merely projects itself into a space, only pertains to us and is *subjective*. You cannot say: Write down this rule, then that, and you'll be able to distinguish. They don't exist and you learn gradually by developing. Properly differentiating between what only concerns ourselves and what manifests as an external vision pertaining to a being can only be reliable when one has oneself suffered the continually-biting attacks originating in those lethal subconscious processes. By then you will be equipped with a reasonable amount of certainty. Yet it can always happen that one can cause a vision or Imagination to appear of which one queries: Can I, through the power of my spiritual sight, *see through* it? Does the vision remain static under scrutiny by the active power of my evolved gaze? If so, it corresponds with an objective fact. If the active force of my gazing obliterates the vision, then it pertains only to my subjective self.

Someone in this situation who is not alert in this sense can—as far as I'm concerned—array thousands of pictures from the Akasha Chronicle; if they do not apply the test as to whether the image is extinguished or not under active gaze, then the Akashic images, however endless the knowledge they impart, can only be seen as relating to the inner world of that person. It might happen—I say *might*—that a person sees nothing more than their own interior and that this is projected in many dramatic images, which they might expand, say, throughout the Atlantean world and over generations of human evolution. This could under certain circumstances be nothing more—however objective it might appear—than a projection of their own internal domain.

When a person has gone through the gate of death, the situation always arises in which those hindrances, through which their inherent subjectivity became objective vision or Imagination, are no longer present. In normal present-day lives, what people experience inwardly and unconsciously—what they transmit to their subconscious—are not always visions and Imaginations. They become Imaginations through regular training, visions in the case of atavistic clairvoyance. When someone has gone through the portal of death, the sum total of their inner life instantly becomes an objective world; it is right there.

Kamaloka is fundamentally nothing other than a world, built up all around us, of everything that we have experienced in our souls. Only in Devachan is this positively reversed. So we can easily understand that what I said about the consequences of sympathy and antipathy present in visions, Imagination, Inspiration and premonitions or inklings does always—in every circumstance—affect the objective elemental world. I said that, in the case of a human being incarnated in the physical world, only what they have elevated to vision or Imagination has an effect on the elemental world. In someone who has died, those forces—which used to exist in their subconscious and which they subsequently brought with them when they passed through the gate of death—always do have an effect, working into the elemental world.

Thus everything a person has experienced entirely pervades the whole elemental world. Just as surely as you create waves in a stream when you hit the water are the experiences of the dead perpetuated in the elemental world—with that very same inevitability as waves replicate themselves outwards from the point where you hit the water's surface. Or: they are perpetuated in the elemental world with the same certitude as a flow of air regenerates itself. This is why the elemental world is constantly filled with everything that human beings have incited in their subconscious and which they bring with them when they die. So it is always only a matter of being in a position to create conditions for seeing and perceiving things in the elemental world. One need not be at all surprised if a seer correctly recognizes and describes what appears in the elemental world as being the consequential effects of the dead. As you will see, one can also pursue these effects of the deceased's experiences right into the physical world—albeit under particular conditions—as they begin to work into the elemental world. If the seer has him- or herself undergone all that I have described as relating to the elemental world, they can attain over time to having remarkable experiences.

Imagine a seer goes through the following process: firstly, let's say he can see a rose. He looks at the rose with physical eyes. Looking in this way, the seer has a sense impression. Imagine further that the seer has trained him- or herself to have a particular feeling on encountering the colour red. This is essential, otherwise the process ends there. Without associating colours or tones with certain nuances of feeling, clairvoyance directed at external objects cannot progress. Imagine the rose is laid aside. If they were no clairvoyant, such a feeling would descend into their subconscious and down there would act upon their health or sickliness. If they are indeed a seer, they will now perceive what effect the Imagination of the rose is having in their subconscious; in other words they will have an Imagination of a rose. They will simultaneously perceive whether it is working supportively or destructively on their physical or ether body.

Having this Imagination, they will now be able to exert a force of attraction on the being we may call the group soul of the rose. They will see the group soul of the rose inasmuch as it exists as such in the elemental world. If the seer now goes further—having started by looking at the rose, set aside the rose and followed the inner process of surrender to the rose and its ensuing effect, then arriving at the point of seeing the trace of the rose in the elemental world—thus seeing in the space the rose appeared to them a quite wonderfully radiant picture as part of the elemental world.

Having followed the process this far, something occurs. One can refrain from seeing what is in front of one; one can instruct oneself: Do not view with your inner gaze what you have extending from you into the world in the form of a living etheric entity! Then the strange phenomenon arises that the seer sees something going through their eye which shows them how those forces work which build up their eye from out of the human ether body; they see the forces concerned with constructively forming their own physical bodies. They really see their physical eye as if it were an external object—this can happen.

You can make your way from outer object to the point where you are in an otherwise totally dark room—you cannot allow any other sense perceptions in—and you see what the eye looks like as a spiritual image. You yourself see your inner organ. With this you find yourself in a realm which in truth creates the physical world. You only perceive this creative physical world by first perceiving how you are physically constituted. So you are retracing a path back to yourself. What transmits such forces into our eye that we positively see our eye as if radiating rays of light were streaming from it, rays that most readily correspond with the essence of our gaze? We see the eye bordered by a sort of yellow glow; we see the eye enclosed within us. This has been caused by the whole progression of forces which have ultimately brought human beings to their present stage.

The same course is now taken by the forces which may emanate from someone who has died. They take with them the contents of their subconscious into the world where they tarry after going through the gate of death. In the same way as we penetrate our own physical eye do the forces radiated by the dead return from the elemental world into the physical plane. The deceased may feel a particular longing for someone they have left behind. This particular longing is initially in their subconscious, but it swiftly becomes a living vision, through which they affect the elemental world. Here, in the realm of the elements, what was mere vision now becomes a power. This force makes its way, as given by the longing for the living person and, if the opportunity arises, it rumbles, it 'polters' and bumps around in the physical world in the vicinity of the person still living, who hears certain sounds of disturbance, which they perceive in the same way as they sense any physical effect.

These events—hailing as they do from a source such as this—would more readily be taken for normal were people to take greater note of the times favourable to such influences, which are when falling asleep and waking up. Not only do people pay no attention to these events but there can hardly be anyone who has not encountered manifestations from the spiritual world in that transition between falling asleep and waking, whether polter-activity or even words.

I wanted to point this out to you today for the purpose of demonstrating, in actual reality, the connection between human beings and the world. What a person derives with mundane consciousness from the objective sense world itself is powerless and seemingly without genuine context in that sense world. But, no sooner have that person's experiences sunk into their subconscious, a connection with reality is forged. The swooning or unconscious state of the previous level of awareness turns into a fine sort of magic. And once that person has gone through the portal of death, is freed from their physical body, their experiences are such that they work into the elemental world and—under favourable conditions—have an effect right into the physical world, where they can be perceived by normal consciousness.

I have portrayed this in the simplest form in which it can take place, because one has to begin with the simplest of cases. Obviously—and having as always left sufficient time to gradually work further on the matters about which we need to know—we will move on to more complex issues, which will in turn lead us into the more intimate connections between the human being and the world.

LECTURE 7

STOCKHOLM, 16 APRIL 1912

Three Soul Paths to Christ (in Two Parts)
First Part: The Path via the Gospels and the Path of Inner Experience[29]

O VER the next two, more intimate evenings, we will talk about a question concerning humanity which, in a twofold manner, impacts our souls quite extraordinarily deeply. Firstly, the enigma of Christ has occupied countless souls across the Earth over the past two thousand years, and also because it has flowed into innumerable earthly souls as their spiritual lifeblood, their strength of soul, comfort and hope in their suffering, as fortitude and certainty in their actions. Not only this but, if we take into account everything surrounding us by way of external culture, created over many centuries, then on deeper consideration we see that all this would have been impossible had Christ's impetus not gripped a large swathe of humanity. This is one thought which shows with what strong interest the question of Christ must take hold of us if we are to approach it with anthroposophical knowledge.

This is just one aspect of the attention we bring to this enigma; the other originates specifically in the soul- and spiritual conditions of our time, of our epoch. We need only look around in the world, hoping to understand the yearning, the questing of human souls, and we will reflect: ever increasingly do human souls search for what has been connected with the name of Christ among souls over the centuries; ever more do souls become convinced that renewing the pathways, renewing interest, deepening our knowledge are essential if the needs of human souls—as they increase ever more in relation to Christ—are to be satisfied. Though we find on the one hand a craving to discover Christ, on the other we find in many souls of the present some hesitation and uncertainty as regards the means so far employed. Hence one of the most burning issues of today is that of finding an answer to this longing and—in relation to the uncertainty—experiencing the truth.

It is therefore obviously the task of a spiritual movement, which enters further into spiritual foundations, to create some clarity around such queries. If matters appear like this at present, they will in a relatively short time—in fact in a very short time—look completely different! If we look somewhat unselfishly at what our descendants will need in future in relation to Christ, we will have to admit: even if multitudes of people nowadays derive fulfilment from what already exists, more and more souls will feel uncertain, longing for answers. When we speak about Christ today, we are speaking about what we foresee will be essential for people of a very imminent future. Anthroposophy would not be fulfilling its task were it not to place itself where it could create clarity on these issues—insofar as this is possible today—through its findings.

My point of departure will be to show three ways in which—over the course of human evolution—souls can reach the Christ. When speaking of three paths, I have to mention briefly that one of those paths no longer exists, though it did earlier for millions of people over the centuries. Yet today it cannot be an esoteric path in the way that anthroposophy can be, particularly for our times.

This *first* path is via the Christian records, the Gospels. This was the route for millions upon millions of people and continues to be the only option for them. The *second* way for human souls to seek the Christ is what we can call the path of inner experience, which countless souls in the present and in the near future will have to tread due to their particular configuration and their unique characteristics. The *third* pathway is one which can at least begin to be understood nowadays and which emanates from the anthroposophical movement: the path of initiation.

So there are three approaches to Christ; firstly via the Gospels, secondly through inner experience and thirdly through initiation. The first path, via the Gospels, only needs outlining here. We all know that the Gospels have, over the centuries, nourished the hearts and souls of countless people. We also know that the most enlightened, the most critical of natures—and these are not the non-religious—are starting to lose their connection with this path under the prevailing view that external knowledge cannot be sure which realities actually stand behind the historical events described in the Gospels.

Had people of previous centuries read the Gospels in the same way as today's academic reads them—having undergone a modern scientific education—they would not have had the vast, life-changing effects they have exerted. If they were not read in this intellectual way in past centuries, how were they in fact read? What took place in Palestine at the beginning of our calculated era would not have been at the forefront of consideration by a Gospel reader of earlier centuries and this is still the case for many reading the Bible. Those who start trying to align what took place in full view of the people of Palestine at the start of our calculated era with what appears in the Gospels are sent mad by the historical nature of events in Palestine. Earlier readers did not read them in this way. They would read them by allowing pictures—such as the Samaritan at the well[30] or Christ preaching to his disciples on the mountain[31]—to sink into their souls. Questioning the external, physical reality of events was not their prime concern.

The central focus for them was the way in which their hearts lifted and their feelings were moved by such vast and mighty pictures and, further, what took shape in their hearts, how they were granted strength and a sense of purpose in their lives. They felt that spiritual lifeblood and strength flowed to them from these pictures. When they allowed such images to affect their souls, they felt strong; they sensed that they would be weak without them. Then they would feel a lively personal bond with what was recounted in the Gospels and questions as to its historical accuracy would not further concern them. The Gospels themselves constituted reality. They existed as a power and questions as to whence they originated were of no interest. They knew that people had not written them by earthly means but through stimuli from the spiritual world. I am not claiming that one should also feel like this nowadays—what one has to do depends on human evolution—I am just saying that people felt in this way over past centuries.

How could it be like this? Only now can spiritual science tell us. If we start understanding the Gospels through spiritual science and try to make our way into what has flowed into them from spiritual worlds—is contained within them—we face the Gospels saying: Independently of these Gospels, we learn from spiritual-scientific sources what took place in the evolution of humankind as the Christ impetus and thus we find what is contained in the Gospels independently of them. How can we conceive of the Gospels spiritual-scientifically?

If I may make a simple comparison, I'd say: Imagine someone had clarified something to themselves. They encounter a second person with their elucidation and start a conversation. The first person doesn't initially want to assume that the second person knows about their enlightenment, but during their conversation they notice that the second person knows as well as they do what the issue is. What can be sensibly deduced? It is sensible to assume that the second person acquired their lucidity from the same or from similar sources.

It is just like this with the Gospels and we can do likewise, depending on the perspective from which we approach them. An association of people who read the Gospels in the way described could be formed, one which included opponents of the Gospels who claim: If we check these Gospels within the context of external scientific methods, we find that they were written far later than the events they describe could have taken place in Palestine. Accounts contradict each other. In short, these Gospels cannot be seen as historical documents.

People of such a persuasion could exist in an association of this sort, yet one could say: Leaving the Gospels in peace for now, let's research into spiritual worlds! If we carry out truthful spiritual research, we will reap true supra-sensory knowledge. We would be able to ascertain that a mighty impetus from out of the spiritual world entered into human evolution and exerted an immense influence on the development of humankind. Then we would see that this impetus took powerful hold of an individual who was particularly suited to this task at the beginning of our calculated era. We would then be in possession of this and much else by way of related knowledge, which can only be gained through spiritual research. Then those not wanting to have anything to do with the Gospels could still access what the others have. Then we could approach the Gospels and say: Fine, we have so far not bothered about these Gospels; it's amazing that, when we read them carefully, we see that they contain what we find independently of them in spiritual-scientific spheres. Now we appreciate their worth from a different perspective and we can be certain that their source can be none other than the very source the writers of the Gospels drew upon, but revealed for humanity through this spiritual movement.

This is exactly where we stand as we face what will increasingly come to pass and which will justify every reverence for the Gospel documents. That being so, we will have to state that people will be able to find via other means what can be learnt from these manuscripts. In this way does such knowledge start to become ever more holy for us through today's spiritual understanding. It already used to affect people through the power of the Gospels; it is because the Gospels are so thoroughly saturated with the most sacred wisdom, the most spiritual motivating force of humanity, that they also moved those who accepted them naïvely.

Spiritual impulses do not just work abstractly, theoretically, but where they exist they work as life forces and lifeblood for human souls. Ever increasingly will it be recognized how comfort, strength and certitude will flow from such spiritual findings. However, when we speak of an inner path to Christ, we will encounter ever more content there that can at present only be understood and felt when approached with the correct spiritual-scientific understanding. An attempt will be made to speak of the inner Christ experience in such a way that it will be possible to see how it can arise in any person, quite regardless of the means of transmission. For this we will admittedly have to view the human being with the knowledge we have garnered from spiritual science. Immersing ourselves in such knowledge, we find that even the most basic grasp of this approach will bear fruit when applied to life.

It shows how we can transcend schematic abstraction beyond the seven constituent elements of the human being when we focus on the genesis and evolving of humankind. The human physical body undergoes its particular development in the first seven years of life. We also noted that during the second seven-year phase—between the change of teeth and reproductive maturity—the forces of the etheric body are chiefly active. Thereafter, astral forces come to the fore and only around twenty or twenty-one—depending on the over-all deployment of forces within the organism—does what manifests as the I arise with the forces it maintains throughout its life as bearer of the human ego. Actually, it is barely noticed nowadays how the bearer of a human I only becomes fully viable around age twenty or twenty-one because the present is not inclined to pay attention to things of this nature. What does it in fact signify that the ego only becomes properly active around the age of twenty or twenty-one?

We need to observe the evolving human being and their deeper organizational forces by spiritual means. These forces are in perpetual change: from birth to seven, from seven to sexual maturity, from reproductive maturity to I-evolution. They change in a way that cannot be tested by conventional physiology or anatomy. They can, however, be recognized very well by spiritual means and one can confirm that around the age of twenty, human beings evolve such powers that a complete entity, suited to itself as a bearer of an I, is present. Before this, it is not fully formed as the bearer of an I, human physicality being—also at a supra-sensory level—no proper carrier for an ego.

So when we observe the constituent elements of human beings in terms of great world principles we would need to say: Human beings are only capable—through the uniqueness of their organisms—of their I evolving to fully matured form, from out of itself, at around age twenty and no earlier.

We can contrast this fact with another, namely that in our first years—and with normal consciousness—we practically dream or sleep our way into life and only from a distinct point onwards do we start to have our own memories. Our parents or older siblings tell us everything before that point; from then onwards we say to our inner selves: I am the one I am. From then on—when we say *I* did this, *I* thought that—do we identify our I within our souls. What went before is lost to soul gloaming. Our memory only reaches as far back as the point described. With what are we presented when we juxtapose both these facts?

Firstly, that the actual bearer of the human I is only born around the age of twenty or twenty-one and, secondly, that our souls only designate us as an I from around age three or so. This is so because, in the present phase of their evolution, human beings have an opinion or a feeling about themselves that does not correspond with their inner configuration, such as it has become. An awareness of an I sets in around age three or four while the constitutional support for an I only appears around age twenty or twenty-one. This discrepancy is of fundamental importance for an understanding of human beings. If you present this fact abstractly as spiritual knowledge, nobody will be particularly excited; but because this fact is true, countless well-known experiences are available, which are still not viewed in light of this fact.

Everything humans experience as the dichotomy or discrepancy between external organism and inner experience, in life's suffering and pain as a result of certain things not being possible due to their constitutions, in the disharmony between what they wish or want and what they can actually achieve, the fact that they can have ideals that are beyond their capabilities to fulfil, all this leads back to the reality that the consciousness of our I takes a path quite different from the bearer of that I.

We are twofold beings in the respect that we are organized as external entities whose ego-nature matures around twenty or twenty-one and an inner being of soul whose inner soul existence is already freed from its external constituents from around the age of four or five. This emancipation of ego-consciousness from its external components takes place during childhood. We undergo something in our souls which takes place independently of our outer elements and which can actually come into harsh conflict with those outer components. As regards inner consciousness of our I, we tend to ignore our constitution and what exists down in our bodies. We evolve in soul quite differently from the way in which our bodies develop.

The course of inner human evolution is therefore twofold. The course of our development goes from our first to our seventh year, then from seven to fourteen, from fourteen to twenty-one as has been described. The course of inner development is quite independent of this, in that consciousness of our I is freed from earliest childhood onwards, making its own way independently through life. What are the consequences of this unique fact of human evolution? Only a spiritual scientist will be able to tell you that.

If we bear in mind all that spiritual research can teach us, we arrive at an extraordinary insight: namely that illness, organic human frailty, everything constituting sickliness, age and death alone make possible—and are results of—the fact that we are actually a dichotomy. We die because, in a certain sense, we are constituted not to take account of the evolution of our I. We are reminded of the fact that our ego-consciousness takes a self-dependent route that is concerned with our organism only when that organism sets itself up as a hostile hindrance to that ego's development during illness, infirmity and death. Then we are reminded that our I progresses, quite sundered from our bodies. Where does this strange twofold human nature originate?

If we look at the human being and all this in their true context, we are shown that, had only progressive forces intervened in human evolution at a certain point in Earth evolution—namely during the Lemurian epoch—childhood and youth would now proceed quite differently: they and the development of the I would remain in step with each other. Soul and body would develop in exact congruence. It would then have been impossible for human beings to grow up differently from the ideal, as represented, for instance, in my book *The Education of the Child in Light of Spiritual Science*.[32]

Had only progressive forces been active then, the curious circumstance would have pertained that, for their first twenty-one years, humans would have been far less self-reliant than they are presently. This lack of self-reliance is not meant in any negative sense; the state of dependence is meant in a sense with which you would all agree. It is human nature to rely purely on imitation in the first seven years of life. Had only benevolent forces been active in Ancient Lemuria, grown-up people would not have done anything shameful and children between birth and seven would not have been able to imitate anything disreputable. In the second seven-year phase, the principle of authority would have held sway, whereas now it is not only a national- but a world-scourge that young people aged between seven and fourteen want to be—and are even brought up to be—independent and to have autonomous opinions. Adults would naturally have been the obvious authority for children. Between fourteen and twenty-one, young people would have been far less introspective, focusing more on externals than on themselves. The power of ideals, the strength to live life's dreams, would have become immensely meaningful to them. These dreams would have burgeoned from their hearts and then full self-consciousness would have dawned at age twenty or twenty-one. So one would have had an age of imitation from birth to seven, in the second seven-year phase a deference to authority and in the third phase the heartfelt burgeoning forth of ideals, which would lead people to full I-self-consciousness around age twenty-one.

A certain segment of powers deviated from this course over evolutionary ages, thwarting its progress, and these we call *luciferic* powers. Since Lemurian times they have been tearing human I-consciousness adrift from its foundation in our bodies. That we are conscious of our ego in our earliest years is attributable to luciferic powers. How did luciferic powers intervene? These luciferic powers are beings who remained behind on the Moon and who for this reason have no sense of the Earth's mission nor for what should have evolved on Earth from age twenty-one onwards: the human I. They took humans to be just as they had been when they transmigrated from the Moon and planted the seeds of self-sufficiency into their souls' development.

Thus behind the prematurity of ego consciousness—that idiosyncratic dichotomy in human nature—lie luciferic forces. Only now can anthroposophy enable us to recognize this fact. Anyone who is in tune with their nature can feel it, because anyone can feel that they contain something that separates them from their full humanity. Everything we can call unjustifiable egotism in our natures, all insularity from the true activity of humanity, derives from the fact that our I does not follow its true course in accompanying our bodies. This is how the human being presently appears to us.

When we are capable of feeling: I could be different from the way I am; I contain an element which disagrees with me—when we feel this, we become aware of the antagonistic conflict of progressive powers against luciferic powers within ourselves. This reality had to be created over the course of human evolution. It was necessary because—otherwise, and without those luciferic powers—humans would never have become truly free and would have remained forever bound to their bodies. The very thing that causes human beings to diverge into dichotomy, on the one hand, offers them, on the other, the potential to be free. Yet one thing is lacking from this dual constitution in a normal life. As evidence for this, we sense that our I has become impoverished, unable of its own accord to transform our bodies.

If we survey in a wider context all that constitutes the human being, two forces are described: the organic forces of our human nature, which are intended to develop up to seven years and, on the other side, luciferic forces. Were there nothing more in the course of human evolution than nature and spiritual life, human beings could never create any harmony between their emancipated egos and their own natures. Were nothing further generated from the furthest reaches of Earth existence, then that evolution could only result in human beings becoming ever more alienated from their bodies, their constitutions becoming ever sicklier, ever more desiccated and the dichotomy necessarily growing ever wider.

If only people could manage to really feel this as an instance of spiritual-scientific knowledge, a momentous point would be reached in which they said: Here I am with my human disposition, which has been given to me by progressive spiritual beings working in seven-year cycles—they wouldn't need to say this in actual words, just *feel* it—but because my bodily nature contains a counter-force that evolves independently, it sickens, gets old and eventually dies.

Human beings feel this in the depths of their souls and only need to sense the discrepancy between their inner I and their external features. If they can live in this feeling, without even knowing anything about anthroposophy, then yes!—from whence? They don't at first know from whence—something enters their soul that prompts them to feel: I myself, with my I, that I towards which I can think back, I can do nothing much to counteract my constitution because I have not grown into it. Yet there is something I can absorb into my consciousness as a conviction. Directly from out of the spiritual world, something approaches that is not inherent in me but which permeates my soul. Something from unknown worlds is able to flow into my soul. If I accept it into my heart, if I suffuse my I with it, then it can help me directly from spiritual worlds. Call it what you will, it makes no difference, it just depends on the perception or feeling.

Let's take someone who was not coping well in life. They might say to themselves: I need to look far and wide throughout the world for a force that will enable me to overcome the duality within me. It is in the nature of things that people no longer turn to the old religious denominations, nor can they connect with outmoded ecclesiastical concepts which cannot provide them with the strength they seek.

Let's say—to take a concrete example—that a person were to turn to one of the ancient, holy religions, such as Buddhism, and would immerse themselves in its extraordinary teachings. If such a person naturally experienced in all its force the dichotomy described—I am not saying due to some theory but with an indistinct feeling—they would sense that in the personality, in the individuality of Gautama Buddha there lived something which could only exist on the basis of a lengthy evolution. This individual had undergone many incarnations, reaching ever higher and loftier levels of development until finally, at the age of twenty-nine, he rose from Bodhisattva to Buddha and as such had no further need to return to a physical body. How did what flowed from this individual come about?

Anyone with an open mind can feel what issues from the Buddha, what grew for the first time in Earth evolution in the Bodhisattva, what evolved over many incarnations. All this contains, in the most beautiful, sublime sense, forces to be found in the periphery of the Earth, in the interplay between constitutional and luciferic forces. Because they persisted from incarnation to incarnation, the forces flowing from Bodhisattva to Buddha—stemming as they do from the same source as those of humanity—they have the effect that the unbiased soul does not feel the full harmony that can be brought about between the human I and its attendant body. The soul feels that something must exist which does not persist from incarnation to incarnation, but which flows directly into each human soul from spiritual worlds.

When the human soul feels that it must have a direct relationship with what streams downwards from spiritual worlds, then it begins to have an inner experience of Christ. Then it comprehends that in Christ Jesus something had to arise that was quite different from everything that had gone before. That is the fundamental and radical difference between the life of Christ and that of Buddha.

Buddha evolved from Bodhisattva to Buddha with the forces that allow human beings to advance from one incarnation to another, just as is the case with all the great founders of religions. In the life of Jesus of Nazareth something was working directly from the spiritual world into the individuality of Jesus of Nazareth over three years, something that had nothing to do with human evolution and which had never previously been connected with a human life. This is a difference we need to make quite clear to our souls if we want to grasp why—in the fourth post-Atlantean epoch which named him Christ—something existed which was completely different from all the other religious impulses and why those other religions had always directed humanity towards this Christ.

If we look back over post-Atlantean ages to the hallowed ancient culture of India, we see the emergence of the seven holy rishis, whose souls encompassed elements of direct vision into spiritual worlds. Had one asked one of the seven holy rishis about the underlying mood of their soul, they would have answered: We gaze aloft to spiritual powers from whom all human evolution has issued forth. This reveals itself to us in seven rays, but above this is something far more exalted than our sphere. Later they called what the seven holy rishis experienced Vishvakarman,[33] and they were speaking of a power which had not evolved with the Earth. This was followed by the culture of Zarathustra. When Zarathustra directed his gaze towards the

Spirits of the Sun, he spoke of an element which would flow into human evolution by streaming out of spiritual worlds. Zarathustra said: What we can grant humanity is not what will one day stream from far spiritual realms of the Sun. The spiritual element in the Sun was the being whom later Persian culture called Ahura Mazda.

As a result of a particularly tragic impact did the Egyptian mysteries experience the question of Christ. It was experienced in the deepest possible way, if by 'deepest' we understand a form of human perception that inscribes into the soul a consciousness that humanity stems from what is spiritual. An Egyptian initiate would say: Wherever we turn our gaze, we experience in what surrounds us a fall from our spiritual origins. Nowhere can we find direct, unalloyed spirituality in our physical surroundings. Only when human beings go through the gate of death will they encounter the realm of their origins. One first has to die—as regards inner experience not as regards initiation—in order to be united with the Osiris principle, as the ancient Egyptians called the Christ principle.

This does not happen in life, where the mismatch of duality reigns. Nothing within the compass of Earth leads to Osiris; a soul has to be beyond the gate of death to be united with Osiris. In death the soul will become a part of Osiris, will itself become a sort of Osiris. The outer world has become such that his enemy has dismembered Osiris; in other words everything belonging to the outer world has carved him up. An initiate of the Egyptian mysteries would have said: The human beings of our present culture are a sort of recollection from ancient Moon existence. Just as the humanity of the seven holy rishis is like a memory of ancient Saturn existence and Zarathustrian culture reminds us of ancient Sun existence, so does Osiris culture remind us of ancient Moon evolution, when the Moon and all its attendant beings first separated from the Sun, on which, however, those beings remained from whom humanity originates. This is where humans were separated from the benevolent forces of their constitution, from the fount of their life forces. But the time will come, through all that humanity will have suffered by way of longing for—and privation of—a spiritual dimension, when Osiris will descend and will manifest as the fresh stimulus that is bound to appear, one which has not previously existed on Earth because it had already separated from Earth during ancient Moon existence.

Everything referred to by the seven holy rishis and Zarathustra, and which the Egyptians believed the people of their times could never during their lifetimes attain, this was the force, the incisive impetus which for three years manifested in the body of Jesus of Nazareth. All the great religions spoke of him and he was revealed in Jesus of Nazareth, the being whom all religions had presaged. Thus not only did Christians speak of Christ but so did the believers of all the old religions. In this way an element entered over the course of human evolution of which human beings had great need and which can be reached through inner experience.

Suppose that someone grew up on a remote island. They were told nothing of what was going on in the rest of the world as regards the name of Christ, nor about the Gospels, but only told about prevailing local culture, without mention of Christ or the Gospels. What had developed in their culture under the influence of Christ—but now divested of Christ's name—was introduced to this person. What would happen? The following mood would have to arise; one day they would muse: I have within me something that is in harmony with my entire human makeup, but I cannot at the moment access it. For the place in which my ego consciousness exists appears to me to be lacking something, something which I cannot receive through human culture, some impetus from the spiritual world which will once more strengthen my I in my constitution, from which it has become detached.

If such a person were to feel strongly enough what humans need, something would come over them, enabling them to recognize: something had to stream directly from the spiritual world and wholly settle within my I. They do not know that the name of this is Christ, but they know that they can infuse their consciousness with it, that they can cherish in their I what flows to them from spiritual worlds. Then a sense would come over them of which they could say: Well, I may be ill, I may be weak, I could die, but I can strengthen my I by my own efforts; I can send something into my constitution which will make me stronger, which will give me strength directly from the spiritual world. What they call it is of no consequence.

If a person arrives at this feeling, they are suffused with the force of Christ. It is not the person who claims that they can expect to gain from a teacher who has undergone incarnation after incarnation, but the person who senses in their feelings that waves of power, of strength, can come directly from spiritual worlds; this is the person who is seized by Christ's impetus. Human beings can have this inner experience; without it they cannot live, without it human beings of the future will not be able to live. They can have this experience because for three years this impetus, issuing directly from spiritual worlds, lived objectively within Jesus of Nazareth. As truly as one can plant a seed in the earth and from it many other seeds will issue, just as truly was Christ's impulse laid into humankind. Since that time, something exists within humanity that did not previously exist.

It is for this reason that Egyptian life is so tragic: it was felt that, during one's lifetime, one would be unable to reach Osiris, that one would have to go through the portal of death in order to be reunited with Osiris. This applies only to *inner experience* and not to initiation, which we will speak of later. However, since the time of the Mystery of Golgotha, what was previously impossible is now possible for human beings—of their own accord and on the basis of their unique incarnation—to seek a connection with the spiritual world.

This has come about because the impetus that was given by the Mystery of Golgotha can light up within every soul and, since that time, can inhabit every human being through their inner experience; not the Christ who walked on Earth—the soul is not concerned with this figure—but the Christ who is attainable through inner experience. Since the Mystery of Golgotha it is possible—within a single individual incarnation—to gain a union with what is spiritual. And because this is so, something took place with that single deed of Golgotha which can radiate throughout humanity, which is not granted through the achievements of succeeding incarnations. For this reason it is not possible for Christ to manifest in a way that is the result of many incarnations in the same way as Buddha emerged from his incarnations as a Bodhisattva.

Tomorrow we shall see how, for the future, the path to Christ can be found amid human evolution.

Lecture 8

Stockholm, 17 April 1912

Three Soul Paths to Christ
Second Part: The Path of Initiation

I f in a few words attention might be directed towards the high point of what was presented in yesterday's lecture, I would like to say that, as a result of that point, the opportunity ought to be available to every individual—by deepening their being correspondingly and through a trusting belief in spiritual worlds—for a mood of soul, an attitude of soul, to arise in them whose message is: Not only do those things of the surrounding world—stemming as they do from Earth evolution itself—flow into the human soul, but it is possible for human beings to condition their souls such that they receive into themselves beneficial forces, flowing from spiritual worlds, which can bring about a compensatory balance—one which has flowed into Earth evolution—between the individual's egotistical I and the totality of their constitution, if it is open to this prospect. Whoever can muster confidence in this influx from the spiritual world will have an inner experience—by whatever name they call it—that is a personal, inward Christ experience. Everything else on this subject will emerge once we proceed with the third path to Christ: the path of initiation.

In introducing the path via the Gospels and the path of inner experience, we have set out both routes towards Christ that are available to every single person. Certain preparations are involved in the path of initiation, as anyone will understand. If we want to understand what the path of initiation is—and nowadays this includes real, not just theoretical, immersion in the truths of genuine spiritual science—then this at least must be the starting point in modern times.

Now, it would be good to say a few words in advance about the essence of initiation. Initiation is the highest to which a human being can attain over the course of Earth evolution because it leads them to a certain comprehension of—and insight into—the secret mysteries of the spiritual world. What proceeds in spiritual worlds is the content and the object of initiation; genuine knowing and direct perception of processes in spiritual worlds are achieved on the path to initiation. Even in describing initiation in this way, anyone allowing this characterization to take effect in their soul ought to notice something quite particular. Basically, it has been said that initiation is—if you will allow the expression—a supra-religious path. All the great religions, which have spread across the face of the Earth throughout human epochs—and still exist amongst humanity—have, if we study their origins, all been founded upon initiation and endowed by initiates. They flowed from all that the great initiates were able to confer upon humanity. Religions were founded for humanity in such a way that their content related appropriately to their epoch, ethnicity and even the region in which populations were living.

In terms of human evolution, we are now living in quite an exceptional era, and it is precisely the task of spiritual science to understand how this is the case. The way in which spiritual science is being brought to our contemporaries and is capable of being spread abroad has never before been possible in bygone epochs. Anthroposophy as such could never have been communicated in public. It is only now, in these times, that anthroposophy can be openly imparted. Religions were the way in which the secrets of initiation could flow into humanity in a form suited to a given group of people. But nowadays we are in a position, through anthroposophy, to share something that is not tailored to a single people nor region, nor to any specific group, but which can bring something of the mysteries of existence to any human being, wherever they find themselves on Earth. Souls yearn for this knowledge, which they must receive if hearts are to be strong in their work on Earth. This already shows that in anthroposophy something is being conveyed that ought to occupy higher ground than the point at which religious views stood, still stand and from which they are currently declared. In a certain

sense it is anthroposophy that is tasked with spreading the mysteries of initiation in a pan-human way, whereas in the various ancient
religions across Earth this was always in a distinct manner that was
differentiated according to individual groups of people; only in these
groups could the secrets of initiation be spoken of.

What are the consequences of this? It follows that we find the
most varied religions spread across the globe, all leading back to their
respective religious founder. First we find a religion of Krishna, leading back to Krishna himself, secondly a Buddhist religion, originating
with Buddha and thirdly the ancient Hebrew religion originating with
Moses. Then, too, Christianity, leading back to Jesus of Nazareth.
Because religions flowed from initiation, we need to be quite clear
that today we cannot occupy the same ground as that occupied by
religious philosophers wishing to appear enlightened. Comparative
theologians have a secret view of religions, considering them all false
or simply childlike phases of human evolution. We can take a stand
as anthroposophists—because we learn to recognize that religions
are just differentiated manifestations of initiation wisdom—on the
grounds of recognizing the truth, not the falsehood, within all the
varied religions. We allow religious systems their full right to exist
alongside each other and see them as equally eligible manifestations
of the great truths of initiation.

An extraordinarily important consequence follows from this for
our practical feeling and practical activity. What is so important?
That out of an anthroposophical attitude, a full understanding, an
inner respect and a complete recognition of the core of truth in all
religions will follow and that those who ponder the world and its
evolutionary phases on the basis of anthroposophy will respect the
verities existing in each and every religious system. The greatest reverence will result and the highest respect will claim its place. Yes, my
dear friends, this will be the result to flow from the spiritual stream
of anthroposophy for all the religious faiths on Earth. You will go to
the believers of the different religions of the world and you will *not*
believe you can graft onto them nor instil in them other beliefs. We
will moreover go towards them and—on the basis of our own religious convictions—we will cultivate the truth we find in their beliefs.

And if you are born into a region where a particular religion predominates, you will not denigrate nor reject other religions intolerantly but will be able to go into what can be found by way of truth in its content.

Let us take an example. An example such as this can only be understood by those who are, in their souls, deeply serious about an anthroposophical attitude and about the consequences of knowledge about the nature and basic conditions of initiation. Take a western individual who grew up within Christianity. They may have come to know Christianity by absorbing the mighty truths of the Gospels. Maybe they have reached what we called the path to Christ through inner experience, maybe they have already experienced Christ inwardly. Imagine that they come to know another religion, for instance Buddhism. They learn from those living within the sacred truths and knowledge of Buddhism about what westerners consider a nuisance but which we, as anthroposophists, can understand, namely, that the founder of their religion, having undergone many incarnations on Earth as a Bodhisattva, was reborn as the son of a king, the son of Shuddhodana;[34] further, they learn that, in the twenty-ninth year of his life as a Bodhisattva, he attained to Buddhahood, which in this religion stems from initiation, the *one* great truth, which applies not only to Buddhism but to all humankind, which every initiate will recognize, as will all human beings who understand Buddhism; they learn to acknowledge what believers of Buddhism rightly state: If the Bodhisattva can, in one human incarnation, become Buddha, then this incarnation, undergone by Buddha on Earth, must be his last; then he will never again return to a human body.

Those within Buddhism would be deeply pained, were anyone to claim that Buddha would return to a corporeal body. Deep sorrow would be felt by a follower of Buddhism were some power to question the axiom that the Bodhisattva, having risen to Buddha, could never again return to corporeality and appear on Earth. As anthroposophists, we try to recognize the truth at the core of every religion, standing on terrain that seeks the truth—rather than the errors—among diverse religions. So, we go to those who understand Buddhism and learn to recognize—or learn from initiation to recognize—that it is true: the individual who lived on Earth as Bodhisattva has, since that time, reached spiritual heights from which he need not descend again to the physical rounds of earthly incarnations. From this moment onwards—if we are standing on foundations of reincarnation teachings—we will no longer hold up to a Buddhist the claim that Buddha could return to a physical body.

Genuine, true knowledge will create an understanding for any religious form originating in initiation. We respect all forms of religion that have evolved across the Earth *by acknowledging* the truths they have to offer. Yes, I confess it sincerely and honestly, just as the strictest Buddhist would be able to believe in this verity: that the Bodhisattva who lived on Earth and rose to become Buddha attained the pinnacle of human development, which made it possible for him no longer to need to descend to Earth. That is what it means to have an understanding for the most varied of religious forms here on Earth.

Let's take the reverse case: that a follower of Buddha were to bring themselves to acquire an anthroposophical awareness. They would focus—either on the basis of a real knowledge of Christianity or knowledge of initiation principles—on the fact that for different regions of the world there are different forms of religion, where those who understand religious forms are in agreement that there once lived an individual who actually belonged to no single nation—least of all to the Occident—and that, between their thirtieth and thirty-third year, this personality was inhabited by such an impetus, a force, of spiritual life, to which we referred yesterday, to whom the seven holy rishis referred as their Vishvakarman, to whom Zarathustra referred as Ahura Mazda, to whom the Egyptians referred as their Osiris and whom the fourth post-Atlantean calls Christ.

But this is not the crux of the matter, which is to recognize in Christ what lived as a force for three years in the personality of Jesus of Nazareth, an entity which had never before lived on Earth, had descended from spiritual heights into the personality of Jesus of Nazareth, underwent the Mystery of Golgotha in this personality and, as such, this Christ impulse is a unique spur for Earth that does not have anything in common with a normal human incarnation. Thus the being who was on Earth as Christ—*once only*—and cannot return in human form but, as the Bible relates, will come in the clouds of heaven;[35] in other words, who will reappear as a spiritual revelation to humankind. *That is a Christian belief.*

This person, living within Buddhism, who is permeated with the gravity and dignity of spiritual science, will have to confess that they need to respect and show some reverence for this Christian faith, too, just as a Christian will need to respect their Buddhist faith. The Buddhist who has ascended to spiritual science and who takes it seriously will say: Just as you, being a Christian, bring trust towards the doctrine that the Bodhisattva-who-became-Buddha cannot return to Earth and—appropriately, as it strikes me—you know that Buddha cannot return, so I, as a Buddhist, recognize that the being whom you call Christ cannot return to physical incarnation, but lived as a unique force for just three years in a physical body.

If we can find in anthroposophy such mutual understanding between religions so that the source of initiation can enter into human hearts, such that no one person would impose an alien concept on another, then we arrive at a concept that unites peoples across the Earth, then we are conferring peace among individual religious beliefs.

Jesus of Nazareth lived as the founder of Christianity. Christian initiation tenets apply to the founder of a religion, to Jesus of Nazareth, only as to a fact, a fact that can be investigated by occultists as a verity, as a deed. The life of Jesus of Nazareth can be researched with the same love, with the same care, as would be the life of Buddha or one of the other founders of religions by those who know the ethos of initiation. A description of the life of Jesus of Nazareth appears, purely on the basis of occultism or spiritual science, in my booklet *The Spiritual Guidance of the Individual and Humanity.*[36] However, the actual principle of Christian initiation is concerned with recognizing Christ and deals with the path to Christ. This Christian religious determinant has for many centuries been preparing for what we refer to as the concept of freedom across the world, inasmuch as it does not in the least radiate from the founder of a religion as such, but rather from a factual deed which once took place on Earth.

That is the fundamental difference between Christianity and other religions: the path of initiation leading to Christ has a task—within its worldwide mission—that differs from cultures emanating from other religions, in that it emanates from a deed, from an event, and not from a personality. To understand this we will first have to deal with a few pre-conditions.

A single sentence, a single indication, a single point of origin—albeit externally characterized—describes Christian initiation: It is death that is experienced in the union of Christ with Jesus of Nazareth. The fact of this death, which we know as the Mystery of Golgotha, is the sole basis on which we are to understand Christian initiation. One can only gain a real understanding of this death if one is clear about the mission of that death within Earth evolution. Yesterday we mentioned that fragility, failing health, disease and death are connected with the disjunct between our luciferically-permeated I and our dispositions.

Ultimately, this luciferic aspect is connected with death, but in a most particular way. It would be completely wrong to assume that Lucifer was the bringer of death. Lucifer did not cause death. He brought what we can call the risk of error, including moral error, the differentiation of humanity into ethnicities as also the chance of freedom. That is due to Lucifer. If what Lucifer brought were the only principle active among humanity, and had nothing opposed him, this luciferic activity would have resulted in humanity falling away—breaking away—from divine onward evolution. Humankind would have spiritualized itself, however in a completely different direction from divine onward progress.

To maintain humanity within its divinely-ordained onward course and not to allow it to become lost to divine direction, a particular situation had to be brought about: that human beings would thenceforth, for ever more, be warned of the consequences, were they to misuse the potential for error and for freedom. All illness, frailty, sickness and death are warnings that human beings would be distancing themselves from divine-progressive evolution—even if they were healthy and strong—by relating to the luciferic option of freedom. Thus illness, sickliness and death are not the gifts of Lucifer but gifts from benevolent, wisdom-filled divine powers who, in giving these, have set up ramparts against the influences of Lucifer.

Thus we must say: Everything continually approaching us in the world by way of external evils, be they illnesses or death, all exist so that we humans remain chained to the Earth for as long as is needed for us to take the opportunity of making good, and so that we are taught, the better to adapt to our constitutions. We suffer so that, through our suffering, we create experiences that rebalance our luciferically-permeated I and our divinely-permeated constitution. Our disposition fails us as often as is required for our I to be fully suffused with the laws of divine progress. Every death is therefore the point of departure for something else. Nobody can die without taking with them the potential for one day overcoming death in their future incarnations. All pain exists so that, from that suffering, we create experiences that instruct us how best to continually align with—or adapt to—our divinely-constituted bodies into the future. This issue cannot be dealt with without reference to evolution as a whole.

We can study this matter best if we test, by occult means, the relationship of humankind with the realm just below it, with the animal kingdom. We know that, over the course of evolution, humans have always caused animals pain, that they have killed animals. Those who have learnt to recognize the importance of karma in human life often experience it as very wrongful that animals, who do not reincarnate, should suffer, should experience pain, and even, as far as higher mammals are concerned, undergo death with a certain level of consciousness. No karmic compensation will take place! Human beings naturally experience karmic rebalancing during Kamaloka for the pain they have inflicted on animals—about which I am not going to talk at the moment—I am talking about compensation for animals. Let us be quite clear about this thought: When observing human evolution, we see how much pain humans have inflicted upon the animal kingdom, how many animals they have killed. What does this pain, what does all this death, signify throughout evolution?

Occult research shows us that all pain experienced by sentient beings—apart from humans—and every death sows seeds for the future. Just as animals are willed by advancing divine evolution, they are not intended to have incarnations in the same way as humans. But if change is introduced into this wise cosmic plan, if human beings interfere and meddle in animals' evolution, not leaving it in peace as it would evolve without us, what happens then?

Occult research tells us that all pain and every death perpetrated by humans upon animals, all return and are restored, not through reincarnation, but because harm and pain has been caused to animals. Such pain and suffering elicits once more, or restores, their animality. Animals that have been dealt pain are not restored in the same form but the element in them which feels pain does return. It returns such that the sufferings of animals are rebalanced, each painful experience being replaced with its opposite sensation. This pain, suffering and death are seeds sown by humankind; they return in that their opposite sensation is adjoined in future.

To take a concrete example: when Earth is replaced by Jupiter, animals will no longer appear in their present form, but their pain and suffering will awaken the sentient forces of that pain. These will live in human beings, incorporating themselves as parasitic creatures. The senses and feelings of human beings will create the compensation for that pain. That is the occult truth, which can be spoken of in unvarnished and objective terms, even if this is unpleasant for people of today to hear. Human beings will suffer and from it animals will derive a certain pleasant sensation, will have a good feeling as compensation for their suffering.

This is already beginning to happen slowly and gradually over the course of our present life on Earth, however strange it may seem. Why is it that people are plagued by organisms that are actually neither animal nor plant but somewhere between the two, entities somewhat related to bacilli, which derive a sense of wellbeing from human suffering? We have created this destiny in earlier incarnations because suffering and death were inflicted on animals. Because entities experience this throughout the ages, albeit not in the same form, they sense its compensatory rebalancing in the pain which human beings have to undergo. Thus all suffering and pain is absolutely not without consequence. It is the seed from which ensue the results of what has been caused through pain, suffering and death. No sorrow, pain nor death can occur without it activating something which later arises, bearing fruit.

In view of this, let us review the death on Golgotha, which followed the union of Christ with Jesus of Nazareth. What is first made clear to anyone undergoing an initiation of this kind is that this death on Golgotha was no ordinary death, human or otherwise, to take place on Earth. Those who do not yet have faith in a supra-sensory world cannot conceive of this death on Golgotha at all. Because, even from an external perspective, this Mystery of Golgotha is fraught with exceptional features, from which much can be learnt by human beings. No contemporary description tells of this death and critics of the Gospels claim that the Gospels do not count as historically authoritative documents. Initiation principles are those applied to what cannot be described in historical terms. What took place on Golgotha can still today be observed by initiates; people who have undergone initiatory processes can see this in the Akasha Chronicle.

The writers of the Gospels only wrote what they retrieved from the Akashic Record. An event is described but the original Gospel writers did not think to draw on perceptions of the physical plane. Consciousness was still such that they knew they were dealing with events of the spiritual world and that the most important aspect was to achieve a relationship with those spiritual worlds. No genuine rapport can be established with these events from the sense world. Initiation makes clear what came to pass. One could say: At the start of our calculated era, Jesus of Nazareth lived and in the thirtieth year of his life a momentous change took place through the assimilation of Christ and he was crucified three years later—and this would constitute an event in the continuing history of humanity. Were one to state it in this way, it would be the opposite of what an initiate would find. It would remain a concern of earthly humanity, however much one tried to spiritualize it. This is not something with which initiation concerns itself.

Fundamentally, one can say—and you must not misunderstand me—one can state it radically: Initially, what took place on Golgotha was not an event that concerned humankind inasmuch as they exist on the physical plane. Initially! Not in the sense that one can relate

how a man lived, one Jesus of Nazareth, at the beginning of our calculated era who, in the thirtieth year of his life experienced a decisive
change through the assimilation of Christ and who was crucified
after three years—this is not how the initiation truth of Christianity
would be framed. One would need to say something along these
lines, as the one to be initiated into Christian principles experiences
the following.

The Earth previously underwent a Moon condition. During this
Moon state luciferic entities remained behind. These luciferic entities developed alongside the forwardly-motivated, progressive divine
spiritual beings. During Lemurian ages Lucifer approached humanity
and insinuated himself into human terrestrial evolution, causing what
was characterized yesterday. In this way Lucifer became enmeshed
amongst the entire evolution of humanity. Had human evolution
continued with Lucifer, it would ultimately have resulted in Earth's
mission failing to reach its goal. Humanity would have dried up, the
human I would have detached itself, breaking away from divine-spiritual evolution. On ancient Moon a whole array of beings belonging
to supersensible worlds had, as it were, discovered that Lucifer had
fallen and was opposing them in enmity. Thus the Gods had to see
how Lucifer had become an enemy of progressive evolution. We can
leave aside for now how this affected humankind. Let's view this as
a matter for the Gods and their adversaries, the luciferic beings, and
humanity, as a creation of the Gods. That was the situation.

Now there is a certain unique feature of supersensible, spiritual
worlds. Something is not on hand there that exists on Earth. Death in
all its manifestations is absent. In spiritual worlds one is transformed
but one does not die. Metamorphosis—not birth nor death—exists
there. Group souls, for instance, existing in spiritual worlds, do not
die. Instead they transform, they morph. Birth and death do not pertain in this realm, where the physical world has never exerted its influence. Only where qualities of the physical world have to some extent
transferred to the beings of supra-sensible worlds is there anything
that can be compared with death, such as with nature spirits; but we
cannot take that further today. In the actual spiritual realm there is
no birth nor death, just transformation, metamorphosis. In the case

of those divine-spiritual beings who can be called the creators of humanity, birth and death do not come into consideration. Neither does Lucifer incarnate on Earth as a physical human. He works in humans, through humans, using human beings as his vehicle.

Thus we are dealing with the Gods and with luciferic entities who, as it were, gaze down upon their creations. Had evolution proceeded in this way, had nothing taken place in the world of the Gods, then the intentions of those Gods for humanity would not have reached fulfilment. Then Lucifer would have thwarted the Gods' plan. The Gods had to make a sacrifice—that was their situation—they needed to experience something that was infiltrating their spheres in a way that Gods are actually incapable of experiencing while remaining within that sphere. They needed to send a being of their ranks to the physical plane in order to experience what Gods cannot experience in spiritual worlds. The Gods had to send Christ to Earth in order to do battle with luciferic principles. Over the course of time, when the time was fulfilled, the Gods—who can be collectively called *the divine world of the Father*—sent Christ downwards to learn of humanity's endless pain, an aspect which signifies something quite different for a God than it does for a human being. In this way did the Gods enter into the sphere of Earth in order to do battle with luciferic spirits. A God had to undergo death on the cross, the most punishing, abusively ignominious death, as St Paul in particular emphasizes.[37] For just once in Earth evolution, we were permitted to become witnesses in that we could, as it were, gaze through a window into spiritual worlds at a divine circumstance.

Initiation lore of old stipulated that human beings must, under all circumstances, rise to divine-spiritual heights in order to participate in the determinants of initiation. In sight of all humanity, a principle of initiation was laid bare in the Mystery of Golgotha, an event that was both sense-perceptible at a physical level—to those who had wanted to see—and also supra-sensibly as an event intrinsically of the Gods. That is the essential core: that a God underwent death as a single, unique deed as a balance to Lucifer, and it was granted to humanity to witness this. This is what initiation lore shares as Christian wisdom; it is a source of trust in the truth that to human beings, in their human state, a force could flow which can raise them above and beyond the sphere of Earth and death: because, just once, the Gods carried out their works on Earth and human beings were allowed to witness them.

This is why what flows from the Mystery of Golgotha is pan-human, universal in nature, given for all humankind. Just as every pain, every sorrow, every death has its effect—including those inflicted on animals by humans—this death too had its impact. This death was a seed, sown by the Gods; it was something that remained bound to the Earth, a seed that has ever since endured, bound to Earth to the extent that each human being can, through trust in—and through love of—spiritual worlds, find it. They can find it! The initiate knows that this is so; the believing and trusting human being feels that help with their striving comes from spiritual worlds if only they can nurture sufficient faith and trust. That will develop in a quite specific way.

There lived those who were contemporaries of Egyptian initiation. As part of their initiation, those initiates instructed their pupils in the whole tragedy of the Gods' conflict with Lucifer by symbolically embedding in their mysteries the myth of Osiris and Seth. Yesterday we observed the feelings elicited in Egyptians by this myth of Osiris and Seth. In it there lived the divine-spiritual, towards which humans were striving. This was named Osiris. Yet on Earth human beings could not find a union with Osiris; for this they needed to have gone through the portal of death. Osiris could not live on Earth and was immediately cut into pieces; Earth was no place for what was embodied in Osiris. The last cultural epoch before that of Greece looked towards a hereafter as if towards Christ, towards a Christ-Osiris principle.

Then followed the Greek era, which was entirely permeated by the feeling that it is better to be a beggar in the lands of the living than a king in the realm of shadows.[38] This was still the feeling in Greece in the years of the heroes, when the full weight of the discrepancy between the human I—permeated as it was by Lucifer— and its underlying physical disposition was felt. People felt, as the fourth post-Atlantean cultural epoch ran its course, that they had to grapple with much that could only be experienced on the face of

Earth. Hence the abnormal and exceptional nature of those times. No other age encompassed as many extraordinary consequences of incarnation as did the fourth post-Atlantean epoch.

People had to carry out a great deal here on Earth as a result of focusing more on Earth than on yonder realm—far more than in the previous cultural age. The Greeks did not greatly value this embodiment in Osiris, focusing more on themselves, filling human incarnations with as much as possible, living life to the full. Hence the remarkable fact that Pythagoras—that great initiator of a particular direction in Greek culture—lived in an earlier incarnation as a Trojan hero, fought on the Trojan side, saying of himself that he had been that Trojan hero, as described by Homer, identifying himself as a foe of the Greeks by later recognizing his own shield. If Pythagoras relates that he was once Euphorbos,[39] anthroposophy teaches us fully to understand his avowal. The Greeks set great store by the significance each physical incarnation bestowed on them, even the greatest among them.

However, the fourth post-Atlantean epoch was to lead human beings to feel spiritual worlds in their full significance, because in this timeframe occurred the Mystery of Golgotha. While Greek culture was valuing the outer world above all else, in a far, unknown corner of the world the Mystery of Golgotha was proceeding; in a place where humans were going about their affairs, the Gods were staging, on an earthly arena, their own affairs.

If the Egyptians looked upwards to death when thinking of Osiris, then those in the fourth post-Atlantean age learnt of a contemporary form of religion which contained the impetus for bringing to human beings a sense that in the physical world a divine process was being enacted, which would refute what the Greeks had hitherto believed: that it is better to be a beggar in the land of the living than a king in the realm of shades. For the Greeks would now learn to recognize the one who, as king among the Gods, had descended to Earth and, as a beggar, lived out his destiny among human beings. This was the answer to that feeling during the fourth post-Atlantean epoch. It is also the very nexus of feeling from which light can radiate into the future evolution of Earth. The Egyptian looked aloft to Osiris—

who Christ was for him—so that he could unite with him after death. In the fourth post-Atlantean epoch the Mystery of Golgotha was seen as a contemporary deed that taught humanity how an event had been enacted on Earth in which matters of the Gods were visible.

We live in the fifth post-Atlantean epoch. In our fifth age since Atlantis, human beings will add the great teaching of karma to other beliefs; they will learn to understand their karma. In our fifth post-Atlantean age people will experience the third deed which follows on from the deed of Osiris and the deed of the Mystery of Golgotha. They will learn to grasp the concept: I was placed on Earth through birth. My destiny is on Earth. I experience joy and sorrow and I must understand that what I experience as joy and sadness does not randomly approach me as my lot; it is my karma, my great educator. I look at what existed before my birth, what placed me into this incarnation because this, my destiny, is important for my future development. Who sent me here? Who will keep me on this Earth in my destiny until I have discharged my karma? For this I will thank Christ, that human beings can repeatedly be called to experience their destiny until they have worked off their karma on Earth.

This is why Jesus of Nazareth could not say to humanity, speaking as Christ: Try to take leave of your physical bodies as quickly as possible. Instead he had to say to people: I will send you to your destiny on this Earth until you have disbursed your karmic debts. You need to repay your karma. The nearer we come to the approaching future, the more will people realize that they were united with Christ before birth, that they have experienced being granted his mercy to fulfil their karma through incarnating on Earth.

It was in this way that the people of the fourth post-Atlantean era looked towards Jesus of Nazareth as to the bearer of the Christ. In this way will the people of our time discover that Christ will manifest in ever more spiritually supra-sensible ways and will increasingly hold sway over the threads of destiny among earthly affairs. They will learn to see in that mighty Power the Fate which the Greeks could not yet recognize: the power which will lead humankind, in fitting manner, to discharge their destinies over subsequent incarnations. As they experience them in future, people will look up to Christ as if to a Judge, as to the Lord of Karma in the sequence of their incarnations.

Thus people will relate to their karma such that they are challenged to deepen their souls ever more and more, to the point where they can reflect: I have not been dealt this destiny through an impersonal Power; I have been dealt my lot by an element with which I feel related in my inmost being. In my karma *itself* do I perceive what is related to my being. I like my karma because it makes me a better and better person. This is how one learns to love one's karma and it then becomes the incentive whereby one recognizes Christ. Human beings first learnt to love their destiny through the Mystery of Golgotha. This will proceed ever onwards, ever further and human beings will increasingly learn that Earth could never have reached its goals under Lucifer's influence alone; that human evolution would have become ever more degenerate were it not for Christ.

Yet Christianity does not view Christ as a personality, as the founder of an abstract religious system. In our present times, a founder of a religion would establish—in relation to the needs of this time—only non-peace, only strife. Christian initiation does not proceed from a single personality but from a deed, from a non-personal act of the Gods, which was enacted in full view of humanity. This is the enigma of Golgotha: how what took place at the beginning of our calculated time was transmitted, and that from this unique death the seeds were sown, which now arise as humanity's love of their destiny, of their karma.

We have observed how the death humans have inflicted upon animals has definite consequences. The death on Golgotha acts as a seed in the human soul, in souls who feel within them their relationship to Christ. It was like this with the Mystery of Golgotha: the One died so that we can take that seed and set it into the ground, that it may spring up in the field and that what has risen from the seed may increase. The death of a God on the cross was made reality in this way. The seed was sown on Golgotha, the ground is the human soul; what springs up is the relationship of human souls to the supersensible Christ, who will never more vanish from Earth evolution and who will appear to human beings in the most diverse ways. Just as people saw him physically at the time of the Mystery of Golgotha, so will they, in the near future, elevate themselves to encounter an etheric image of Christ. They will see Christ as St Paul saw him.[40]

What was veiled in Christian initiation was enshrined in the emblem of the Holy Grail and was brought into the community which conferred Christian initiation. For those who receive this Christian initiation, what is said here is no mere abstract theory, is not some hypothesis, but a fact of the spiritual world. The ministration or preservation of Christian initiation was entrusted to those who were protectors of the Holy Grail and, later, to those who served the community of the Rose Cross.

It is in its very nature that what is disseminated from Christian initiation is intended to be impersonal. All personal elements were to be excluded, because what is personal has brought only strife and dispute to humanity, and will increasingly cause disharmony in future. For this reason there is a strict rule among those who—symbolically speaking—serve the Holy Grail or—speaking realistically—who serve Christian initiation, that none of those in leading roles in the upper echelons of Brotherhoods of the Holy Grail or in Rosicrucian communities, that neither they nor those living in their environs are permitted to speak of the secrets that govern their lives until a hundred years have passed after their deaths. There is no possibility of obtaining any sort of explanation from a leading person among the first rank until a hundred years have elapsed since their death. This has been a strict rule within the community of Rosicrucians since their inception. Nothing is ever gleaned externally about anyone who is a leading figure in the Rosicrucian fraternity until a century after their deaths. By that time, anything shared will long have flowed into humanity and will objectively have augmented the common good. This is why all personal elements are eliminated. It will never be possible to identify any personality as a bearer of Christian mysteries while they are in physical incarnation. This would only become possible a hundred years later, and this rule is adhered to by all Brothers of the Rose Cross. Nobody from among Rosicrucian Brotherhoods would ever confirm a living figure as being a leader of the first rank in relation to what is to flow from Christian initiation into humanity.

It could be prophesied in ancient times who would in future come, in the way that prophets were forerunners of their followers or prophets indicated future founders of religions—as, at the time of Jesus of Nazareth, a person then living such as John the Baptist could point to one who was his contemporary—but spiritual provisions for humanity had of necessity to change after the Mystery of Golgotha. Prophecy can no longer tell of one approaching nor indeed indicate one already present. Instead, only a hundred years after they have gone through the portal of death can a personality who has borne the secrets of Christian initiation—that spiritual reality gauged by human hearts—be identified.

All these matters are not decreed by human will but because they have to be thus. They have to take place because humanity is on the brink of times when love, peace and understanding must spread in the process of human evolution. They can only spread if we learn to take matters in a non-personal way, if we learn to represent truthfully everything bequeathed to humanity throughout human evolution.

Never again will we, as westerners, approach a Buddhist with the aim of persuading them to become a Christian because we believe that what they have been given as the deepest aspects of their religion will necessarily lead them to Christ. Above all, we will believe in *their* own truth. We will not hurt the feelings of a Buddhist by claiming as untrue that the founder of their religion, having lived among people as a Bodhisattva, as Buddha no longer needs to incarnate physically. In this way we foster peace among religious beliefs. In future, a Christian will understand a Buddhist and a Buddhist will understand a Christian. The Buddhist who understands Christianity will say: I understand that Christ is related non-personally to his religious principles and that the fact of the Mystery of Golgotha is an impersonal fact, a circumstance of the Gods, which a human being is allowed to witness and adopt and which can connect them with the divine. No perceptive Buddhist will claim to a Christian that Christ can be physically reincarnated. They are more likely to see a breach of true religious principle. No new, strife-instigating faith with a personality-based religious leader will be instated in the world. Instead, the initiation principle itself—with its peace, harmony and promotion of understanding—will enliven mutuality between religions without pitting the truth of one religion against that of another.

In the same way as an eastern Buddhist would reply to a westerner who claimed Buddha could reincarnate: You do not understand the nature of a Buddha, a Buddhist who had grasped Christianity's core and who professed sincere, dignified spiritual knowledge would reply to one claiming Christ's future reincarnation: You do not understand Christianity if you believe Christ will reincarnate in a physical body, you would then understand Christianity as little as someone understands Buddhism who thinks Buddha could reappear in a physical body. What a Christian who is an anthroposphist will always credit a Buddhist with—if they are an anthroposophist—the Buddhist will also credit the Christian with. And likewise the followers of all the religions in the world. In this way will anthroposophy be a great and empathetic force for unity, one which can synthesize religious faiths across the world.

Lecture 9

COLOGNE, 7 MAY 1912

Mysteries of the Kingdoms of Heaven in Parable and in Real Form

T HE increasing significance of theosophy for the people of today and of the near future will only slowly and gradually be appreciated. It will be understood once one has settled into an understanding of certain things which are at present hinted at in religious and occult writings, but which are not usually taken seriously enough. One could point to thousands of places in such religious or occult literature whose depths are simply not recognized because people only skim through them superficially. Today I would like to paraphrase a deeply, deeply significant place in the Gospels: 'Those who stand outside, to them will the mysteries be revealed in parables, so that they see and yet do not see, that they hear and yet do not hear, that they understand and yet do not comprehend. To you, however, will be revealed the mysteries of the Kingdom of Heaven without parables and in their true form.' [Matthew 13: 13-17]

It does not usually occur to us what endless depth of meaning a passage like this contains. What does this mean? Where are the most important parables in which Christ is speaking to his Apostles? The most significant parables are those which one does not normally take to be parables.

Human beings take what they see in the mineral, plant and animal kingdoms around them in the physical world as factual reality, as things which simply exist. They see this animal or that plant and imagine that they are things which are really there, which really exist. They see processes taking place in air and water and imagine these are processes that actually exist. In fact, they do not. Because all these processes in the kingdoms of nature around us, everything taking place in air and water are in fact processes taking place in spiritual realms, revealing themselves through what takes place on a physical level. They are manifestations of spiritual processes, and they are the true reality. Nothing other than the spiritual world is real and only when we can recognize the spiritual in all things and processes have we in truth recognized reality. Everything in the physical world only has the value of a parable, an allegory, a cipher standing for the spiritual world that exists behind everything. We will have to learn to view every process in the animal and plant realms—and everything we encounter in the human realm—everything that makes an impression on our minds and intellects in this way too. They are all nothing more than allegories and only those who learn their true meaning reach actuality, arrive at reality.

Human beings make their way through the world, watch all the processes taking place and do not understand that they are merely tokens. Human beings are directly spoken to through allegories; reality is only mentioned when we speak of the spirit. Christ Jesus speaks to his disciples in images taken from nature, explaining processes which belong to the spirit. He speaks of grains of wheat being sown and diverse outcomes resulting. This can only be a parable because the things of nature are themselves parables. Then, when he explains to his disciples that he is one with all that is the spiritual nature in all existence, that he must undergo death, that what lives within him must sink down into death in order to arise as a force in human hearts and souls—to be bestowed by him on all humankind through this death—then he is speaking of reality because he is speaking of the spirit and of what is to take place through the spirit. This is why real knowledge is only won once human beings have gradually forged ahead beyond the mysteries of the world by learning to recognize all that approaches them externally as tokens, as emblems of spiritual processes. Human souls can only be fruitfully enriched when this attitude to the outer world is established.

If the outer world gradually becomes suffused with spirit for human beings, they will embed themselves differently within it from the way in which they did so beforehand, and will find spiritual traces everywhere in its rhythms. We can note in ourselves an ever-repeating rhythm: that of falling asleep and waking up. We know that humans need to repeat this igniting of day consciousness and fading into sleep consciousness every twenty-four hours or so. If we then ask ourselves with what this alternating human rhythm of sleeping and waking can be compared in the external world, many might imagine alternating states in the plant kingdom such as growth in spring and wilting in autumn. We see the burgeoning sprouting of plants, growing into summer and in autumn see the fruits ripening through the power of the Sun, which has been streaming inwards to Earth over that time. Everything appears to be extinguished during winter, only to regrow again in spring. People might compare their own waking up in the morning with this awakening of physical nature and their own falling asleep with autumn's wilting. But this would be a grave mistake, one to which we must not subscribe if we want to see what is true.

What do we experience when we fall asleep? Our astral body and our I take their leave. They leave our physical and ether bodies. Were we to see what our physical and ether bodies were doing during the night, we would be able to observe that they are quite otherwise engaged from anything that could be compared with autumnal wilting. This can only be observed by looking down onto physical and ether bodies from the spiritual world. They can be seen behaving quite differently from the way they do during the day because, during the day, they are seen to be depleting themselves so that when we are tired of an evening, this is only a sign that we have exhausted our physical and etheric bodies. Living life in full day consciousness entails ruination—death-dealing—to our physical and ether bodies. By evening they are largely drained; and at this point we fall asleep. If we look at them spiritually, we see that a purely vegetative activity begins in physical and ether bodies, which can be compared with what takes place in spring. Physical and ether bodies begin as if to sprout new green growth, as if something were happening within the person that could be compared with spring in outer nature.

The moment of falling asleep needs to be compared with spring and, the deeper into the night we sleep, the more what is happening within can be compared with what happens in external summer.

Vegetative activity becomes ever stronger within our bodies, and by the time we wake up, our condition can be compared with autumn in outer nature. Waking consciousness is subject to forces like those that bring summer vegetation to the point of withering. Over the course of the day, a condition of such barren desertification of physical and etheric forces is reached, which can be compared with winter dreariness, when plants have withered and vegetative activity has died down. Thus, in a spiritual-scientific sense, we should equate falling asleep with spring and waking up with autumn.

When falling asleep—that is, in a spring-like condition—astral body and ego leave their physical and etheric counterparts. Outside in nature it is in fact so that the spirits of the Earth, which are connected with the plant kingdom, as it were, free themselves in spring from what is physical in the plant world and that only then do they rouse themselves into a state of activity. In summer, those spiritual beings connected with the plant kingdom fall asleep, waking up in winter to permeate the entire planetary mass.

One could say: While it is winter in one half of the Earth, it is summer in the other half. Well, rhythmical interplay is such that the spirits of the Earth—when they leave the northern hemisphere—move to the southern hemisphere. They course through the Earth and encircle it rhythmically. The same happens in human beings. We believe our thinking and consciousness to reside only in our heads. When we are outside ourselves at night, we may believe that nothing remains in us that thinks. Yet in truth it is a fact that in the lower part of our bodies a sort of thinking and consciousness that differs from the human is active, so that there, too, a rhythmic circulating is taking place in human bodies.

In spring we can say: Now the spirits of the Earth are beginning to fall asleep; they have withdrawn from the area of Earth where it is summer. Here a vegetative life continues, which is similar to when human beings fall asleep and vegetative processes start in their bodies. In winter, however, Earth spirits wake up. They are united with the Earth in a way that is similar to humans' wakeful consciousness in daily life. When we stand on the ground in summer we are surrounded by physical nature as it jubilates in its physicality. All plant life sprouts and burgeons, as do all the lower spiritual beings of the plant kingdom who are the active builders of growth. In winter, on the other hand, when a covering of snow is spread across the land and over slumbering vegetative activity, we know that the highest divine beings are creating, working and weaving throughout the universe, that they are all around us, that the loftiest cosmic life and consciousness is active in the Earth. This is how it is in winter—and not in summer.

True spiritual science teaches us to be clear about this. Spiritual science, which is able to penetrate these matters with fully clear consciousness, knows that people who retain this, not only theoretically in their heads, but who can feel it in their hearts, too, will reflect: Oh, you approaching forces of spring and summer, you cause everything in nature to flourish and bloom, you call elemental beings forth from the Earth to work. At the height of summer, around midsummer, these elemental beings are celebrating in ecstasy, almost in a frenzied eruption. This is when the solstice and St John's tide are celebrated. Then follow autumn and winter and humans should feel in the depths of their souls: with the withdrawal of external, physical Sun forces, with the approach of winter, when outer nature dies back, as it grows ever darker and darker, it is then that the highest celestial forces are again uniting with the Earth in which we live; and we feel ourselves as if enfolded within those lofty spiritual forces, we feel as though belonging among them in the most profound depths of our souls. We may feel the deepest reverence on becoming aware that, with the onset of winter, we may watch forces—spiritual kindred since primeval times—as they manifest in our immediate surroundings. It is theosophy or spiritual science's task to acquaint you with them and to explain their existence to humankind.

We know that a task of spiritual science is to recall what humans once experienced in the dim and dreamy clairvoyance they once possessed. We are reconquering humanity's primeval heritage. This was a dreamlike, primal, clairvoyant revelation for human beings and there are witnesses to this fact. The festival of St John is placed near midsummer so as to direct human consciousness to experience: now physicality has unfurled to its zenith, now lower elemental beings are revelling to near-ecstasy in the power of their most potent forces. The festival of St John is set by primeval human consciousness that, in this ecstasy of physicality, human beings forget their spiritual element, giving themselves up to the pressing resplendence of physical nature. Yet just as surely did those ancient seers know that in winter the most elevated of spiritual forces are united with our earthly bodies. This is why that ancient consciousness—wherever it could be active—placed the festival most intended to signify that humankind felt at one with the spiritual in the Earth, near midwinter, at Christmas. This feast of a divine being—of the spirit of the Earth—could never have been set in summer by a clairvoyantly cognisant humanity. It had to be celebrated in winter. At the time of the winter solstice did human souls feel connected with divine-spiritual forces then permeating the Earth. The festival of Christmas belongs in winter, just as St John's celebration belongs in summer.

Once one is aware of how the festivals speak to us in lively manner, in the sense that ancient human consciousness fixed them as it did, one can feel spiritually united with their significance. On can then appreciate how the human soul is intended to be enlivened by such knowledge.

The way external physical sunlight arrives, bringing with it celestial-physical forces to Earth in springtime, and the way spirits withdraw to sacred spheres—just as the spirit of each human being withdraws into spiritual worlds at night—all this is wonderfully expressed in the festival of Easter, which is set such that Sun, Moon and constellations are decisive in its setting. The way in which spiritual powers visibly fall asleep in spring is expressed through these constellations.

It is typical of our materialistic age to consider fixing the Easter festival—thereby abandoning precisely what gives Easter its meaning—to facilitate the materialist demands of industry or commerce. What an expression of present-day materialism! It may be handy for finalizing accounts that Easter does not fall one year in March, the next in April, but precisely the fact that celestial constellations determine the setting of Easter expresses how Heaven and Earth work together in concert. Great primeval human wisdom resides in the setting of festivals. Commercial considerations may well prevail and Easter may be set by external criteria, but forgetting Easter's true meaning would be a dire blow to all that humanity should cherish dearly. This is why spiritual science feels called—even if Easter is to be fixed by criteria of superficial interests—to continue counting Easter a moveable feast, one which can only be set according to Sun, Moon and stars.

Alongside any materialistically-fixed Easter, a spiritual Easter will continue to be celebrated, one which we can continue to celebrate in our hearts as being consciously connected with spiritual worlds. A spiritually-celebrated Easter festival will be a parable for the spiritual process which, in spring, is witness to the consciousness of higher spiritual beings as they fall asleep while the consciousness of lower spiritual entities comes to the fore. However, in autumn those lofty spiritual powers, whose consciousness has remained with the Earth, awaken. Once you have felt this deeply, you will gradually come to understand that human beings do entirely belong to the spirit and that external nature is but a parable. People will ever increasingly want to discover how they relate to the spirit—not to outer nature—within this parable.

We are living in the fifth post-Atlantean epoch and attention has often been directed to the fact that this age is a recapitulation of the third post-Atlantean epoch, of the Egyptian age.[41] In the way we now live, something of Ancient Egypt re-emerges in our thinking, feeling and willing. A principal aim of the Egypto-Chaldean epoch was that people were to develop their sense of interrelatedness with the realm of stars.

Astrology was founded and especially cultivated in that era. People knew clairvoyantly how the constellations were related to human life and destiny. They could see deeply into the mysterious connection between the realm of stars and human fate. There were some extraordinarily great spirits in whom this faculty continued into more recent times. They were also incarnated in the Egypto-Chaldean epoch and, in subsequent incarnations, were illumined in their deeply intuitive astrological knowledge as if by an intuitive power emanating directly from within their souls.

This was the case with Julian the Apostate,[42] who was reincarnated as Tycho Brahe.[43] He shed light on the mysterious connection which can be thought of as existing between human destiny and the arcane structures formed by the constellations. It is considered scientifically irrefutable that Tycho Brahe[44] was a great astronomer who discovered a number of new stars in the heavens and who drew a map of the constellations. Scientists therefore consider it forgivable that he was also an astrologer who peddled all manner of prophecies to people on the basis of the stars. They forgive him for predicting the death of Sultan Suleiman[45] on the basis of his deep astrological knowledge[46] when he was teaching at the University of Rostock. They also forgive him for stunning the world with this pronouncement, saying that prophecy was just a weakness to be overlooked in an otherwise great man. They even forgive him for the fact that the Sultan did die at the very moment Tycho had predicted! In Tycho Brahe we see ancient Egyptian wisdom reigniting, and this must shine into our own times, as they are a recapitulation of the Egyptian age.

Nowadays we also need to seek out connections between the divine and earthly worlds. This involves not only seeking in heavenly realms but also studying parables about—analogies with—divine realms which are to be found in physical kingdoms. We can find them in both the greatest and the smallest matters. If we, for example, study leaf spurs in various plants, we will find that, by following on the stem the line made by the sequence of budding leaf spurs, we arrive at a spiral. We notice that leaves grow in a rhythmic spiral sequence around a stiff stem. In other plants, such as Bindweed (*Convolvulus*) it is the stem itself that creates the spiral. Most people do not notice things like this. Were you to study something of this kind, you would make new discoveries.

You would discover that such spiral formations are dependent on forces not present on Earth, but which exert their influence downwards from the planets. These planets inscribe spirals in space and cause plants to make similar spirals around their stems. Yet the stem grows upwards from below and this motion bisects the spiralling forces. This is the force that concludes at the tip, preparing the blossom to emerge. This force radiates outwards to the Sun and back.

Each species of plant is assigned to one planet or another and their respective movements. A time will come when we will know how Venus or other planets move. This will not be discovered by external astronomical data but by studying how those plants, which are entities of Venus, reflect in their microcosmic spirals Venus' unequivocal track. Up yonder Venus inscribes her great spirals into cosmic space and the plants mimic her movement in their own small spirals. The planets inscribe their script, imprinting it into the Earth, and the Sun forms their conclusion, pouring itself over everything and reigning supreme over what the planets have created. The co-operative work between Earth and celestial realms will be studied in the spiral growth of plants. The growth of plants is a parable for facts concerning spiritual beings in cosmic space.

In this way cosmic correlations will be found between each physical entity and cosmic space. One will be able to link them to events in the cosmos and in this way one will gradually find one's way as to where minerals, plants, animals and even humans—in their deeds and destinies—find their corresponding realm of affiliation. We will study such things in their small beginnings—as we have done today—in the light of spiritual science. It will be a long time before science travels these paths, till it studies such things in their true contexts, on the basis of occult sources. But happen it must.

If one relates to the world in the context of present-day evolution and takes everything outward as a sign, allegory or parable, a guideline will be found in our *Soul Calendar*. But you should not think that the signs for the zodiac images represent those constellation themselves. The sign of Capricorn does not represent the constellation of Capricorn, but means that the Sun or the Moon stands in a certain relationship to this constellation, activating particular forces there. These signs do not represent things placed in space but forces that are active there, be it in this or that way. What we call space is mere make-believe. Spiritual forces exert their influences from everywhere and *how* they do this is expressed in those signs. When the Sun rises of a morning above, say, the constellation of Pisces, this constellation is the expression of distinct forces emanating from spiritual beings and raying down to Earth.

We can feel all this and we can transform it into imaginative knowledge. What can burgeon forth from our souls when we really feel what radiates towards us from the spiritual world, this is what we were trying to express in the *Soul Calendar*,[47] brought out this year within the theosophical movement. In it you find signs that differ from the old, traditional calendar symbols in an attempt to express what souls of today need to learn anew. They arose as a result of following in feeling—not intellect—what we observed as those alternating rhythms on Earth: how spiritual beings connected with Earth fall asleep in spring and reawaken in autumn. A renewal of aspects such as this—festivals into which age-old clairvoyant wisdom has been poured—is essential. Festivals have to be renewed because, in this fifth post-Atlantean age, the heritage of wisdom from the third age is to be resurrected.

It must strike outsiders as highly irrational to start our *Calendar* in 1879. We simply wanted to emphasize how exceptionally important it is to place the Mystery of Golgotha as the starting point of our calculated time and not the year of Jesus' birth. The Mystery of Golgotha took place on a Friday, the 3rd of April in the year 33, at 3 o'clock in the afternoon. And this is the time of the birth of the I, in the sense that we have often referred to it. It does not matter where on Earth a person lives, nor to which religion they adhere, what entered the world through the Mystery of Golgotha is for all humankind. Just as the particular day Caesar died is applicable the world over—and not on another day for the Chinese and a different one for Indians—so it is a simple fact of spiritual life that the Mystery of Golgotha took place at that time and that here we are dealing with the birth of the human I. It is a matter of international fact. One has to wonder that from some quarters it is claimed that what goes on here in our Rosicrucian theosophy—which places the Mystery of Golgotha at the very centre of everything—should be cut out solely for German consumption and be unsuitable for other peoples.

Where things of this kind are stated, no inclination is shown to get to grips with the matter in hand. Nothing is understood about Christ and the Mystery of Golgotha. Distortions are put out into the world and unfortunately distortions are believed. Yet it is a sacred duty to protect people from error, even though it can be no pleasant task telling them such truths. But it has to be done. In other places it is said that the same rights apply to everyone, yet one breaks this rule oneself. It is not a matter of saying this or that and printing it, but that truth should prevail amongst us and that truth becomes our sacred law. We want to bring the birth of the I to expression in our *Calendar*. But this means actually taking the moment of that birth as our starting point. This is why we counted from Easter to Easter instead of New Year to New Year. Were this to cause further annoyance, derision and sneering, this need disturb us little because we know that, had we only ever wanted to repeat old, well-worn traditions, no new life would ever come about. Sameness, endlessly repeated, is death; differentness, slipped into sameness, is life. Our *Calendar* is a project for life. And if we have done it badly to date, we will do it better next year.

Most important, however, is part two of *The Soul Calendar*. There I tried to assemble, week by week, meditations formulated in such a way that souls can live through them inwardly, meditatively, and which have the effect on souls of making the connection between their own inner experience and what is directed over the course of time by divine-spiritual beings. These meditations can lead to truly experiencing these spiritual beings if they are carried through seriously and with devotion. Lengthy occult experience and research have been compressed into these fifty-two formulations, which can serve as time-blueprints for an inner life of soul, linking it to processes in divine-spiritual experience. They constitute something timeless that can represent the correlation between what is spiritual and what is sense-perceptible. Anyone will be able, over time, to appreciate the value of this *Soul Calendar*, and will retain its meaning for ever, gradually finding their way from the human soul out to the spirit, which inhabits and weaves throughout the universe. It will not be easy to make these meditations one's own in their deepest significance. Souls will take years and years to do that. This *Calendar* doesn't merely document notions that suddenly cropped up, but is a deed, which relates organically to our whole movement, where it will eventually be seen why some of its contents are created in one way, while others are done differently.

LECTURE 10

COLOGNE, 8 MAY 1912

Prophecy and Heralding Christ's Impetus
The Spirit of Christ and its Sheaths: A Whitsun Message

ToDAY's talk calls for an introduction on the theme of our observations. It is, after all, the day which we in the theosophical movement call White Lotus Day,[48] which each year reminds us that Mme
Helena Petrovna Blavatsky, now having left the physical plane, was
the founder of the theosophical movement in recent times. It will
need little encouragement to adopt a tone, which is surely within
every soul here present, to elicit feelings of admiration, devotion
and gratitude towards the individuality who sojourned on Earth
in Mme Blavatsky and who refocused and renewed humankind's
view of the ancient Mysteries, from which has flowed every motivation towards—and strength for—spiritual development needed by
human beings. Understanding and grasping the task of recent times,
H.P. Blavatsky could share, in popular form, the Mystery wisdom to
which she had access, such that this popular form diverges from the
ways and means—through secret channels and streams—by which
Mystery wisdom once percolated into human work and creating.

Precisely this is the recent significance of the fact that what used to
be given to the few now has to be disseminated in more general form.
To be among the first to act along these lines became the mission
of Mme Blavatsky. She directed human attention towards something
which has indeed for ever been holy to those who knew about it.
That this is so will now be the starting point for today's remarks and
it will bring us nearer to our subject: the poetry of a thinker whom
the mass of educated people know—or, rather, do not know—as a

dry, conceptual thinker, as a foreman, as a master builder of far, far removed forms of ideation. What this thinker supposedly only transmitted in crystalline mental constructs belied the warmest of feeling and proved that ideas alone cannot clothe what stems from the heart. He demonstrates this in a poem addressing sacred Mysteries.

Hegel[49]—who one can say is the thinker of Europe—who has become so well known to modern scholars that today many of his books remain unopened in libraries, has left us a poem written with his heart's blood. I am referring to the poem 'Eleusis',[50] which will now be recited by Miss von Sivers. With this poem we would like to pay tribute to the memory of H.P. Blavatsky.

Hegel's 'Eleusis'—dedicated to his friend Hölderlin, August 1796:

> Around me, within me, reigns peace.
> The unrelenting cares of busy human beings now sleep.
> I am granted freedom and ease.
> Thanks be to you, my liberator, O night!
> The Moon shrouds the uncertain outlines
> Of the distant hill with a bloom of mist. The bright strip of lake
> Glints genially across at me.
> The memory of the day's tedious clatter
> Recedes, as if long years lay between it and now.
> Your image, dear friend, now rises before me
> With the joy of days long flown.
> Yet soon these yield to the sweeter hope of our reunion.
> I paint even now the opening scene:
> Of our long-anticipated, fiery embrace,
> Later, the more inward questions, the secrets,
> The mutual querying:
> To discover what, in bearing, countenance, sense or feeling,
> Time has since wrought upon my friend.
> Then the delight of certainty on finding
> That faith in the old bond remains, now truer, firmer, riper than before,
> Not sealed by any oath save: *by free truth alone to live,*
> *Never, never to make truce with any convention*
> *That would regulate our feelings and opinions.*
> Then does thought parley with drear reality,
> And that thought, which lightly bore me to you
> Over mountains and rivers,

Announces with a sigh its discord, and with it
Flees that sweet dream of fantasy.

My eye is raised to the eternal dome of heaven,
To you, O radiant stars of night!
And forgetfulness of all hopes and wishes
Streams down from your eternity,
Erasing all thought in the beholding,
And what my I named I vanishes.
I give myself up to the immeasurable.
I am in it, am everything, am it alone.
But returning thoughts estrange,
Horrified at the endlessness and,
Amazed, fail to grasp the depth of this beholding.
Imagination brings thought closer to the eternal,
Marrying it with form.
Welcome, you sublime beings, lofty shades,
From whose brow fulfilled perfection rays,
I am not daunted. I feel it also as my home,
That gleam, that gravity, which around you flows.

Ah! Were the portals of your sanctuary now to spring open,
O Ceres, you who were enthroned in Eleusis!
Now drunk with exaltation, I feel the festive nearness of your presence,
And would comprehend your revelations.
I'd interpret the lofty sense of the images,
Would hear the hymns at the Gods' banquets,
And the sublime axioms of their counsel.
But your halls have ceased to echo, O Goddess!
The circle of Gods has fled to Olympus.
Fled from their desecrated altars.
And from the tomb of profaned humanity
Is fled that genius of innocence who enchanted them here.
The wisdom of your priests is silent. Not a note of the sacred
Rite is preserved for us—and in vain do they strive,
Those scholars, their curiosity greater than their love of wisdom.
They possess the seekers and they disdain you.
To master them they dig for words,
To find the graven imprint of your exalted mind
In vain! Mere dust and ashes do they seize,
Wherein your life eternal returns never more to them.
Yet, even under mould and un-ensouled, they preen

Themselves, th' eternally dead, the self-satisfied—in vain!
No sign remains of your celebrations, no trace of an image.
For the sons of initiation, the abundance of majestic teachings,
The depths of that ineffable feeling, are far too sacred
That they should dignify it with desiccated symbols.
The very thought of it seizes not the soul,
Which, submersed beyond time and space in intimations of infinity,
Forgets itself and once again
Awakes to consciousness.
Were any to want to tell of this to others

—were they e'en to speak in angels' tongues —
They'd feel the poverty of words.
Recoiling in horror at the sacred being thought so small,
Having made it so small
That speech to them seems a sin,
Thus, quaking, their lips they seal.
That vow the initiate bade himself,
A wise law forbade those poorer spirits
From making known what they had seen, heard, felt
Throughout the sacred night.
That not even the further advanced themselves
Should be disturbed in their prayers by the clamour of their mischief,
Their hollow chatter stirs to anger that holiness itself
Should e'er be dragged through filth, yet be still
Entrusted to memory, so that never would it become
A plaything, nor wares of the sophists,
Who would sell it for an obol[51] coin,
Nor become the mantle of eloquent hypocrites, nor
The cane to a mirthful youth, nor yet to become so empty in the end
That only in the echo of foreign tongues would its life's roots be found.
Your sons, O Goddess, stinting in your honour,
Flaunted it not through lanes and markets
But nurtured it in their breast's inner sanctum.
Thus did you *not* live upon their lips,
And thus did their lives honour you.
In their deeds you still live on.

Only tonight, holy Goddess, did I hear you.
And oft do the lives of your children reveal you to me.
I divine you time and again as the soul of their deeds!
You are the exalted signifier, the true faith
In the single Godhead who, when all else founders, does not falter.

I feel myself to be in complete harmony with the individuality of H.P. Blavatsky, especially when, if I may say, over the next few days a few words are spoken about her in clear and frank truthfulness. It was her way, when she was fully herself, to wish to be true. That is why we honour her best when we send our grateful thoughts to her and speak a few words of the purest truth.

H.P. Blavatsky showed in her totality, in her individuality, what inner strength, what a strong impulse she had in relation to the spiritual movement we know as the theosophical movement. To underline this one only needs to be directed to her first larger work, *Isis Unveiled.* On the average reader, this book really makes a chaotic impact in that it goes, as it were, above and below. Yet if someone who knew that its contents represent ancient wisdom, protected in the mysteries, knowledge that has been guarded over many ages from profane view, and who also knew that this wisdom is not disseminated through external human works but via secret societies, they will nevertheless find much chaotic material in this book—but also something else. They will also encounter, for the first time, a work which, staunchly and fearlessly, lays certain secrets of the Mysteries bare before a profane world. Anyone who understands such things will find vast tracts that are correctly interpreted, in a way that only those initiated can do.

The chaotic impression remains and can be explained in terms of the following, sensible observations: the outer personality of H.P. Blavatsky, to the extent that she was incarnated in her physical body, with her intellect and with her personal traits, her sympathies and antipathies, demonstrates to us, in the way *Isis Unveiled* is written, that it was utterly impossible for her—on the basis of her personality, of her soul—to produce what she gave to the world. She communicates things she herself could not possibly understand. If one follows her train of thought, it becomes proof that higher, spiritual individualities made use of the body and personality of H.P. Blavatsky in order to communicate what necessarily had to flow into humanity. Just because one cannot ascribe to Blavatsky what she gave does one have lively proof that those individualities who are with the theosophical movement are the Masters of Wisdom and the

Harmony of Feeling, who found in her an instrument. Those who see this clearly know that matters do not issue from her but that they flowed through her from high spiritual individualities. Today there is no time to speak of this in detail.

One could raise the question—and it is often raised: Why did these exalted individualities choose Mme Blavatsky as their instrument? Because she was, in fact, the most suitable. Why was one of the scholarly gentlemen who study comparative religions not chosen as this instrument? We need only focus on the most eminent and respected of experts in oriental religious systems, the great Max Müller,[52] and we will see why, in his own words, he could not announce what had to be communicated through the human instrument of Mme Blavatsky. He expressed a curious opinion about what Mme Blavatsky had to say about oriental wisdom: If you encounter on a road a pig who grunts, nobody finds that remarkable. But if you encounter a human being who grunts like a pig, people find that very remarkable. It should be said: Those who do not corrupt eastern religious systems in the sense mentioned by Max Müller equate with a human who grunts like a pig. Neither do I see much logic in the comparison, for what grounds would one have to be so surprised that a pig grunts? However, when humans grunt, that is an art not everyone can master. This is a slightly lame comparison, but the fact that it could be made at all shows that the personality of Max Müller was not the appropriate one.

A personality had to be chosen who was not particularly gifted intellectually and this naturally entailed all sorts of disadvantages. In the event, Mme Blavatsky brought with her all the passionate sympathies and antipathies of her character into this great communiqué. Now she felt a strong antipathy towards those worldviews which flowed from the Old and New Testament records; she had a strong reaction against all things Hebrew and Christian. One thing, however, is essential to recognizing the ancient wisdom of humanity in its original form, and that is to face the revelations emanating from spiritual worlds with absolute *symmetry* of feeling. Antipathy and sympathy create a sort of fog, obscuring our inner eye. It was in this way that Mme Blavatsky felt increasingly constrained by this mist existing in her vision and could only see with any clarity what was transmitted via the so-called purely Aryan tradition. She saw this in its spiritual depths with peculiar clarity but became one-sided and so it came about that, in her second great work, *The Secret Doctrine*, she depicted the ancient, Aryan proto-religion in a biased, prejudiced way.

One should not seek for the Mysteries of Sinai and Golgotha among Mme Blavatsky's oeuvre because she brought antipathy towards them. It was because of this that she was led by powers which could—with great clarity and power—endow her with anything but Christian content. You can find this in the wonderful *Dzyan Stanzas*, which Mme Blavatsky included in her *Secret Doctrine*. Yet, through it, she was forced from the path of initiation in the physical world, and this emerges through *Isis Unveiled*, if only in fragmentary 'rays'. In the latter book Mme Blavatsky could only portray—on account of her incomplete initiation—this one-sided stream, which was being led by a view of the world that excluded Christianity. Thus did an idiosyncratic book, *The Secret Doctrine*, come into being, a book in which there are the greatest revelations that humanity could at the time receive. It contains things that are emphasized in other books, such as the letters from the Masters of Wisdom and Harmony of Feelings, the so-called *Letters from the Masters of Wisdom*.[53]

Here again you find some of the greatest things revealed to humankind. But there are other parts of *The Secret Doctrine*, such as a detailed theory of mass. It is precisely those who—from a correct understanding—value among the highest what her *Dzyan Stanzas* and her *Master* letters could convey to humanity who also gain the impression that the long drawn-out tracts on the theory of mass issue from someone suffering from graphomania, from someone who just jotted down whatever came to them and who couldn't put their pen down. Other parts speak out of a deeply passionate nature about scientific things, yet without comprehension of any precision.

Thus *The Secret Doctrine* is an intermixed assemblage of things best disconnected, yet which does contain high wisdom. It becomes understandable when one takes alongside it the remarks of one who knew Mme Blavatsky well and was highly knowledgeable.[54] He said:

Mme Blavatsky was actually a threefold being. Firstly you encounter a small, ill-favoured woman of illogical thought, with a passionate character, who was always annoyed about something, yet who could be good-naturedly loving and compassionate, but definitely not what one would call a talented woman.

Secondly, when wisdom would pour through her words, she was a pupil of the great Masters; then her expression and gestures would change, she became someone else, out of whom spiritual worlds spoke. She was also a third personality, a royal apparition: awe-inspiring, towering above her surroundings. These were the rare occasions when the Masters spoke directly through her, giving tidings through her words and writings. Souls inspired with a sense of truth will always differentiate meticulously in Mme Blavatsky's works and know what is at issue. No greater service could be offered to Mme Blavatsky—to whom we turn our gaze today—than that we recognize her in light of the truth; no greater reverence could be offered her than to lead the theosophical movement in light of the truth.

Clearly, at the inception of the theosophical movement, an individual direction had to be taken. But it has grown and become more significant, and it also became necessary to feed another stream into this theosophical movement. It has become essential to add to the theosophical movement what has been flowing from occult sources through Rosicrucian elements since the fourteenth century and against which Mme Blavatsky was implacable.

Today we have fulfilled the intentions of the theosophical movement in that we have not only recognized the oriental wisdom and view of the world but have also added to them the outlook that finds expression in the revelations of Sinai and the Mystery of Golgotha. Maybe especially today a question might be inferred: Does the comprehensive scope in understanding the true impetus that should be contained within the theosophical movement consist in adding to the world outlook of H.P. Blavatsky what could not be included at its inception? Or does 'comprehensive scope' consist of elevating a most questionable and specialized opinion to the level of dogma and wishing to disseminate this as that very comprehensive scope of the theosophical movement?

For my part, I say unapologetically: I know that we would be dishonouring the spirit of H.P. Blavatsky, who is now in the spiritual world, were we to follow the latter course. I know that it is not to transgress against this spirit—but rather to accommodate it—if one does what it wills today: if one adds to the theosophical movement that which this spirit—while in their physical body—was not capable of adding.

I also know that I am in full harmony with Mme Blavatsky in what I am telling you when I say the following. I wish for one thing: that our western stream should be brought to bear on this theosophical movement.

Some additional knowledge and certain supplementary truths have been introduced over the last few years. Let us imagine—let us really imagine—that in fifty years everything would have to be revised and corrected; let us suppose that not a single stone of our spiritual building—in the way presented today—could remain standing upon another, that occult research would be obliged to rectify everything, from the ground upwards, in fifty years' time. I would have to describe it only thus: that may be the case, but one thing among what we want here will remain, and it is towards this end that the prime thrust of our occidental theosophical movement is aimed. May this be the one thing that can be said: That there was a theosophical movement which wanted nothing other—in the field of western occultism—than to show to advantage what issues from the purest, most unclouded truthfulness. Our aim is that this can be said. It is better not to say dubious things at all than that people should somehow deflect from that which—in the purest sense of the truth—we can stand for responsibly in the face of spiritual powers.

There may be other upshots from this, namely that someone may feel called upon to object: Why do you reject this or that issue as it appears in the theosophical movement? That is hardly tolerant! Others may associate tolerance with differing concepts, but we use concepts such that we feel obliged to protect humanity from anything that cannot stand the test of unalloyed truthfulness. Some may distort what we do but we will not give ground; we will try to fulfil our task to the point where we reject everything that needs to be rejected while serving what has just been said. Then—but only then—when something causes our sense of truth to be in disharmony with it, only then can we reject it. We do not recognize any other reasons nor feelings. We will not get involved in trivial turns of phrase and talk of opinions being of equal value, of brotherliness and so on, because we will know that even love among human beings can only flourish when it is truthful and sincere. Let this wish to be ensouled by truth—permeated by a pure sense of truthfulness—be the expression of this festive day.

Because a new feature has been added today, more has come to light that can serve as a contribution towards explaining the mysteries of the universe. These things are not said to denigrate in any way other great cultural or religious movements among humankind nor to compare one with another. How often has it been mentioned that, when we look back to the first post-Atlantean epoch, with its spiritual culture of the holy rishis, there was during that first period a culture of loftier spirituality than all that followed? Just as little does it occur to us to disparage Buddhism; rather do we highlight its virtues, knowing that it has endowed humanity with qualities, which Christianity will only in future have to attain. Yet it is immensely important that we repeatedly point to the differences that exist between eastern and western cultures.

Eastern culture speaks only of individuals who have—over many incarnations—undergone advancement. Oriental culture speaks, for instance, of Bodhisattvas as individualities who have completed their human development more quickly than others. However, they focus on the individuality who goes from incarnation to incarnation and that, in a particular incarnation, that Bodhisattva attains Buddhahood. When such a Bodhisattva has become a Buddha—something that can only take place on Earth—they are no longer required to return to a physical body. In other words, the further back one goes, only the individuality remains in focus and their incarnations are less emphasized. Buddha is more frequently spoken of in terms of a stage or a virtue, which other Buddhas also attained over the course of their lives, than of the historical Buddha, Prince Shuddhodana.

By contrast, it is different in the West. We have undergone an evolution in which we do not speak of the individual who moves from incarnation to incarnation but value is placed on the personality in western culture. We speak of Socrates,[55] Plato, Caesar, Goethe, Spinoza, Fichte,[56] Raphael[57] and Michelangelo[58] in their single incarnation, not as individualities passing from incarnation to incarnation. We speak of *the* Socrates, about *one* Plato, Goethe and so on as the particular expression each individual has found. Western culture was conditioned to emphasis the individual qualities, characterizing them afresh and ignoring what the individual undergoes over many incarnations. Now we have reached the point where we are gradually recognizing how an eternal individuality proceeds through separate lives. Now we are experiencing how humanity is striving to see what lives from personality to personality. This will entail inspiring human souls anew with light that brings understanding and this will spread throughout human souls. The way in which individual personalities will be conceived in future and how this will transpire can be illustrated in an example.

Let us turn our gaze towards a figure such as the prophet Elijah.[59] First one observes the prophet Elijah as himself. The primary feature concerning us is that Elijah in a certain sense prepared the ground for the Mystery of Golgotha. He pointed towards the fact that the impetus of Yahweh-Jehovah could only be understood and conceived of by an I or ego consciousness. He was not able to predict the full meaning of the human I, being himself at an intermediary stage of ego consciousness between Moses' idea of Jehovah and the Christian idea of Christ. In this way the prophet Elijah appears to us as a mighty harbinger, as a forerunner of Christ's impetus, of what took place through the Mystery of Golgotha; thus he appears great and mighty to us.

Let us now move on and look at another figure. From a western standpoint, we are used to seeing him as a single individuality: behold John the Baptist. Western outlooks see him as a finite personality. But we learn of him as the herald of Christ himself; we know him in his life as a forerunner of Christ, as the first person to utter the words: Change the condition of your souls, for the Kingdoms of Heaven are nigh—indicating wholly towards what would become the impetus of Golgotha: that in the human I a totality, a God, could be found, that the Christ-I would ever increasingly inhabit the human I, and that the stimulus towards this was at hand.

Now we learn through spiritual-scientific knowledge that what the Bible hints at is true: that the same individuality as lived in the prophet Elijah was then living in John the Baptist. So that the one who was to be a harbinger for Christ lived as Elijah, returned as John the Baptist, and was once again a forerunner of Christ, as befitted those times. Now these two figures are connected for us. Western culture goes about things differently: it goes straight to an individuality, thereby neglecting the individual personality.

Looking further, we find an extraordinary figure in the Middle Ages, born—as if to hint that it stands in a particular relationship with the spiritual world—on Good Friday in 1483, and who returned thither as a young man in his thirty-seventh year—one who so mightily influenced the world through what he was able to bring humanity: the figure of Raphael. He was born on Good Friday, as if to betoken his connection with the event celebrated on Good Friday. What can western views learn from spiritual science in relation to the figure of Raphael?

If we observe this figure by means of spiritual science, we can learn that he accomplished more for the spread of Christianity, for embedding inter-confessional Christianity in the hearts and souls of humanity, than all theological interpretations, than all the popes and cardinals, of his time. Raphael may have had in his mind's eye what history writes about the Apostles: one among the Athenians stepped forward and said:—even the gesture is captured in the painting— You people of Athens, you have brought offerings to the Gods in outer signs. But there is knowledge of a God who lives and weaves in all people. That is Christ, who went through death and arose again, thereby granting humanity the stimulus towards resurrection.

Some listened to this, others found it strange. Within Raphael's soul this became the painting we find in the Vatican, which bears the incorrect name of *The School of Athens*.[60] It actually depicts the figure of St Paul, teaching the Athenians the fundamental tenets of Christianity. In this Raphael was bequeathing an image, as if heralding what transcends the denominations of Christendom. The profound meaning of this painting has met with little understanding until now and its full significance has still not dawned on humanity.

If we look at other paintings by Raphael, we would need to say: Truly nothing remains of what popes and cardinals achieved for humankind in those days. Yet the effects of what Raphael attained are only now really coming to life. How little he was understood in times gone by is evident from the fact that Goethe, when in Dresden, did not even go to admire the *Sistine Madonna*[61] because he had heard from museum officials that general opinion held that the Jesus child had something mean in his expression; the two angels in the foreground could only have been added by some lumpen artist; the Madonna herself could not—in the form we now see it—have originated in Raphael and must have been repainted. One can trawl through the entire art history literature of the eighteenth century and find barely a reference to Raphael; even Voltaire[62] does not mention him.

And today! Today Protestants and Catholics alike—or indeed anyone at all—can be deeply moved by Raphael's paintings. It can be appreciated how in the *Sistine Madonna* a great cosmic mystery exists, one that imprints itself deeply on human hearts and one which will in future be able to take this quality further if humanity can be inspired towards an inter-denominational, widely-encompassing Christianity, as portrayed today through spiritual science. One will be able to build upon the experience that something as wonderfully mysterious as the *Sistine Madonna* has affected human souls. I have often mentioned that, if you look into the eyes of a human child, you can be sure that from those eyes radiates an element that has not yet stepped through birth into existence and which allows the depths of the human soul to gaze out. Anyone looking at the children in Raphael's Madonna paintings will see that his children's eyes radiate the divinity, mystery, super-humanity, with which all children are still connected shortly after birth. This can be seen in all Raphael's paintings, except one. Just one painting cannot be described in this way and that is the Jesus in the *Sistine Madonna*. Anyone looking into this child's eyes knows that far more than can be contained in one human being is looking back at one from this child. Raphael created this difference so that, in this one *Sistine* child, something should live that is purely spiritual, foretelling Christ-like qualities.

So, Raphael is a harbinger who announced the spiritual Christ and who is conceived of anew in spiritual science. Through spiritual science we learn that here again is the same individuality who lived as Elijah and John the Baptist, now living in Raphael. We also learn to understand that the world in which he was John the Baptist is resurrected in Raphael through the fact that his birthday on Good Friday implies his relationship towards the historical Christ.

Here we find a third harbinger after Elijah and John the Baptist and can understand some aspects that someone seeking more widely around questions of John the Baptist would uncover. John died a martyr's death before the advent of the event on Golgotha; at the time of the Mystery of Golgotha he experienced the red dawn at sunrise, the time of prophecies and presaging, as also the times of jubilation, but he does not accompany the time of cruel persecution and suffering. If this mood of soul is now transplanted into the personality of Raphael, can we not fathom why Raphael painted so many paintings of the Madonna and child with such devotion? Do we not understand why we find no paintings of the betrayal by Judas, no bearing of the cross, no Golgotha, no Mount of Olives? Such paintings as exist of these subjects must have been painted to order and the being of Raphael is not truly expressed in them. Why do such images not reside within Raphael? Because, as John the Baptist, he was not present to accompany the Mystery of Golgotha.

If you view the figure of Raphael in this light, as an individual who has existed for many centuries and still lives today, and turn your gaze to all the works that still survive—and those already destroyed—while considering that all this must go the way of all matter, one knows full well that what is alive in these paintings will be taken up into human souls long before they pass away. There will be reproductions for many centuries ahead but what can only convey an image of Raphael's true personality, what he himself created, that will fade, will turn to dust and his works will pass away. And nothing *temporal*, nothing on our Earth is capable of preventing that.

Yet through spiritual science we can be certain that what lives in Raphael as an individual, all that has been worked upon, reappears in that individual together with what has been transmuted. When we learn that this same personality re-emerges as the poet Novalis,[63] when we first hear Novalis announced, appearing like a roseate dawn as a new, living idea of Christ, then we can reflect: Long before all that Raphael created and attained disappears from the world, here there reappears the individuality within this person, now in a new form to endow humanity with all that it is capable of giving. How good it was that western culture could only view the limited personality for a while, that we learnt to love a personality purely in terms of their single life! How immeasurably are our souls enriched in the knowledge that what is eternal in human beings journeys from life to life! However differing these personalities appear to us, we will nevertheless come to understand much through what spiritual science can teach us—with concrete facts—of reincarnation and karma.

Humanity will benefit greatly, not so much from general concepts and doctrines as from all that can shine light on individuals. Only through intuitive vision and occult research can aspects such as these be added to what is known, and then we will be able to direct our gaze towards the Mystery of Golgotha itself, remembering that in Jesus of Nazareth's thirtieth year the Christ being entered him and underwent the Mystery of Golgotha.

If one speaks today of the fact that the Christ being cannot be embodied again in human corporeality, one must state that this has never actually been claimed. Because, even then, his physical body was merely the sheath provided by Jesus of Nazareth, into which the spiritual Christ being was able to descend. This is not like other human beings, who build their own bodies; but it was only later that the Christ being sank down into the body, which Jesus of Nazareth had prepared, albeit blending entirely with it. Here, too, we can hardly speak of a corporeal embodiment of Christ. These are matters that are obvious to those who know about them.

Now we are aware that, through this Christ impetus, something appeared on Earth, which flowed into humanity, which benefitted all humanity by streaming into all human cultures. Thus the being who went through death is like a grain of corn, which increases, entering into individual human souls and bearing fruit. Now that we know that the Christ being—who underwent death and was immersed in the Earth—was absorbed into the body of Jesus of Nazareth, we can ask ourselves: What will happen when Earth has reached its goal, has come to its end? Christ, who approached the Earth from far distant regions and united himself with the Earth, will become the essence itself of Earth's goal, will become the Spirit of the Earth. He is already the Spirit of the Earth, but in future human souls will be permeated by his being and will form a whole, a totality, with his being.

Now let us frame another question. We have learnt to view human beings—in their earthly guise—as maya. This figure or guise, which dissolves at death, is an image or simulacrum, which appears to humans as the outer form of the human body. The outer form of the physical body does not remain, just as little as will the outer body of a plant, an animal or a mineral remain. Physical bodies will be transformed into what atomizes and becomes cosmic dust. What one presently sees as the physical Earth will have completely disappeared, will no longer exist. And as for etheric bodies? They only retain their relevance as long as physical bodies require renewal. They will also no longer be present. By the time the Earth will have attained its destination, what will remain of all the humans we now see? Nothing, absolutely nothing will exist, nothing of themselves, nothing of the beings of other realms of nature. When what is spiritual will be freed, nothing will remain of material but unformed dust because only the spirit has reality. Yet one thing, which was not previously united with Earth, will have become a reality and human souls will be united with it; one thing will be a reality: the Spirit of Christ. He will be the only real element remaining of the Earth. How does this Spirit of Christ come by his spiritual sheaths? How do those sheaths, in which he will work onwards, come into being?

This Christ Spirit, like the Soul of the Earth, descended as momentum, as a force of impulsion, into the earthly sphere at the Mystery of Golgotha. Even the Christ being has to form elements one can call his layers or sheaths.

From whence does such a being acquire his sheaths? This does not take place in the same way as with other human beings, but Christ, too, will have a kind of spiritualized physical body, a kind of ether body and a version of an astral body. Of what will such bodies consist? These are matters that can only be hinted at provisionally, in an interim sense.

Christ descended through the Baptism in the Jordan into the sheaths surrounding Jesus of Nazareth. He made use of them; he inhabited them; in them he partook of the Last Supper with his disciples, in them he experienced Gethsemane, in them he was berated and scourged, in them he underwent the Mystery on Golgotha. Then he arose, was resurrected, and has lived ever since as the Spirit of the Earth, united with it; he is creating something akin to the elements enveloping human beings.

Gradually, over epochs of time, around the original, purely spiritual Christ impulse, which descended in the Johannine baptism, elements akin to an astral body, an ether and a physical body are being formed. All these sheaths are formed from forces which must be developed by humanity on Earth. Which forces are these?

The forces of external sciences cannot build Christ a body. In them one merely learns about things which will have disappeared in future, which will no longer exist. One thing, however, advances ahead of such knowledge and which has an endlessly greater value for souls than any knowledge in and of itself. It is what Greek philosophers saw as the origins of philosophy: awe or wonder.

Once we have arrived at cognition, what is actually valuable for the soul has already passed. Those who are capable of wonder at the great events and truths of the spiritual world imbue themselves with feelings of awe and wonder. The qualities which they absorb in this way create—over time—a power which exerts a force of attraction for Christ's impetus, attracting Christ spirit. Christ's impulse unites with individual human souls to the extent that a soul can marvel at the mysteries of the cosmos.

Christ's impetus draws its astral body from all those feelings of wonder and awe alive in individual souls throughout world evolution.

The second constituent needed to educate human souls—by which it draws to itself Christ's impetus—are feelings of compassion. Every time such a feeling of compassion or sympathetic joy is nurtured in the soul it creates a force of attraction for the Christ stimulus and Christ connects with the soul through compassion and love.

Compassion and love are the forces out of which Christ forms his ether body, and will do so until the end of Earth evolution.

In relation to compassion and love, one could mention an agenda— to put it coarsely—which spiritual science needs to deliver in future. Materialism has diminished science to a shameful matter even in this area, something that has never before happened on Earth. The most appalling outcome of this is to conflate love with sexuality. It is the most terrible expression of materialism, the most diabolic of our times. What takes place in this quarter needs to be crystallized out. Sexuality and love, in their true senses, have nothing in common. Sexuality can be an adjunct to love but has absolutely nothing to do with pure, pristine love. Science has caused an outrageous disgrace in publishing swathes of literature combining these two behaviours, which are totally disparate.

A third trait attracted into human souls as if from spiritual worlds is conscience, to which it submits and to which it ascribes a higher value than to its own, individual moral instincts.

Christ unites most inwardly with conscience, and from conscience does Christ derive his physical body.

A saying in the Bible becomes very real for us, once we know that Christ derives his life- or ether body out of human feelings of compassion and love: 'What you have done for the least of my brethren, you have done for me,'[64] because Christ is forming his ether body out of human compassion and love until the end of Earth evolution.

How Christ creates his astral body out of wonder and awe and how he shapes his physical body from out of human conscience, in just such a way does he build his ether body out of feelings of compassion and of love.

Why is it that we can now say such things? Because now one great problem will be solved for humanity, namely, portraying—in its reality—the figure of Christ in the most varied quarters in life. This will only be seen as it really is once we have taken into account what spiritual science has to say. We should not look backwards to Palestine: there the Christ availed himself of the sheaths of Jesus of Nazareth. If you immerse yourself over a long time in the spiritual-scientific conception of Christ and try to depict Christ, you will arrive at a figure in the nature of whose countenance you recognize all the qualities towards which art can aim, must aim and will aim. His countenance will contain an expression of forces victorious over all other forces in the human form.

Once humans are able to form an eye that is alive and radiating pure compassion, a mouth not made for eating but for speaking only such words of truth as issue from human tongues of conscience, and if a brow can be imagined which is not just high and beautiful but whose contours express clear beauty in the way it tautens forward towards what we call the lotus flower between the brows—if all this could be created, one would understand why the prophet said: He is without form and what is beautiful.[65] This does not mean without beauty, but it denotes that which triumphs over decay; the figure of Christ consisting solely of compassion, of love and the moral imperative of conscience.

In this way can spiritual science serve as a seed that is planted into human feeling, into human sensing. All the teachings that spiritual science is able to share do not just remain static but are transformed directly into *life* within human souls. The fruits of spiritual science will eventually become conditions of life—manifesting in souls as if they are external embodiments of spiritual knowledge itself—over the course of future human evolution, as it is destined to become.

It is with thoughts such as these that I hope to have put something to work that can be effective in your souls, not merely with dry words but when one would like to speak with feeling-ideas, with nuances of feeling, to those striving for spiritual knowledge, so that these nuanced feelings and ideas can live and work, so that they can exist out there, in amongst the world. If nuanced feeling can live in hearts, it can become a fount of warmth, which can stream outwards into humanity. And those who believe in this will also believe in the effect of their good feelings, will believe that every soul can feel in this way—even if karma does not allot to them the means of express-ing this outwardly—and also engender invisible effects so that what needs to come into the world through spiritual science can really be brought about.

This is what I so dearly wished to elicit from you as a feeling on the occasion of my present visit to Cologne.

LECTURE 11

Synthesizing Worldviews
A Fourfold Herald

S PIRITUAL science must become an instrument of mutual understanding, a means by which we can—right across humanity and
deep into souls—learn to understand one another. This learning-
to-understand-deep-into-each-soul must permeate us, must be alive
in us as an anthroposophical attitude and ethos, otherwise those
occult truths which must flow into humanity through spiritual science will be unintelligible also to us. In this sense spiritual science
can—because it is like the key to understanding our most inward
aspects—create peace and harmony on Earth. How can it do that?

Let us demonstrate this in a concrete example. Take the relationship of two people in the world who have two differing religious
beliefs, let's say Christianity and Buddhism. What can be said of
Christians and Buddhists—as a classical example—can, of course,
also be said about the worldviews and beliefs of two people living
next to each other in Europe. For what applies to the great also
applies to the small within spiritual knowledge. If we take a Christian
and a Buddhist in their traditionally orthodox beliefs, how do they
relate to one another?

Well, in the way that the Christian is actually convinced that Buddhists can only attain happiness if they adopt Christianity in the
form in which they themselves have adopted it. This is how Christian missionary activity takes place among Buddhists: they transport
their particular beliefs to them. In similar vein do orthodox Buddhists behave. Imagine that both of them become anthroposophists.

How can the Christian, as an anthroposophical Christian, relate to the Buddhist? Let's say they hear all about the main tenets of Buddhism, which can only be rightly understood by someone fully within Buddhism. Nowadays, there are two ways in which one hears about various religious beliefs: from those who study comparative religions and from those who learn about differing beliefs through spiritual science.

Focusing for a moment on those engaged in comparative religion, one has to admit that they are extremely diligent and active people engaged in academic evaluations of differing religious creeds. When they carry out these comparisons, something odd transpires: what they are seeking—even though they do not admit to it—actually turns out to be non-truths about those religious beliefs. They seek out what is untrue, what was believed by various religions in more child-like times, in other words, what is not true. A spiritual-scientific researcher will look for the primary core in each religion, will seek for what albeit exists as a single nuance, but which is a nuanced perception, in this or that religion. Put differently, they will look for what is true in each faith rather than for what is untrue.

In this respect, it can turn out strangely. Isn't it the case that nobody in possession of the facts will have anything but respect for the most prominent among comparative religion academics, perhaps the greatest expert in his field, Max Müller? Even he did not produce much apart from what can be called the falsehood of oriental faiths. Yet he believed that he was conveying everything comprehensively. At this point H.P. Blavatsky stepped forward, speaking in quite different terms. She spoke in such a way that one could see that she was conversant with the core truths of oriental faiths.

What did Max Müller make of that? His judgement is somewhat grotesque and proves that an academic does not need to be exactly clouded by logic. He opined that people flocked after 'the Blavatsky', that she gave them an utterly false, distorted depiction of eastern religions, in total disregard of true portrayals such as, for instance, those promulgated by himself, Max Müller. He made the following comparison:[66] when people on the street see a normal pig grunting, they are hardly surprised, but seeing a person grunting like a pig causes quite a stir. Wishing to compare what oriental religious systems naturally bestow—namely his version of comparative religion—that is, the naturally grunting pig (needless to say, I am not making this comparison!) with Mme Blavatsky's contribution: that of a human being grunting pig-like. Now, I don't wish to comment on the refinement of such a critique, as it doesn't seem particularly cogent to me. I might be slightly surprised at someone grunting convincingly. But I would not—absolutely not—couch the discipline of comparative religion in terms of the said animal. It is strange that Max Müller himself should do so.

Spiritual science acquaints us with the true core of the various religions. Let's take Buddhism as our starting point. A Buddhist knows—if conversant with the roots of their faith—that Bodhisattvas exist, that these Bodhisattvas, starting as individualities, make a swifter ascent than other human individuals in attaining Buddhahood. Buddha is a general term for all those who, during a corporeal incarnation, rise from Bodhisattva to Buddha. One among them who is especially identified by the name of Buddha is the son of Shuddhodana: Gautama Buddha. One has to recognize in him one who, in the twenty-ninth year of his life, attained to Buddha virtue, that the incarnation during which this occurred would be his last and that he would no longer be obliged to return to Earth in physical incarnation. All this is perceived by the Buddhist as being true.

A comparative religionist would see this as childlikeness. To anthroposophists familiar with the mysteries of religions in different fields, Buddha does not appear in such a guise, because they recognize the truth in this. In this respect anthroposophists relate to Buddhism in the same way as a believing Buddhist, saying: Yes, I know that Bodhisattvas exist who rise to Buddhahood and no longer need to incarnate. This is an item of faith in your community and I recognize it just as you do and, inasmuch as I do this, I too can look upwards and revere Buddha. The anthroposophical Christian starts fully to understand what Buddhists profess and shares the same feelings and sentiments; they understand one another—at least in this respect.

Let us now take the contrasting case, in which the Buddhist has become an anthroposophist, who now understands what Christians who have gone beyond the earthbound orthodoxies familiar to denominational Christianity also know about Christianity, assuming from the outset that this anthroposophical Buddhist has heard what a Christian of this kind has to say about Christ's impetus itself. They hear that, within esoteric Christianity it is understood that, in the course of Earth evolution, what is known as Lucifer approached humankind, as part of their human evolution. They hear that, through this, humanity descended further than would have been the case without such luciferic influence. Further, they hear that we look aloft as if to a circumstance of the Gods when we focus on Lucifer's rebellion and outrage in face of the progressive Gods. We are actually looking at a circumstance of the Gods. And then we hear from the Christian who really understands their faith that the compensatory balance for this divine situation—playing out as it does between the progressive Gods and Lucifer—had to be what we know as the Mystery of Golgotha. Why was this so?

Well, in its present form, death and all that pertains to death, really came about through luciferic influence. Death is something which can only be found on physical Earth. There is no death in supersensible worlds, inasmuch as it is accessible to human beings through clairvoyant consciousness. Not even do the group souls of animals die; they merely transform, they metamorphose. Metamorphosis exists, but not what we call death. Death in the form of decay and dissolution of parts of an entity only exists in the physical world. By way of a compensatory force, supra-earthly beings had to choose—and this can only be hinted at—an experience of undergoing death in order to establish community or common circumstance with human beings, something that would create a balance for the luciferic outrage. In order to triumph over Lucifer, divinity had to undergo death. For this to take place, divinity had to descend to Earth.

What took place through the Mystery of Golgotha is therefore a concern of the Gods, through which recompense for Lucifer's activities could be created. This is the only divine situation that has played out in full view of humanity. This unique impetus can be portrayed in no other way than that a divine being underwent death on the physical plane and that Christ's force has been streaming out into the Earth's atmosphere ever since. This is now seen as the original and fundamental element of Christianity by the Christian who understands their faith.

What distinguishes Christianity—when grasped in its deepest aspects—from all other religions is that other religions view their genesis in the figure of an original founder or instigator, in a personality. But in Christianity the founding core is not the personality of Jesus of Nazareth, but the fact that this personal founder is only the bearer of the Christ impulse; that Christianity sees as its central fundament a deed. This can only be grasped with all possible intensity: as a deed that had to be fulfilled just once in all Earth evolution; in a divine God undergoing death. This constitutes the exceptional nuance of truth in Christianity: that its origin was not an individuality but a deed, an event, an experience.

For this reason it does not concern us if someone says: Just look, Jesus of Nazareth had all sorts of passions, all sorts of qualities which—let us say, in the manner of eastern views—someone advanced should no longer possess. This is not what matters. In Christianity Jesus of Nazareth is not at issue, but the deed, the event on Golgotha is the issue. Just let the founders of other religions have their personal qualities, let their merits please other folk better than those of Jesus of Nazareth! But those who, as Buddhists, become anthroposophists will see that everything in Christianity hinges upon the event on Golgotha and they will reciprocate in kind the respect they were given. They will say: Just as you concede that there are Bodhisattvas who self-develop as individuals and rise to Buddhahood, never again to reincarnate, so we concede that once in human evolution a God underwent death. You grant us the nuanced truth of our religion, likewise do we grant you the nuances of truth in your religion; both understand each other.

However, they would not understand each other—and peace would not break out—were Christians who deemed themselves to have become anthroposophists to say: I don't believe that Buddha will never reincarnate; I assume he will, at some point, return to a

corporeal body. That would be an impossibility for one who understood the very kernel of Buddhism. A Buddhist might reply: You do
not understand Buddhism. It is quite obvious and beyond discussion
that, just as little does someone who states that Buddha will return
in the flesh understand Buddhism as the other who states that Christ
will return in the flesh[67] comprehend Christianity as a unique life of
a divine being whose purpose it was to undergo death on the physical
plane—and nothing else.

We are talking about mutual understanding right across the world,
about real comprehension and, through it, peace. Strife would be
the result of claiming to a Buddhist that Buddha would return to
physical existence. Strife would result from claiming Christ could
return to physical life. Such claims would need to retaliate at a deep
level, because they are impossibilities in terms of what really lives in
human evolution. It would be grotesque to suggest that Christ would
return and that people would understand him better than they did
then, and would prepare themselves better for his return and this
time would not need to kill him. Such a view would be unaware that
it was precisely a matter of death and that without it there would
be no Christianity! Goodwill towards understanding really does lead
back to *mutual* understanding and we see that spiritual science can be
an instrument for finding the prime core of all religious faiths everywhere. If one has the will to find it, one will surely do so. This makes
it a message of peace across the Earth.

Spiritual science will add to the material-cultural body—today
consisting of industrial and commercial relationships worldwide—a
cultural soul element, which can span the globe. It is precisely
because we can recognize the manifold ways in which the various
religious faiths have endowed humanity that we continually apply to
them all what spiritual science can furnish us with in terms of their
core truths. Precisely by these means do we arrive at a kind of synthesis, a union, a consolidating fusion of varying worldviews in our
time. This is underlined in just one point.

It has never been the intention within the anthroposophically-
orientated movement we are creating to portray the differences
between religious faiths in such a way as to apportion merit to one

to the detriment of another. They are simply characterized. How often has it been said that the spiritual heights attained immediately after the catastrophe of Atlantis in the culture of the ancient Indian rishis has not even now been reached? Such heights—in the form that they now exist—have still not been attained in Christianity. We are not apportioning merit nor fault when we describe each religion in its very essence. We are merely describing when we draw attention to other differences.

If we follow a more oriental way of thinking such as that adopted by most people of a Buddhist faith, you will notice one thing: the main focus of interest is on what one can call the passage through many incarnations. One speaks of a Bodhisattva; but a Bodhisattva is not one who lives only between their birth and their death but one who returns ever and again until eventually attaining to Buddhahood. One speaks of Bodhisattvas as if they appeared in varying numbers within human evolution. There one tends to generalize, seizing more upon each enduring individuality. What has been the prevailing tendency hitherto within western conceptions? Precisely the opposite. When people spoke of Socrates, Plato, Raphael or Michelangelo, they were denoting personality; western views placed each individuality centrally within the limits of their circumscribed personality. That had its advantages in that it educated towards chiselling out, exploring individual human personalities. This was fundamentally the case in outlooks which H.P. Blavatsky did not understand, such as the ancient Hebrew and New Testament perspectives.

Look, for instance, at Elijah. Occult research uncovers something surprising about him. I need only say that his uniqueness is notable in that he appears as a forerunner of what needed to take place through Christ's impetus. He still conceives of the matter as the divine being expressed through the folk-ego. Yet he already draws attention to the fact that the most worthy means of recognizing this lies within the I itself. In this sense, Elijah is to be thought of as a forerunner of Christianity, and no prophet other than Elijah seems to me to be a similar herald. He still retains Jehovah-overtones in his words; yet in Elijah's words Jehovah has moved as close to the human I as was possible.

Let us look at another figure, another unique personality: John the Baptist. We see how he foretold Christ's impulsion, how it is John the Baptist who characterized in words this stimulus of Christ. He enjoins us to change our ways, not to look back to the times of ancient clairvoyance but to seek the Kingdom of Heaven inwardly within the human soul! John the Baptist frames in words what constitutes Christ's influence in reality. He is a herald of Christianity in the most wonderful way. What lives at the heart of John the Baptist appears to us as a sort of advanced teaching—advanced spiritual schooling—by contrast with what lived in Elijah.

Let us now turn to Raphael and we see him as seemingly quite a different figure from John the Baptist. But in looking at Raphael— we only need to immerse ourselves in him a little on a human level— we again find in him a herald of Christianity.

Take the following. Let's open the Acts of the Apostles where Paul is amid the Athenians and where it is related: [Acts 17: 22, Ed.] Then Paul stood …and said: 'Ye people of Athens, I perceive that in all things ye are too superstitious … you have an altar with the inscription: *To the unknown God!* God that made the world and all things …dwelleth not in temples. But [in words to the effect that] I say unto you that the unknown God is not told of in his reality by outer signs nor symbols but resides in all living things in creation. He is the God who lived on Earth and arose and, through his resurrection, will lead humankind itself to its own resurrection.' The Acts of the Apostles tells further—and we still see Paul amid the Athenians—how some believed and others did not. Among the first to believe was Dionysios the Areopagite.

Then we can look at a painting by Raphael, which is hanging in the Stanza della Segnatura in Rome [now called the Stanza di Raffaello, Apostolic Palace in the Vatican] and known as *The School of Athens*. We can assume—as was quite natural in those days—that Raphael had the passage from the Acts of the Apostles just mentioned in front of him. It came alive within him. Now look at the various faces he gave the Athenians and, right down into the hand gestures, we see stepping forward among the Athenians a figure whom we can recognize if we can only focus on Paul in the Acts of the Apostles.

We could examine the most varied aspects of Raphael in this way. If we look at his series of Madonnas, we might wonder: Isn't there one strange feature about Raphael? He is great when he paints scenes depicting becoming, developing and growing in the beginnings of Christianity; the small Jesus child as if containing the germ of all future Christianity. However, we find none of Judas' treachery in Raphael's paintings and no bearing of the cross, as his painting of this subject[68] appears as if assembled in compilation, and not at all like other works by Raphael. On the other hand, his *Annunciation*, his Ascension and the like, all point to what is in process of becoming in Christianity.

How do these speak to people? They speak in a highly singular way. You know that one of Raphael's most glorious works can be found in Dresden: the *Sistine Madonna*. Short-term thinkers might imagine this painting to have arrived in Germany like a victor. It made little impression on Goethe[69] because he had heard what most people thought at the time. As a young man, Goethe was not as confident in his judgement as he was in his maturity and was susceptible to what others believed. What did museum officials tell him in Dresden? That the child wore a mean expression, that the Madonna had been overpainted by some amateur and that the little putti had been added by a handyman. This was the general consensus on the *Sistine Madonna* when Goethe visited Dresden in his youth.

But look at it now! See what Raphael has become for people! He worked in Rome at a time when articles of religious dogma were fiercely debated. The way in which Raphael paints Christian mysteries is inter-denominational. If we take the later great Italian painters, we see religious mysteries painted in a way that makes us imagine: this is the Christianity of the Latin peoples. Raphael paints in such a way that we are clearly dealing with the most universal representations of Christian mysteries, which transcend cultures or ethnicities. Thus we see that within a short time the *Sistine Madonna* had, even in Protestant areas, settled into souls. If anthroposophy is to work towards understanding Christian mysteries, it will find its best access through souls in whom sensitivity is alive, souls who are moved by paintings such as the *Sistine Madonna*, in souls who are prepared in this way. And if we say nowadays that Christianity is only in its developmental infancy, that its true stature will only be understood through the spiritual key which anthroposophy can provide, then we know that Raphael stood as a herald in relation to this Christianity.

And now we can turn our gaze towards yet another figure and in so doing we turn to someone completely western in outlook: let us turn to the German poet Novalis. If we look at his work, we find throughout his oeuvre predictions of the purest anthroposophy—right into the details—one just needs, as it were, to disentangle them. One sees how Novalis is permeated with anthroposophical Christianity.

Today we have brought four figures into focus as personalities. That was a western approach. Now we come to a process of spiritual-scientific deepening. Through this we can experience, for instance, why Raphael felt as if magnetically drawn to being born on Good Friday, so that his birth would signify externally that he had something to do with the mystery of Easter. Such things can only be hinted at today; in only a few decades people will see such things as are being stated here in the same light as scientific facts are viewed: namely, that it is the very same individuality who inhabited Elijah, John the Baptist, Raphael and Novalis. First they will recognize the personality and then the individuality who has persisted throughout. Now we can grasp this fourfold harbinger, this herald and its ascent. Now we can relate to something of this nature differently from before.

Nowadays there is an awareness that the paintings in Rome's Stanza are no longer in their original form but have been spoiled by hands other than Raphael's. In a few centuries they may not exist. Even though reproductions may give them a longer life, what that individuality created will be lost at an atomic level. Though Raphael's works may turn to dust over time, we know that the individuality who created them was present again in Novalis and treated their content in renewed form.

So we see how what a western perspective made of the limited personality can be augmented by the individuality; how what is best in western outlooks can be enhanced by what is best in eastern viewpoints. This is the way evolution strides forwards over time. To the extent that humanity marches onwards and gains insight into these matters will the spiritual world not remain silent but will also speak to humankind in their more everyday phenomena. People will not, as it were, just need to advance themselves towards the spiritual world through types of knowledge, but will increasingly transform such knowledge into what one can call lived experience.

For this to happen, a truly spiritual movement is essential today. That this is vital is shown plainly by the fact that even the simplest things are no longer evaluated correctly. One detail will be highlighted today. Human beings—if they are healthy—go through a cycle of waking and sleeping over twenty-four hours. We know that, on falling asleep, physical and ether bodies remain lying in bed and that astral and ego take their leave. What happens to what remains in bed? When the clairvoyant looks back from their astral body onto what is taking place in ether and physical bodies, they see how a more vegetative life begins, a life that is actually disturbed by day consciousness. Tiredness is balanced; in other words, blooming and burgeoning now thrives in ether and physical bodies when astral and ego are withdrawn. When these sink back into ether and physical in the morning, it is their task to tire them once more: they allow what has grown and burgeoned during the night to be grazed down and to wilt.

Everything in the microcosm also exists in its macrocosmic form. When we see how in spring the Earth is clothed in green, how plants thrive, how leaves and blossom burst forth, preparing for fruit, what are we witnessing? Someone used to making external comparisons will say that waking up in the morning is like nature waking up in spring. Yet the opposite is true! We should be comparing the flourishing in spring with falling asleep. We should be likening the springtime burgeoning and sprouting of plants with what takes place in human physical and ether bodies on falling asleep. When nature becomes ever more verdant towards summer, this is like human physical and ether bodies in the midst of sleeping. Autumn is similar to the human being diving back into their physical and ether bodies, causing wilting in what had flourished during spring. One needs to associate correctly what takes place within and without, avoiding superficial metaphors that link spring with waking up and autumn with falling asleep. Quite the reverse.

So, we can say: Those who are the Spirits of the Earth fall asleep in spring and awaken as Earth Spirits in autumn and winter. In winter they are bound up with the Earth as Earth Spirits in order to arise in spring and summer into the heights of the heavens, into astral heights and onto the other side of the world. When we experience spring again, they return to sleep.

This does not contradict the fact that the Earth is asleep now in this hemisphere, now on the other. Something similar also applies to human beings. Those who can follow these processes clairvoyantly will see that spring resembles humans falling asleep, where each individual spirit withdraws into the astral world; they see how in spring what we have called Earth Spirits withdraw into the astral world, and vice versa. Yes, today's humanity—those present excepted—would probably burst into hilarity on hearing about the Spirits of Earth as they wake and fall asleep; you can credit modern humans with doing everything possible to prove that they haven't the faintest idea about real-world processes. This hasn't always been the case—by no means!—and was once quite different.

A primal clairvoyance used to see such things as they really were. It saw that Earth Spirits withdraw in spring and rise to cosmic heights, descending again in autumn. This was visible in ancient times, when it was natural in mid-summer to point to something like an absence of actual Earth Spirits from the Earth. Conversely, elemental nature spirits shoot upwards, paroxysm-like, leaving behind a terrestrial-corporeal part of the Earth, which manifests through what is sense-perceptible. One can do no better than to place the festival of St John precisely at this time to illustrate how the upwards-rushing nature spirits are at work and how the actual Spirits of the Earth—who are the I and the astral body of the Earth—are absent.

How do matters stand at the approach of winter? The Earth wakes up and is connected with its astral body and I. Festivals associated primarily with human spirituality are therefore best set during this season. This is why Christmas takes place in winter. Then, when the Earth Spirit leaves for the heights—which is the implication at Easter—people would ascribe this taking leave of the Earth—this entering into astrality—to the relationship between Sun and Moon.

In looking into all these questions, we are united in a wondrous way with ancient clairvoyance, showing us what can be seen when elements of ancient times jut into that human connection with primal divination. Materialistic perspectives find it natural to opine that they need only to nurture their bodies. They say that it is inconvenient for us, in terms of banking procedures and suchlike, to have the Easter festival sometimes early, sometimes late in the year and this should be regulated so as not to disrupt commerce and industry. They say let's insist that Easter be celebrated on 1st April every year! That would just suit a materialistic age devoid of all connection with a spiritual world. Just as it suits materialism to foster such ideas, it is equally true that a spiritual movement must protect the connection with the time-honoured setting of humanity's festivals. We will not in any way be prevented—especially with regard to practical activities—from doing what is commensurate with a spiritual view of the world.

This needs to be expressed in everything that is planned for you in our *Soul Calendar*, which will of course seem risible to the world at large. Nor do we wish to deprive them of it, even though they consider us fools. The *Calendar* expresses how we need to hold fast to our connection with ancient times. In the illustrations—created by one of our dear and honoured members[70]—you will find a renewal of what had become dry and barren: imaginative depictions relating to Sun, Moon and the constellations of the zodiac, revitalized for modern souls and rendered—if you observe the sequence of weeks and days—so as to convey something of this vitality.

Were you to ask yourselves: How can one conceive of this oneself?—just look at the *Soul Calendar*, whose mediations are the result of many years' occult research and experience. If you activate these verses in your souls, you will see that what constitutes the connection between the potency of spiritual worlds and your souls will be established over the course of time.

What we call the Mystery of Golgotha has been treated exoterically, externally, so that it would not shock on first viewing. We created an arc all around it, on which 1912-13 is marked, but inwardly the *Calendar* is designed so that the birth of the human I stands at the beginning, in other words with the Mystery of Golgotha. In addition, the way the year has been reckoned makes it uncomfortable for commercial purposes, but as it is necessary for spiritual life: from Easter to Easter!

In this way something has been created which has grown out of our way of thinking and which is useful to those who, by using it, can devote themselves more closely than via other means to this path towards the spiritual.

It will become ever more obvious—working from a base of unified principles and common fundamental motivation—how issues undertaken within our anthroposophical movement are actually thought through; how each person here is not merely present on a whim but is disposed—like single building blocks—to connect themselves with and to join in the totality of our work. For this to happen it is of course vital that—in more and more members—the light of awareness for this co-operative work is activated and that every one of us transcends our specialist interests and personal ambitions to direct ourselves increasingly to what unites us.

It is, of course, understandable that members have many personal wishes and aims, things which one person or another wants to bring to the anthroposophical movement. But particularly here, in this place, where selfless co-operation will be needed if we are actually to bring to fruition what is planned, it must become deeply rooted in our hearts that we can only work productively if our niche interests do not take precedence over what we can contribute to an overarching success, to what benefits the whole, in the manner of the building-block simile. Otherwise no composite whole can be created. This is so exceptionally important! In this context I believe it would also make real what ought to happen, forming a blueprint for the way in which the anthroposophical movement should evolve.

Today I tried to present to you some aspects of our anthroposophically-orientated outlook and in doing so we have created something of a substitute for what was to have taken place this time, but which could not happen because not all the contractual consents were available: namely, for laying the foundation stone for our *Johannesbau,* our St John's Building. Let us hope that we can make up for this at a none-too-distant point. Perhaps we will also—at the same time—be able to lay a foundation stone to revivify the anthroposophical movement as it is intended within the western world. If we succeed in doing what is right in this respect, then we will be able to offer proof that—in every authentic sense of the truth, with which alone we wish our souls to be filled, and without any bias towards sensationalism—we can adopt as our own such occult striving as is needed by today's humanity for its onward development.

LECTURE 12

Love and its Significance in the World

WHEN we speak about human beings at their present evolutionary stage being in need of an understanding of Christ's impetus, the thought may arise as to how it might be for someone who has not heard about Christ's impulse, who has perhaps never even heard the name of Christ. Will such a person have to forego Christ's influence just because they are unaware of Christ's name? Does one have to know what the Christ impulse is in theory for Christ's power to descend into one's soul? Let us clarify these questions through the following observations of human life between birth and death.

Human beings step into the world. At first, in early childhood, they are half asleep. We have to learn to experience ourselves—to find ourselves—as an I or ego, and our soul life is ever more enriched by absorbing all that is allotted to this I. When nearing death, this soul life is at its richest and most mature, which is why we can ask the weighty question: How do matters stand with our souls when our bodies decline?

It is a characteristic particularly of our physical body and our life of soul that what we have garnered in terms of life experience and knowledge become ever more meaningful the nearer we come to death, and certain traits increasingly come to the fore while others recede; these vary, depending on the individual. In our youth we gather knowledge, accumulate experience, harbour hopes, which we can usually only realize later. The nearer we come to old age, the more do we begin to love life's wisdom. This love of wisdom is not egotistical because such love grows ever greater the nearer we are to death; it grows in inverse proportion to the prospect of us profiting from our wisdom. We love this soul content ever more.

Spiritual science can even become something of a temptress in that people may think that their next life depends on knowledge acquired in this life. A good deal of egotism can accrue beyond this life on the back of spiritual science, and therein lies a danger. So it can happen that—wrongly conceived—spiritual science can become a soul temptress. That is a temptation in spiritual science and is integral to its nature. We can observe how love of life's wisdom sets in, like the blossoming of a plant, when the time is ripe; we can observe how love develops for something that exists within us. There have been countless human attempts to raise to a higher level that impulse of love for something that is within us.

Among the Mystics, for instance, we find the attempt to elevate the urge to self-love into the love of wisdom and to allow it to bask in a good light. By immersing ourselves in our own soul life, we attempt to find the divine spark, to experience our higher self as this divine spark. In actual fact, people only create the seed of their next life from out of their life's wisdom, just like seed after the plant has gone through the whole year. Just as seed endures, so does wisdom of life; the human being goes through the portal of death and what ripens there as a spiritual kernel becomes the seed for the following life. Some sense this and may become Mystics, mistaking what is merely a seed for their next life as a divine spark, as something absolute. They may interpret it in this way because they are embarrassed to admit that this spirit seed is but their own self. Meister Eckhart[71] and Johannes Tauler[72] call this the God within us because they knew nothing of reincarnation.

Once we take the law of reincarnation into account, we recognize the meaning of love in the world, both in its micro- and in its macrocosmic dimension. As karma we understand a cause in one life translating into its effect in a subsequent life. As human beings—and in the sense of cause and effect—we cannot rightly speak of love in the sense of deeds of love and their recompense. It would be a matter of a deed and its rebalancing, which has nothing to do with love: loving deeds are those that do not seek equalization in a subsequent life.

Let us imagine, for example, that we are working to earn. This could be different: we could be working but taking no pleasure in it because we are working to pay off a debt rather than for wages per se. We can imagine how we have already used what we are now earning through work. We would prefer not to have run up debts but now need to work to pay them off. Now let's transpose this example onto our human behaviour in general: that everything we do out of love turns out to be repayment of debts! Seen from an occult perspective, everything done out of love brings in no pay packet but is liability for goods already used.

The only transactions for which we receive no reward in future are those deeds we do out of genuine, true love. This might be a shocking truth. Luckily, people are unaware of it in their everyday consciousness. However, everyone knows this in their subconscious, which is why they do deeds of love so grudgingly. This is a reason why there is so little love in the world. People feel instinctively that deeds of love reap no future rewards for their own ego. A soul must be far advanced in its development for it to experience pleasure in loving transactions, from which it will derive no personal gain. The motivation for this is not strong in humanity. Yet, out of occultism one can indeed derive strong motivation towards loving deeds.

Our egotism gains nothing from deeds of love, but all the more does the world profit by them. Occultism states: Love is for the world what the Sun is for external life. No human souls could ever thrive without love in the world. Love is the moral Sun of the world. Would it not be absurd for a person who delights—and is interested—in the growth of plants in a field to wish the Sun to vanish from the world? Transposed into moral terms this would mean: one has to have an interest in beneficent evolution succeeding in struggling through into human relationships. It would be wise for us to have spread as much love as possible across the Earth.

What can spiritual science give us? We learn facts about Earth evolution, about the Spirits of the Earth, about its surface and its changes, about the development of the human body and so on; we learn in detail about what lives and weaves throughout evolution. What does this mean? What does it mean if people do not wish to hear anything about spiritual science? They are not interested in what is there. Because whoever doesn't want to know about Saturn or the nature of the Sun or ancient Moon also doesn't want to learn about the Earth. It is lack of interest—the crassest egotism—when people do not have the interest to find out about the world. It is a human duty to be interested in all existence.

Let us long to love the Sun with all its creative power, with its love for the Earth and for human souls to flourish! Learning how the Earth has matured ought to be spiritual seed-sowing for a love of the world, because a spiritual science without love would be a danger for humanity. We should not preach about love, but this love must and will enter the world by means of us knowing about and spreading what is really spiritual. Spiritual science must be one and the same as genuinely loving action and loving deeds.

Sense-based love is the origin of what is creative, of what is in the becoming. Without sensory love nothing sensory would exist in the world; and without spiritual love nothing spiritual arises in evolution. When we practise love, when we nurture love, forces of genesis, forces of creativity, are poured out into the world. Should we justify this with reason? After all, forces of creativity have had to cascade into the world before us and our reasoning.

Certainly, as egotists, we can deprive the future of creative pow-ers; but we cannot extinguish those deeds of love and those powers of creation from the past—for we owe our existence to past deeds of love. However strong we are as a result of these deeds of love, just as strongly are we indebted to the past, and however much love we can muster is debt-repayment for our existence. We will therefore understand the deeds of a highly evolved human being because a highly advanced human being will have greater debts towards the past. It is wise to repay one's debts through deeds of love.

The impetus towards love grows with the advancement of a person; wisdom alone does not suffice. We'd like to bring before our souls the significance of love in the way the world works. Love always points to our life's indebtedness to the past. And because we gain nothing from paying our debts to the future, we ourselves do not benefit from our loving deeds. We need to leave our deeds of love behind us in the world where they are, though, incized onto spiritual world events. We do not perfect ourselves through our loving deeds—only through other deeds—but the world is enriched by our deeds of love. Because love is the creative element in the world.

In addition to love there are two other powers in the world. How are these to be compared with love? One power is strength or might, potency. The second is wisdom. In terms of strength, one can speak of weaker or stronger power and of almightiness or omnipotence. Similarly with wisdom, where there are stages of wisdom on a gradient up to all-knowingness, to infinite wisdom. To speak of love in such graduated terms makes no sense. What is all-lovingness, a love of all things?

We cannot speak of escalations of love in the same way as incremental steps in wisdom or power ascending to infinite wisdom or omnipotence. Our own being becomes more complete through such enhancements. But this is not the case if we love a couple of beings or more; this has nothing to do with the completion or augmentation of our own selves. Love for everything alive cannot be compared with almightiness; concepts of size or increase cannot readily be transposed onto love. Can one assign to the divine being who works and weaves throughout the world the predicate of Almighty? Judgements on a feeling level need to be silent here: were God almighty, he would do everything that is done and human freedom would be impossible. God's almightiness would exclude human freedom! The omnipotence of God is doubtless not present if humans can be free.

Does divine being possess all-knowingness? Since the striving for God-likeness is humanity's loftiest goal, our striving ought to aspire to omniscience. Is omniscience our ultimate prize? If omniscience is the ultimate asset, then each moment must surely open up a vast gulf between human beings and an all-knowing God. Humans would be continuously conscious of this abyss, were it the case that God possessed the ultimate prize of omniscience, yet had withheld it from humanity.

The all-encompassing attribute of divinity is not omnipotence, neither is it omniscience, but it is love, the quality within which no further graduated enhancement is possible. God is full of love, is pure love, is, as it were, born of the substance of love. God is pure and total love, not the highest wisdom nor the mightiest power. God retained the love but shared the power and the wisdom with Ahriman and Lucifer respectively: power with Ahriman, wisdom with Lucifer, so that human beings might be free and, under the influence of wisdom, take their onward course.

When we seek the source of all creativity, we arrive at love; the very basis of all life is love. A different impetus is at work within evolution which leads all beings to becoming ever mightier and wiser. Perfection is reached through wisdom and power. The way in which wisdom and power evolves and changes throughout evolution can be seen in humanity's own development: we have been in continual development and then the impetus of Christ appears, Christ, who entered humankind through the Mystery of Golgotha. Love did not therefore enter the world piecemeal but love streamed in as a complete, perfected unity. Human beings are gradually able to take up this impetus. The divine impetus of love is a unique and singular intervention, one needed as an impulsion for all Earth.

True love is not capable of decrease nor increase. Love is of a completely different nature from wisdom and power. Love awakens no hopes in the future; love is advance payment for the past. It is in similar terms that the Mystery of Golgotha stands within world evolution. Did divinity then owe something to humankind?

Through Lucifer's influence, a certain element entered into humanity in face of which what had previously been present had to be removed from it. What had recently entered led to a downward decline, to counter which the Mystery of Golgotha brought the possibility of paying off all debt. The impetus of Golgotha did not come to absolve us of the sins committed over the course of evolution, but so that what had entered into humanity through Lucifer should receive its counterweight.

Imagine that someone knew nothing of the name of Christ Jesus, knew nothing about what is conveyed in the Gospels, but that they knew the radical difference between the natures of power and wisdom and that of love. Such a person, though they knew nothing of the Mystery of Golgotha is—in a genuinely Christian sense—a Christian. Whoever knows love as being for the paying of debts and not for future advantage is a Christian. Understanding the nature of love is: being a Christian!

Through mere theosophy—with its 'karma and reincarnation'—one can become an enormous egotist if one doesn't also embrace that impulse of love, Christ's inspiration. For only then does one attain to the quality able to transcend the egotism in theosophy. One is able to rebalance this through an understanding of Christ's impetus. It is because theosophy is needed by humanity that it is being introduced now. But it contains the grave danger that, if theosophy is plied without Christ's impulse—without the motivation of love—that people's inherent egoism will be compounded, that they nurture it, even beyond death. We should not conclude from this that theosophy is not to be pursued, but we have to learn that understanding the substance of love belongs to theosophy.

What actually took place at the Mystery of Golgotha? We know that Jesus of Nazareth was born and developed in the way described in the Gospels, that the Baptism in the Jordan took place in his thirtieth year, that the Christ lived for three years in the body of Jesus of Nazareth and fulfilled the Mystery of Golgotha. Many people nowadays believe that they should portray this Mystery of Golgotha as humanly as possible, believing that it is to be designated a deed within the Earth, an earthly deed. It is no such thing. Only from higher worlds can what took place on Earth in the Mystery of Golgotha be observed.

Let us once more place the beginnings of Earth- and human evolution before us. Human beings possessed certain spiritual forces; then Lucifer approached humanity and here we come to the point where we can say: They, the progressive Gods, gave up their almightiness, their omnipotence to Lucifer so that human beings could become free. However, humanity sank deeper into materiality than was intended, slipping from the hands of the progressive Gods and descending further than was willed. How can these progressive Gods now raise human beings back towards themselves? To understand this, we will have to look into the council of the Gods rather than at the Earth.

It is for the Gods that Christ fulfils his deed: to bring humanity back to the Gods. Lucifer's deed is a deed in the spiritual world;

Christ's deed also takes place in the spiritual world, but simultaneously in the sense world. No human being could have carried it out. Lucifer enacted his deed in supersensible worlds. Yet Christ has descended to Earth in order to fulfil his deed on Earth, and human beings are the observers of this deed.

The Mystery of Golgotha is a deed of the Gods, a concern of the Gods, a divine situation, at which human beings are onlookers. The gates of Heaven are opened and therein blazes forth a divine deed. It is the only deed on Earth that is purely spiritual, and it is therefore no wonder that those who do not believe in the supersensible absolutely do not believe in this deed of Christ. Christ's deed is a divine act, an act which the Gods fulfil for their own ends. It is due to this that the Mystery of Golgotha encompasses its radiance and its unique significance and humankind is called to witness this deed. A contemporary witness account of this is therefore nowhere to be found, because human beings saw only the outer manifestation of it. The Gospels, on the other hand, are written from a supra-sensible perspective, which makes them easy to deny if one has no sense of what is spiritual.

The deed of the Mystery of Golgotha belongs to the loftiest experiences within the spiritual world from a certain viewpoint. Lucifer's action took place when human beings were still participants in the supersensible world, Christ's deed takes place in the midst of material life; it is both a spiritual and a physical act. Lucifer's deed can be understood when investigating the world in terms of wisdom.

In order to grasp the Mystery of Golgotha, wisdom alone is not sufficient. We can possess all the wisdom in the world yet the deed of Christ remains incomprehensible because love is needed to comprehend the Mystery of Golgotha. Only when love streams into wisdom and vice versa will this deed come within our ken, and only when we evolve wisdom into love as we move towards death. We need wisdom that has been evolved into love when we go through the portal of death, because otherwise we die if no wisdom has been united with love. Why do we need love? Philosophy is love of wisdom. The old wisdom was not philosophy because this old wisdom was not born out of love but out of revelation. There is no eastern philosophy but there is eastern wisdom. Philosophy in the sense of love of wisdom came into the world with Christ; this is where we find the entry of wisdom from out of the impulse of love. It is through Christ's impetus that it entered the world. Now we must apply the impetus of love to wisdom itself.

The ancient wisdom sought by the seer through revelation is expressed in the exalted words of the archetypal human prayer: *Ex Deo nascimur*, from out of God are we born. That is ancient wisdom. Christ, who stepped out of spiritual worlds, bound wisdom with love with the goal that egotism be overcome. But this had to be independent, freely offered from being to being and it is for this reason that the era of love began at the same time as that of egotism. The point of origin of the cosmos is love; and from it egoism has of itself grown. Yet Christ's impetus—the impulse of love—will over time become that which entered the world to overcome all that divides, all that sunders, so that human beings will gradually, over time, come to participate in this power of love. In singularly monumental words do we feel the love of Christ pouring into human hearts in the words: 'Where two meet in my name, I am there in your midst.'[73] This is how the old Rosicrucian saying sounds into love that is bound with wisdom: *In Christo morimur*—in Christ we die.

Jehovah predisposed human beings to a condition of group-soul adherence, so that love would permeate blood relationships; as a personality he lives through Lucifer. Originally, humans lived in confraternity with others, followed by a time of divisiveness caused by the luciferic principle, which promoted independence and selfishness. Evil entered the world with this selfishness. This had to happen because good could not be embraced without evil.

Through victory over oneself, human beings are offered the opportunity to unfold love. Christ brought to a humanity sinking in egotism the stimulus to such self-conquest and, through it, the strength to overcome evil. Now those divided by selfishness are being united through the deeds of Christ, making true in the deepest sense Christ's words to us, which speak of deeds of love: *What you have done for the least of my brethren, you have done for me.*[74] Flooding back into earthly life came that divine deed of love which will gradually flow throughout all human evolution and, despite physical forces dying back, will revivify them in spirit because this deed is not done out of egoism but purely out of the spirit of love: *Per spiritum sanctum reviviscimus*, through the Holy Spirit we will be resurrected.

The future of humankind will consist of more than love. Spiritual fulfilment or perfection will be earthly humanity's most avidly striven-after goal. You find this described in my Mystery Drama *The Soul's Probation*.[75] Yet nobody who understands deeds of love will say of what they see in their own striving towards perfection: This striving is selfless. Working towards refinement is something through which we wish to strengthen and support our being, our personality. Yet our value for the world is to be found in deeds of love rather than deeds of self-fulfilment. In this respect, we can allow ourselves no delusion. If a person seeks to follow Christ on the path of love towards wisdom, then such wisdom, placed in the service of the world, is only of as much value to the world as the proportion of it suffused with love.

Wisdom that is drenched in love, which both aids the world and helps it towards Christ, such love towards wisdom also excludes falsehood. For lies are the antithesis of facts or deeds, and whoever proceeds in love within facts knows no lie. Lies stem from egoism—without exception. When we have found the path to wisdom through love—through the growing power of overcoming, of surmounting, and through selfless love—then we will also have penetrated right through to wisdom. This is the way someone becomes a free personality. Evil was the underground into which the light of love could shine. This light of love is what makes sense of evil, the position of evil, recognizable in the world. Light has become recognizable through darkness. Only a free person can become a genuine Christian.

* * *

A question about the necessary lie followed:

Remaining silent out of love, an emergency lie, is always a very complex issue. Telling a lie out of love can become a necessity and can, in some circumstances, be a good deed, but it binds us in an extremely complex way. We are karmically binding ourselves to the person in question and are, in fact, bound to their weakness. We will subsequently have something to do with them. We will have to tell them the truth later. And later, due to the fairly unpleasant truth we will have to tell them, we will have to make amends in evolutionary terms. It is good that this is the case because, when we are forced into a 'necessary' lie, this is already karmic, that is: egotistical. A necessary lie is—however necessary—a lie and hence an egotistical act, which has nothing to do with acts truly done out of love. A streak of cleverness always attaches to a necessary lie. It is not always the result of a loving decision. Spiritual science radiates into even the smallest, most intricate details of the human heart.

LECTURE 13

The Birth of the Light of the Earth out of Christmas Darkness

IT is lovely, my dear friends, that circumstances allow us to meet on this festive evening. There are many friends among us who, in a certain sense, are alone, whereas by far the majority are of course celebrating the festival of love and of peace amongst those with whom they are normally connected in the world outside. Yet it is just as understandable that we—those who are not constrained by so many obligations—should meet within the spiritual stream in which we stand and should least of all be excluded from participating in this festival of love and of peace. What could unite us in a more wonderful sense—in the spiritual air of mutual love and the peace that suffuses our hearts—than a movement in service of the spiritual? We can also call it good fortune that—precisely in this year, on this evening—we can be together and can celebrate this festival with a small reflection close to our hearts. We can do this also because this year we find ourselves near the birth of that which—if we understand it rightly—must indeed lie close to our hearts: the birth of our Anthroposophical Society.[76]

If we have lived rightly with this great ideal—which we long to bring to expression through the Anthroposophical Society—and if we are likewise prepared to expend our forces in aid of this great ideal for humanity, we should also wish to turn our thoughts from this, our spiritual light, our means of illumination, towards the dawn of that great light of human evolution on Earth who is celebrated throughout this night of love and peace. We have before us—be it in spirit or in soul—what we may call the birth of the Earth's light;

that light, born out of the darkness of this Christmas Eve, which will yet shine into all human hearts and souls, providing all hearts and souls with what they need to find the path into spiritual heights, the path that is to be taken over the course of Earth's mission. Were we to inscribe into our hearts what we could feel this Christmas, what would that actually be?

This Christmas, what should pour into our souls is the fundamentally human feeling of love. Love that is our underlying feeling, greater than all other powers, than all other forces in the world, than all worldly goods; love is the greatest power, the strongest force, the greatest treasure, the most intensively effective force in the world. The feeling must cascade into our hearts and souls that wisdom is magnificent but love is still greater; that power is something great but love is even greater. Feelings of the power, the force, the strength of love must pour so strongly into our hearts that some of this feeling can brim over from this Christmas into the rest of the year, that something may flow over that expresses what we always feel: we ought to be ashamed if we do something, in any hour of the year, which cannot stand its ground in spiritual face of this night, during which we long for the omnipotence of love to pour into our hearts.

May the days and hours of the year pass in such a way that we need not feel ashamed in face of the feelings we *will* to cascade into our hearts this Christmas Eve! If we can feel and sense in this way, then we are feeling in harmony with all those beings who wish to bring the significance and implications of Christmas closer to us, as also the relationship of Christmas with the entire Christ impetus in Earth evolution.

We face this Christ motive, whose significance we might say is threefold. At Christ's festival we can see in all its stature the threefold form of this Christ impulsion.

One form directs us towards the Gospel of St Matthew. The being born, whose birth we are celebrating this Christmas, enters human evolution in such a way that three pinnacles of humanity, three representatives of exalted magic,[77] approach in order to glorify the regal being who has entered human progress. 'Kings'—in the spiritual sense of the word—arrive to pay homage to the great spiritual king who appears in the form he could attain due to an exalted being—such as Zarathustra once was—having undergone stages of his development in order to succeed to the stature of the great spirit-king, to whom the Magi-kings sought to render homage. This is how that spirit-king of the Matthew Gospel appears to our spiritual gaze, by bringing into human evolution an endless fount of goodness, an endless fount of mighty love, such goodness and love as feels called to action against human evil.

We therefore see—in a second form—the spirit-god stepping into human evolution such that enmity—which must exist towards a spirit-king—feels challenged in the person of Herod, so that the spirit-king has to flee from the opponent of spiritual kingship. This is how he appears to our spiritual vision in majestic, magical glory. For our spiritual eye, to our souls, there emerges the wondrous image of the spiritual king, the reincarnated Zarathustra, that most noble flower of human evolution, and how he progressed from incarnation to incarnation on the physical plane, and the wisdom which fulfilled enlightenment brought about; we see him surrounded by the three Magi, spirit-kings and themselves flowers and zeniths of human evolution.

Christ's impetus can also arise in a different form for our souls: how he appears in St Mark's and St John's Gospels, in which we are also led towards the cosmic Christ incentive expressing how human beings maintain their eternal connection with mighty cosmic forces through being granted understanding of the cosmic Christ; and how into Earth evolution itself a cosmic intervention would come about through the Mystery of Golgotha. As something endlessly greater and mightier than the spirit-king surrounded by the Magi, before our spiritual eye there appears that vast cosmic being who is to take possession of a human bearer, who as spirit-king is the acme and flower of Earth evolution itself. Basically, it is only due to today's short-sightedness that the whole immensity and power of this incision into human evolution is not felt—that incisive event through which Zarathustra became the bearer of the cosmic Christ Spirit—if the whole significance is not also felt of what was being prepared as Christ-Bearer at that moment in human evolution and which we celebrate in a Christian Christmas festival. When we delve into human evolution we see on every side how deep this incision into Earth evolution, this Christ event, is. Let us feel it through suitable reflections this evening, so that from it some elements may radiate into our other anthroposophical deepening and immersive activities.

Much could be added to this. It could be shown how in times when the spiritual was closer, a new spirit entered humanity as distinct from what had reigned over—and influenced—Earth evolution during pre-Christian times. A figure was created, for instance, a figure who actually lived and who exemplifies for us the effect on an early Christian soul exerted, firstly, by complete immersion in ancient, pagan spiritual knowledge and then experienced how everything changed in their soul when all the ancient pagan knowledge was freely and non-judgementally faced with Christ's impetus.

Today we tend to understand a figure such as Faust better. We feel in such a figure, which the more recent poet, Goethe, as it were, re-awakened, how the highest human striving is expressed, yet we also sense that the prospect of the deepest guilt ought also to be expressed. Disregarding the strength wherewith more recent poetry can endow artistry, one could say: The depth and significance once residing in a soul can be felt if one immerses oneself in the poetry of the Greek Empress Eudocia,[78] who revived the ancient legend of Cyprian. This depicts a person still living fully in the world of pagan Gods, yet in whom a persona was interwoven who—some time after the Mystery of Golgotha—was wholly devoted to pagan Mysteries, forces and powers. It is a lovely scene in which Cyprian becomes acquainted with Justina, who is already deeply moved by Christ's influence and is devoted to forces portrayed through Christendom. She is presented with the temptation to be diverted from her path into service of ancient pagan magic. Everything that plays out between Faust and Gretchen is found in the atmosphere of this battle between old heathen practices and Christ-motivation.

Apart from the spiritual aspect, this is taken from the grand tale of Cyprian and the temptation to which he was exposed by the Christian Justina. Even though Eudocia's poetry is not particularly good, one has nevertheless to admit that in the shattering collision of the ancient, pre-Christian world with the Christian world, there is Cyprian, who still feels remote from Christianity and devoted to divine pagan forces. There is a certain forcefulness in the depiction. Only a few passages will be conveyed today as to how Cyprian feels about those magical forces of pre-Christian spiritual powers. Let us hear from Cyprian in the poetry of [Aelia] Eudocia:

> You who care about the mystery of faith in the exalted Christ,
> See my fresh tears, so that you may know from whence my deep pain
>   originates—
> I speak the truth and I know that you know it.
> You who delight in unseemly icons, pay attention,
> Because I will point to their deceptions.
> There is no other human like me:
> So impious, so in league with demons,
> Such a devotee of worthless idols,
> As to learn what they are or their strength.
>
> I am that famous Cyprian, whose parents dedicated me to Apollo,
> While I was still a child.
> At a young age I learned the sacred rites of the Beast,
> The stomach-travelling serpent.
> In my seventh year, I was initiated into the Phaeton Mithras
> And I lived on the Acropolis of the noble Athenians.
> I became a citizen, since this was pleasing to my parents, who raised me.
> In my tenth year, I lit a torch for the God and I committed myself
> To the white suffering of Kore.
> Also did I accomplish the serpentine initiations of Athena
> Who lives on the Acropolis, being dedicated as a temple servant.
>
> I went to the glen of Olympus,
> Which ignorant people claim
> Is the abode of powerless Gods.
> There I heard the echo and sound of certain words.
> I beheld herbs and roots—an amazing sight it was—
> Things over which shameless evil demons hold sway,
> Though without effect.
> In that place I perceived the seasons and the changing winds.
> I learnt about many days, certain rogues, harsh adversaries
> Used to fabricate deceptive illusions.
> I beheld a choir singing shamelessly
> And saw others in a crowd, performing deeds of warring Ares.

I also saw ambushes of others and their malicious habits,
And saw them distraught with fear.
I also saw a vast array of Goddesses and Gods
Because I remained there forty days and another eight after that.
From there, as if from mighty realms, spirits travelling by air to earth
are sent forth
To make all nations do whatever evil they wish.
I ate a meal from high branches of blossoming trees
Once Phaeton had set.
Going into my fifteenth year,
I was thoroughly taught about Spirits and Gods
By seven hierophants and about empty deeds,
The works of lawless demons.
My parents were exceeding eager that I learn
Everything on Earth and in the sea,
Not only things used for the destruction of men
But also matters of lush grass and well-stemmed plants,
And things that oppress man's feeble body.
And things the evil-minded enemy,
The ruler of this earth, discovered,
That swift-minded serpent
Who spitefully disregards the plan of the Immortal Ruler.

From there, I came to Argos, the lush pasture of horses.
There was a festival of Eos the Dawn,
Wife of Tithonos, clad in white,
And I became there an initiate of the air,
Of the heavens with its many spheres [...]
Of the harmony of the waters and the well-fed earth,
From dewy streams to divine air.

In this way, Cyprian learnt all that one could learn when one was initiated, as it were, into the pre-Christian Mysteries. Oh, he describes them
accurately, those forces, to whom those entrusted with ancient Mystery
records could look up at the time when they were no longer legitimate.
He describes them compellingly in all their ill-timed dreadfulness:

... Believe me, I saw the Demon himself and looked into his face.
Having supplicated him with libations and sacrifices.
Believe me, when I saw him I spoke with him and heard his flattering words.

Among much else, he called me youthful,
Beautiful in appearance, resembling Jambres,
Called me an initiate, mighty in deeds, Jambres' equal.
He promised that I would become leader of the cosmos
By working with him, for he knew the deeds of my life.
Honouring me, he granted me a grievous troop
Of heinous demons and said to me on my way out:
'Cyprian, you are a strong mortal.'
Rising from his chair, he sent me forth,
To the amazement of the spectators.
From that time on, all his priests honoured me in like manner to him.
In appearance he was like richly-worked gold,
With flashing eyes and long hair.
On his head he wore a garland layered with precious stones
Whose brilliance and splendour illuminated that place.
His clothing was likewise embellished.
When he turned, he shook the earth.
Around his throne stood many shield-bearers.
Bending their gaze to the ground, prepared in war-like formation.
He illumined the earth like an Olympian God
Gleaming with stars and causing plants to grow.
By doing everything that God does
He contends with the sovereign Immortal and his Saints.
That is how he deceives the minds of men with illusion.

And as temptation approaches him, how all this affects him before
learning of Christ's impetus is also described for us:

When I left the land of the Persians
I travelled to the great city of Syrian Antioch.
There I accomplished many wonders through my terrible supernatural skills.
For some I provided a cure for love,
For others a cure for jealousy, bitter rivalry and evil afflicting their flesh.
In that city a certain lover, Aglaidas, sought me out,
Begging me, as did many others, on his knees for the sake of a maiden
Named Justina, that he might make love to her.
That is when a demon first appeared fickle to me.
The many legions he commanded were gathered
Around the holy virgin, but returned unsuccessful.
The virgin's faith rendered Aglaidas' helpers unconscious,
Rendering him powerless.

Aglaidas suffered many sleepless nights
And used my magic skills and the enemy's attacks
For seven weeks and three further thereafter.
Then the leader of the demonic horde with his servants
Waged war against the virgin.
For not only had Eros tamed the young Aglaidas
But he had keenly touched my heart as well. [...][79]

Out of the confusion, into which the ancient world had entangled him, Cyprian is healed through Christ's influence. What we encounter in Faust had as if been foreshadowed, but is now saturated in greater poetic power: ancient magic is rejected in order to understand Christ's impetus in all its majesty. Such a figure really shows us, in something of a reprise, how, in the first centuries of our era, such a figure of dual aspect was experienced in what we have just brought into focus for our souls.

A third figure, like a third aspect of Christ's impetus, which can show us how we can feel united with everything associated with the word theosophy—with everything that is human—is something uniquely depicted in St Luke's Gospel and which affected those later depicting Christ's influence: how he is prepared as a 'child'. In that love and simplicity—and inherent unconsciousness—which we encounter in the child in Luke's Gospel, Christ's impulse was well suited to being presented to all hearts. Everyone could feel connected with what was presented so simply and with a child's child-likeness, yet which spoke so mightily and powerfully to human beings in Luke's Gospel and which does not tell of Magi-kings appearing to shepherds in the fields.

The being described in St Matthew's Gospel appears at the zenith of human potential, while spiritual-magical kings come to pay homage. The child of Luke's Gospel appears in all simplicity, outside human evolution, initially as a child, unwelcomed by the great and good but adored by shepherds in the fields. The child of Luke's account is not placed within human evolution in such a way as to draw our attention to evil in the world and how it would be challenged by his royal spiritual power. No. What faces us distinctly, if not immediately, is Herod's power and wickedness: that what lived in this child, which was so great, so noble, so meaningful, could not be absorbed into the ranks of humanity, that it existed as poor and outcast from human evolution, as if cast into a corner, yet which by remarkable means reveals to us his supra-human, his divine—which is his cosmic—origin.

And how inspiring was Luke's Gospel for all those many artists who, ever and again, created scenes prompted by Luke's Gospel! Do we not feel—when faced with all these portrayals inspired by St Luke over the centuries—Jesus to be a being with whom every person including the simplest can feel related? The most unsophisticated people learnt about the great event of Palestine through what lived on of this Luke-Jesus-child; they learnt to feel it as a family episode, something that affected each one personally, much as anything to do with a close relative. No other Gospel has affected subsequent humanity in the same way as the gracefully ensouled mood and flow of Luke's Gospel, which creates an intimacy between the Jesus being and human souls. Yet everything is contained within this childlike portrayal—everything which must in fact be inherent to it—the highest quality in the whole world: love.

Wisdom is great, is valuable and beings cannot exist without wisdom, yet love is even greater. The power and the strength underpinning the world is vast and something without which the world cannot exist, but love is even mightier. You only feel Christ's impetus aright if you recognize love's even loftier standing in relation to power, strength and wisdom.

Particularly as spiritual individuals, we should strive for wisdom because wisdom belongs to divine world-stimuli. That wisdom is worth striving for, that wisdom must be the holy trove that makes progress possible, is about to be presented in the first scene of the drama *The Soul's Probation*, showing that we should not allow wisdom to rule us but must tend wisdom in order to ascend the ladder of human evolution. Wherever wisdom exists, two aspects co-exist: the wisdom of the Gods and the wisdom of luciferic powers. In all circumstances do beings seeking wisdom come close to the enemies of the Gods, the host of light-bearers, the hordes of Lucifer. There is therefore no divine, all-wise omniscience because an opponent to wisdom is always present: Lucifer.

The might and the power! It is through wisdom that the world is grasped, is understood; it is seen and illuminated by wisdom; the world is upheld by power and strength. Everything that comes into existence, comes into being through the power and might within being, and we would exclude ourselves from the world were we not to seek our part in the power and might of the world. We witness the world's power and might when lightning flashes through clouds; we perceive it when thunder rolls, when rain cascades out of heavenly spaces, fructifying the Earth or when rays of sunlight pierce the Earth, awakening the dormant seeds of plants. We see power and strength in the forces of nature working downwards into the Earth in the rays of the Sun, bestowing healing, in the powers of rain and clouds. On the other hand, we also see power and might in such as volcanos, as if they were rising up against Earth itself: heavenly force against heavenly force. We look into this world and we know that, if we want to be beings in the universe, in the cosmos, then something of this power and might must also be active in us—we need to have our part in power and might. That is how we stand amid the world: both divine and ahrimanic powers are alive in us; they flash through us. The Almighty is not omnipotent because his foe is forever against him.

Between power and wisdom, love prevails, and we feel—if it is real love—that it is uniquely and totally divine. We can speak of omnipotence, total power, in terms of an ideal, but facing it is Ahriman. We can speak of all-encompassing wisdom, omni-cognizance, as an ideal, but facing it is the force of Lucifer. Saying 'all-encompassing love' seems absurd because it is not capable of gradation when truly practised. Wisdom can be small and can be increased; power can be small and can also be increased. Hence all-encompassing wisdom and almightiness are valid as ideals. Cosmic- or worldwide love—we feel that the concept of all-love, love of all, cannot be included in this, because love is something singular, sole and unique.

The way in which Luke's Gospel describes Jesus to us, he appears as the personification of love; yet he appears as this embodiment of love between wisdom or omniscience and omnipotence. He appears in this way because, basically, he is a child. The only heightening of qualities common to a child is added that of abandonment, of being marginalized into a corner of humanity. The pinnacle of humankind is already visible in his child's disposition. Wherever we may look in the wide universe, there is nothing so singularly created out of wisdom as this wondrous—and quite pristine—form, as this child's organism. Just as all-wisdom appears in this child's physical body, it also appears in his ether body, where the wisdom of cosmic powers is expressed, likewise in his astral body and his I. The child lies there like an extract, an essence, of wisdom. When all this is also abandoned in a corner, as is the Jesus child, then we feel: an image of perfection—concentrated cosmic wisdom—lies abandoned there.

Omnipotence also appears personified, embodied in the child lying there, as described by the St Luke Gospel. The relationship of almightiness to the child's body and infant being can be felt by anyone who has dwelt upon what divine powers and forces can achieve. Bring to mind the power of natural forces and potencies when weather is in control; conjure up those violent forces of nature active in subterranean realms; think of all the simmering and seething of universal powers and forces, all that is combined when benevolent and ahrimanic forces combine, how they rage and thrash. And now imagine that everything storming and stirring is pushed and cleared away from a minute patch so that in this tiny space the miraculous structure of a child's body can lie, apart and in isolation, for it must be protected; were he not for an instant sheltered from the power of natural forces, he would be swept away!

Here you feel what it is to be placed in almightiness. And with this you feel what the human soul can sense when it gazes without prejudice at what the Gospel of Luke expresses: were you to approach the concentrated wisdom of the child with wisdom, were you to advance towards it with the greatest human wisdom: this wisdom is mockery and stupidity! For it cannot ever be as great as the wisdom expended so that this child's body might lie before us. The loftiest wisdom remains stupidity and is obliged to stand in awe before this child, venerating celestial wisdom, but knowing that it can never reach such heights; such wisdom just remains a mockery and must feel itself rebuffed in its own foolishness.

No, we cannot approach the Jesus being described to us in St Luke's Gospel with wisdom. Can we do so with power?

We cannot come near with power either. Using power only makes sense where opposing power is concerned. The child, however, faces us with his powerlessness—whether we want to exert great or little force—and this taunts our power! Such an approach by power would be senseless with only defencelessness as opposition.

This is the wonderful thing about Christ's impetus that its preparation in the child Jesus is placed in just this way in Luke's Gospel so that—however wise we may be—we cannot approach with our wisdom and just as little with our power. Everything that usually binds us to the world cannot come near the Jesus child, as he is portrayed in St Luke's Gospel. Only one single quality can draw near: not wisdom, not power, only love. The only possible thing to bring towards the being of the child is boundless love. The power of love and the sole justification, the unique significance of love is what we can feel so deeply when we allow the Luke Gospel to work upon our souls.

We live in the world and no one should mock worldly imperatives. It would mean denying your humanity and betraying the Gods were you not to strive for wisdom. Every day and every hour of the year is well used in which we convince ourselves that it is our human duty to strive for wisdom. Every day and every hour of the year demand that we become aware how we are placed into the world, how the play of the world's forces, powers and almightiness pulsates throughout creation. There is one moment when we may forget this while remembering the Gospel of St Luke: when we think of the child who is more defenceless yet far wiser than any human child and in whose presence the most exalted love is justified, in whose presence wisdom must halt, in whose presence power must stand still.

Thus we can feel how significant it is that precisely this Christ child, welcomed by the shepherds, is presented as the third aspect of Christ's impetus, alongside its great cosmic aspect, alongside its spiritually regal aspect and its childlike aspect. The spiritual-royal aspect draws near to us, reminding us of supreme wisdom; the ideal of omniscient wisdom is placed before us. The cosmic aspect draws closer to us, showing us that through the child the entire course of

Earth evolution is shaped anew. The highest power is shown to us through its cosmic impact, power so mighty that it can even overcome death.

What has to be added as a third element to wisdom and power—and which must settle in our souls as something surpassing both these—is presented to us as the very origin of human evolution on the physical plane of Earth. This has been sufficient to bring home to humankind—through the ever-recurring depiction of Jesus' birth at Christmas—the vast significance of love in world- and human evolution.

Thus it is on Christmas Eve that we are presented with the birth of the Jesus child, which can be born anew every Christmas by gazing at the birth of this Jesus child in our souls with an understanding of genuine, true and all-surpassing love. And at Christmas an understanding of this feeling of love can be fittingly awakened in our souls, and when we celebrate this birth of Christ—that awakening of love in our souls. So that, out of every moment that we experience this love, there may radiate into the days and hours of the coming year such wisdom as will bless and permeate the wisdom we pursue—on every day and in every hour of the year.

It was through this emphasis on the impact of love—even in Roman times—that Christianity entered into human evolution in a remarkable way: that an element could be found in souls who grow closer, not due to something with which the world has endowed them, but because of what human souls of themselves possess. There has always been the need for human closeness through love. But as the Mystery of Golgotha approached, what had become of it in the Roman world? It had become Saturnalia. In the days following the seventeenth of December, when differences in rank and status were suspended, people mixed with other people, civic strata ceased to matter, everyone addressed each other in familiar terms. External influences were brushed aside. But, for fun and as jokes, children were also given Saturnalia presents, which later became our Christmas presents. That refuge was taken in joking and horseplay to enable social differences usually pertaining to be abandoned—this is the state to which Ancient Rome had come.

Into the midst of this, something new arrived around this time, in which people no longer resorted to japes and jesting but aspired to the spirit, to what was highest in their souls. In this way did equality between people become established at the time when in Rome it took the form of the boisterous Saturnalia. Yet this testifies to the aspect of love—that universal human love—which can hold sway when human beings are fathomed in all their depths. We do this, for instance, when a child on Christmas Eve awaits the arrival of the Christ Child or the Christmas Angel. How does a child wait then? It awaits the arrival of this Christmas Child or—Angel by knowing that he comes not from earthly lands but from spiritual realms! It is an understanding of the spiritual world in which children prove to be the equal of adults. Because they know, like a child, that Christ's impact has come from spiritual worlds into Earth evolution! So it is not only the child in the Gospel of St Luke who appears spiritually to our souls at Christmas, but also what Christmas elicits from human hearts in the most wonderful way—both in children's and adults' hearts—uniting children with adults.

Everything a child can feel—when they start being able to think— is at the one extremity. The other extremity is what we can feel in our highest spiritual states, what we can feel when we devote ourselves faithfully to that highest of stimuli mentioned at today's outset as the origin of the will we can develop—in the impending Anthroposophical Society—towards spiritual light. For there, too, we wish that what is to flow into human evolution be carried by a stimulus from the spiritual worlds. Just as a child feels about the Christmas Angel, who is to bring them their Christmas presents—feeling connected with spiritual worlds in their own naïve way—so can we, too, feel bound to the spiritual element we long for at Christmas, a high, spiritual ideal towards which we can strive. If we in this circle can feel bound by a love that can stream towards us when Christmas is rightly understood, then we will achieve—with our anthroposophical ideals—all that must be achieved in our Anthroposophical Society. We will achieve this if—in our united work—a ray of that love between human beings can fire us on the basis of having understood—and given ourselves up to—Christmas aright.

For those dear friends who are with us tonight, it is largely a matter of the feelings they may have. Even if you are not sitting around a Christmas tree in the traditional manner of these times, yet you, our dear friends, are indeed sitting round a Christmas tree. You, my dear friends, as we gather here to celebrate Christmas Eve around the tree, can try to awaken in your souls something of the feeling which can creep up on us when we feel the reason for our gathering: to make real for our souls the impact of love which, one day in the far future, must grow ever stronger if Christ's impact, of which we are so beautifully reminded on this Christmas Eve, is to grow ever stronger, ever mightier and ever more deeply understood and if it is to intervene in human evolution. It will only intervene if souls can be found who understand Him in all His significance. Understanding in this realm includes love, which we can acknowledge in our souls as the most beautiful element in human evolution precisely on this night when we allow our souls to be pierced with a spiritual view of the Jesus child; that child introduced to us, rejected by most of humankind, abandoned in a corner, born in a stable. Likewise, viewed externally, the child joining human evolution and welcomed by those spiritually simple, poor shepherds.

If we can allow the love elicited by these images to flood into our souls, our souls can beget the strength for what we need to fulfil—for what we *will* to fulfil—to contribute to the furtherance of the tasks we have set ourselves in the field of theosophy and which—in the anthroposophical field—karma has presented as our deep and rightful task.

Let us leave today's Christmas reflections by taking with us that impulse of love, not just for a short while, but in the way we have understood them out of the spirit of our worldview and for all our intended endeavours.

LECTURE 14

COLOGNE, 29 DECEMBER 1912

Novalis—Proclaimer of a Spiritually Conceived Christ Impact

W HEN we hear the resounding heart of our dear Novalis,[80] through which he knew how to announce Christ's mission in such a heartfelt way, we can feel a certain confirmation of our spiritual movement because we feel it in a personality whose entire being is deeply entwined with all the riddles and mysteries of the world and we feel, reverberating from him, something akin to longing for the spiritual world, something which souls more recently arrived have to seek out in worldviews such as those towards which we strive. It is wonderful to immerse oneself in the heart and soul of a personality such as Novalis; how he grew beyond the depths of western spiritual life, being himself deeply immersed in capturing the yearning for the spiritual world. If we allow the way spiritual worlds streamed into his youthful heart—in this incarnation—to affect our souls— and how those spiritual worlds irradiated him with Christ's impetus—we will experience something of a challenge to our souls—to our own hearts—to strive, with him, towards what appeared to him as a higher light, the light towards which he unremittingly dedicated his most recent short existence.

We feel how—in his latest incarnation—he was one of the prophets of what we seek in spiritual realms, and we also feel how best we can be enthused for this search by sharing the enthusiasm in the heart and soul of a Novalis, a soul thoroughly suffused with Christ's motivation. In the present moment of our endeavours when, on the one hand we are seeking to found the Anthroposophical Society— intended to encompass all human riddles—and when, on the other hand, we wish to observe the light, shining so radiantly from the Orient,[81] in connection with Christ's impetus, we may be allowed to connect ourselves with what expresses Christ's impulse in this soul of Novalis.

We know that once, in ancient Hebrew times, the great voice of prophecy rang forth in the momentous words of Elijah, welling forth from out of creation. We know that this was the stimulus present when the cosmic being of Christ descended into the body of Jesus of Nazareth. We know that this was the same motivating force which prophetically announced what was about to be embodied in human evolution. We know further that this spurred the soul of Raphael to magically reveal for human gaze the boundless mysteries of Christianity.

Sensing mysterious enigmas, we turn our longing souls towards the reincarnated soul of Elijah, of John the Baptist, of Raphael, towards Novalis and we feel with this soul how all its vibrancy is charged and irradiated throughout with longing for a new spiritual life for humanity; and then we feel the courage, sensing that something of this strength comes to us, helping us to live towards humanity's new spirituality. Oh, why is Novalis born into these more recent times, prophetically proclaiming a move that conceives spiritually of Christ? Was it not all around him in his spiritual horizon like a resurgence of the great spiritual streams in humanity as a whole? Novalis grew out of circles in which spiritual life itself glowed like a first declaration of a theosophical-anthroposophical worldview in the western world. In the radiance of a Goethe-Sun and a Schiller-Sun did this Christ-longing and weaving soul mature towards Christ's influence.

What sort of spiritual stream was alive in Goethe? How is spiritual Sun-quality expressed through Goethe as it radiates out into his young contemporary? Goethe sought in Spinoza's outlook to identify through feeling everything that might calm his hotly glowing passionate nature, everything that might ensoul him for dedication to the spirit.[82] Among Spinoza's comprehensive worldview Goethe was looking for a view into the widths of the cosmos and to the spiritual beings weaving throughout it, radiating into human souls, enabling these souls to resolve the mysteries of nature and their own souls by feeling and recognizing the creative essence living and weaving in all beings and worlds. Out of what he could glean from Spinoza did Goethe try to elevate himself to purity and vision. He felt, in a spiritual sense, something of the monotheistic outlook which resounds and glows across the ages to us from the words of the Vedas.[83]

If one follows this up, one can hear, in the loveliest consonance of Goethe's renewed Vedic words, as they resound with the warm enthusiasm kindled in Novalis, together culminating in the Mystery of Christ in the world. Light streams out towards us in Goethe's Vedic words; love and warmth flow into light when Novalis' Christ-proclaiming words cascade feeling into Goethe's light-filled words.

In other places, if we grasp Goethe where, in full keeping with the lore of world-unity, he recognizes the independence of each soul, in Leibniz' sense,[84] then we sense something wafting towards us not from Goethe's words yet within the ethos of western Monadology, which is a reiteration of Sankya philosophy.[85]

This all matured in the heart of Novalis, turned as it was towards Christ, as the Weimar and Jena of those years experienced something of a reverberation, an echo, of Sankya philosophy. You can sometimes feel a spirit of this kind, permeated by modern nuances, of a Sankya mood in one such as Fichte with his prim brittleness; you feel how he is made gentler, made into a true spirit of the times when, alongside him, you observe his devoted enthusiasm when he thinks of Novalis. On the one hand you hear, in Fichte's remarkable renewal of the words of Ancient India, that the world surrounding us is merely a dream and that thinking—in its everyday form—is merely a dream about a dream, but that reality is the human soul as it pours its will as a force into this world of dreams. Such are Fichte's renewed words from the Vedantas.[86]

Next to this is Novalis' confidence. Oh, he felt this confidence somewhat like this: yes, physical existence is a dream, thinking is a dream about dreaming, but from this dream there wells forth everything that the human soul deems and feels to be most valuable, and in this feeling and sensing can do what is spiritual.

Out of this dream of life, out of his Christ-inspired I, does the soul of Novalis create magical idealism, as he calls it, which means spiritually-carried idealism. And we feel—as if almost more harmoniously than it can otherwise be in a world-dream—that something seizes us when we see Novalis' loving soul standing next to another spiritual hero of his time, listening, while Schiller tries to elate the world with his enthusiasm, and how Novalis—in depicting Schiller's ethical idealism—himself announces his magical idealism from his Christ-inspired heart.

How deeply it speaks to our souls, this goodness, which we can call Novalis' most inward of inner, occidental kindliness, when he writes with such enthusiasm about Schiller.[87] Its entire integrity, all its capacity for love of a human soul is expressed when we allow ourselves to be affected by the words Novalis spoke when praising Schiller for what he meant to him, for what Schiller meant to humanity. To express this praise, Novalis said something along the lines of the following:

> If those avarice-free beings we call spirits can perceive in the heights such words and such human knowing as flow within Schiller, then may those desire-free beings we call spirits also be filled with the wish to descend to the human world and be incarnated here to work on true human evolution, absorbing such understanding as flows from a personality such as this—Schiller.

Dear friends! Which heart can so revere—which heart can so love— that it is a paradigm heart for all those who wish to surrender to this feeling of genuine, true, devotion-filled reverence and love? Such a heart can express in the simplest words the great mysteries of the world and the human soul. This is why some of the words issuing from Novalis' mouth have such value, as if they lent renewed resonance to what, from out of the threefold stream of humankind, has so longingly—and sometimes in so light-filled a way—been raised to the spirit throughout all time.

He stands before us, this reborn Raphael, this reborn John, this reborn Elijah; there he stands before us and we may revere him, and he may be one of many intermediaries who can show us the way towards the spirit revelations towards which we work in the stream of our spiritual movement; so that, with a true heart, true love, true enthusiasm, real devotion may allow us to succeed in bringing down from spiritual heights what we hope will also flow into the most guileless of souls. Because, whatever may be said here or there about the inaccessibility of modern spiritual research, it is primarily those unworldly hearts and minds who will be damaged by lies about incomprehensibility; for it is they who will understand how our spiritual stream seeks to be a downward conduit from spiritual heights.

The path from spiritual heights must not be sought only for those among whom some may to varying extents have allowed spiritual practices to work on them. We should seek a path for *all* yearning souls who long for truth and the spirit. Whilst our preface should be Goethe's axiom, which only has to be grasped in the depths of its simplicity: 'Truth exists only within truth,' so must our aim be to transform the spiritual life we seek—and about which we hear—in such a way that, through the grace that spiritual powers bestow on us, we frame this spiritual life in such a way that it can find its way to every—to every single—seeking soul. That must be our aim. It is our will to work in truth and actively to find ways to all seeking souls, at whichever stage of their incarnation they may be.

The mysteries of incarnation are profound, as the path of Novalis' incarnations shows us. That is why he, of all people, can lead us ahead like a guiding star, can lead us forwards in such a way that—in feeling him, in following him—we, too, summon the good will to rise with every effort towards him in knowledge, while on the other hand nurturing that life-filled will to reach every human heart seeking truthfully for the spirit. Let what Novalis himself so beautifully says[88]—and which can serve as a kind of motto—light us forward to the decisions we made at the outset of this anthroposophical spiritual stream.

Words are no longer mere words when spiritual words are also the founders of worldviews, because then they are both enlightening and warming for loftier and humbler souls alike, and this must become our longing. It was also what Novalis longed for. He expressed this in the lovely words I wish to bring you—at the end of which I have changed a single word—and which speaks to your hearts, my dear friends. I change this word of Novalis', even though philistines who

think themselves free spirits may be a little incensed. So let our guiding star, among other guiding stars, also be what lies in Novalis' beautiful words:

> When numbers and figures cease to be
> For every creature's thoughts the key,
> When they who merely kiss or sing
> Know more than sages' reckoning,
> When life to freedom will attain
> And freedom in creation reign,
> When light and shade, no longer single,
> In splendid clarity intermingle,
> And one in tales and poems sees
> The world's eternal histories,
> Then will our perverse, herd-like being
> Before *one* secret word be fleeing.

NOTES

*T*EXTUAL *sources*: With almost all of the lectures here, the author(s) of the transcript(s) cannot be clearly determined. However, they were likely always members of the Theosophical Society who took shorthand reasonably well, but on the whole they are not professional transcripts. This is also noticeable in the texts, which seem to be very incomplete in many places. The transcript of the lecture of 15 January 1912, for example, may have some considerable gaps, despite the apparently continuous text. Nonetheless, what has been handed down seems substantial enough that it should not be omitted. For the Munich lectures (11 Jan., 25 & 27 Feb. and 16 May 1912), Georg Klenck may have taken notes, but also Agnes Friedländer. A handwritten transcript of the lecture in Zurich on 17 Dec. 1912 was made by Alice Kinkel. The transcript of the lecture on 24 December 1912 is by Walter Vegelahn, but there is also an almost identical shorthand transcript by Franz Seiler.

1   Refers to the lectures in Munich of 8 January 1912, 'How can Theosophy be Refuted?', and that of 10 January 1912, 'How can Theosophy be Established?'. Only inadequate notes of these lectures exist. Lectures given in parallel in Berlin (between 31 October and 7 November 1912) are published in *Results of Spiritual Research*, CW 62.

2   See previous note.

3   Here the postscript is clearly lacking.

4   Henri Bergson, 1859–1941, French philosopher and professor in Paris. Bergson is at pains to break out beyond the bounds of materialism and naturalism with his philosophy. The relationship between 'I' and 'perpetuity' or continuance is treated of primarily in his book *Time and Freedom*, Paris 1911. Regarding this issue, see also Rudolf Steiner's treatise in the lecture of 18 April 1918 in (currently untranslated volume) 'The Eternal

in the Human Soul—Immortality and Freedom', CW 67; on Bergson's philosophy in general, see the chapter on 'The Modern Person and their World View', in Rudolf Steiner's *The Riddles of Philosophy*, CW 18.

5   Nostradamus, actually Michel de Notredame, 1503–1566, doctor and astrologer. Nostradamus drafted some 1000 prophesies in the form of sayings or proverbs, which he divided into ten books so that each book contained 100 'centuries'. All self-published, the first seven books appeared in Lyon in 1555 and three further volumes appeared in 1558.

6   Max Kemmerich, 1876–1932, art and cultural historian. In his book *Prophecy—Old Superstition or New Truth?*, Munich 1911 (to be found in Rudolf Steiner's library), Chapter 11 is dedicated to the life and work of Nostradamus.

7   In the Introduction to his book *Prophecies*, he says: 'I only approached this question as a historian and this happened as follows: In my examination of length of life and causes of death within the German Imperial and Royal families, in which I for the first time brought the proof—on the basis of historical and statistical data—that life expectancy and level of material culture stand in direct relationship to each other and that people have lived into older age ever since the early Middle Ages, I came across the following instances...' Then follow a few examples of death dates and premonitions of death experienced by German emperors and kings, based in horoscopes. Kemmerich then continues: 'These and other historical—and hence incontrovertible—facts, which I found tucked away in my memory, caused me to become perplexed and I decided to subject them to incisive scrutiny. [...] But how, if I convinced myself of its reality, was I to prove, with the courage of a believer, a truth of which I had obviously become a convinced follower? The following case arose: [...] It was precisely my lack of authority and my urge to be truthful that enabled and encouraged me to test a question which had long been resolved for thoughtless devotees to contemporary dogma.'

8   Followers of Johannes Calvin (1509–1564), Swiss reformer and champion of the doctrine of predestination. Calvin called for the complete separation of Church and state.

9   Paracelsus (Theophrastus Bombastus von Hohenheim), 1493–1541, doctor, natural historical researcher and philosopher. Having served as a surgeon in the Danish War and taken part in the Salzburg farmers' rebellion, travelled from Sweden to Sicily through Europe and into the Near East, had become a professor and city doctor in Basel—

which he had to give up due to his unorthodox lectures and methods of treatment—Paracelsus travelled around Southern Germany. His writings were titled *Bibliographia Paracelsica* (1894) by Karl Sudhoff.

10 In the dedication of his eighth 'century' to King Henry II of France, it is stated that he, Nostradamus, had written his prophecies, 'based on reckoning the course of the heavens in connection with a certain stimulus inherited from his ancestral fathers taking place at certain times' that his 'natural instinct was able to chime in harmony with a long-running calculation, in that he freed his soul, spirit and mind of all troubles, worries and excitement through inner stillness and peace'. (See Kemmerich, ibid.)

11 Wolfram von Eschenbach, around 1170-1220. Wolfram says of himself that he could not read, [words to the effect that:] 'Quite unknown to me is reading, as others are able to do.' (*Parsifal*, Part 2, Verse 1711): '*Swaz in buochen stet geschriben / des bin ich kunstelôs beliben, / niht anders ich geleret bin, / wan hân ich kunst, die gît mir sin.*' ('Willehan' 2, 19ff). See also *The Life and Poetry of Wolfram von Eschenbach* (*Leben und Dichten Wolframs von Eschenbach*), published by San-Marte, 1st volume, Magdeburg 1836; 'Introduction and Education', where it states: 'Of scientific learning there was little of note; those who could read and write were considered highly educated and the first poets, Wolfram von Eschenbach, Wirnt von Grafenberg, among others, understood neither. [...] To wield the pen as a writer or to study learned works was an unseemly occupation for knights.'

12 Friedrich Hebbel, 1813–1863, German poet known primarily for his dramas (*Nibelungen, The Ring of Gyges, Judith, Maria Magdalena* i.a.). The quotation in question (*Tagebücher* or Diaries, publ. by Theodor Poppe, No. 1336) is, literally: 'After the soul's transmigration, it is possible that Plato is now once again being caned at his school desk because he does not understand Plato.'

13 Prince of old Danish saga; known through William Shakespeare's drama *Hamlet* (1603/1604). The quotation in question is from the fifth scene of the first act:

> My tables, my tables—meet it is I set it down.
> That one may smile, and smile, and be a villain.
> At least I am sure it may be so in Denmark.
> [So, uncle, there you are. Now to my word—
> It is 'Adieu, adieu, remember me'. I have sworn't.]

14 Refers to the lecture 'Death and Immortality in Light of Spiritual Science', held on 16 January 1912 in Zurich. No notes of this lecture exist.

15 The Ten Commandments: 2. Mos: 20.

16 This refers to Rudolf Schober. See also Chapter 4 of Rudolf Steiner's Autobiography *The Course of My Life* (1923-25), CW 25, for a detailed description of this scene.

17 *Knowledge of the Higher Worlds. How is it Achieved?* (1904/05) CW 10.

18 See, for example, Plato's *Thaetetos*. Socrates: [...] 'For amazement is the state of the man who greatly loves wisdom; indeed, there is no other origin of philosophy than this.' [...] And Aristotle: *Metaphysics*, Book 1: 'To people both now and when they previously began to philosophise, amazement offered the impulsion to consider immediate problems and, on further study, to consider issues lying further in the past. [...] Anyone who finds themselves in doubt or puzzlement has the feeling that they do not understand the matter in hand and, similarly, do those who move among mythical imaginations to some extent have a tendency to philosophize; [...] The point of origin in all of them is amazement or wonder that the issue should be as it is.'

19 '...but whosoever shall smite thee on thy right cheek, turn to him the other also'. Matthew 5: 39.

20 See note 18.

21 Euripides, 480-406 BCE, Aeschylos, 525-456 BCE, and Sophocles, 496-406 BCE, the three great Attic tragedians.

22 Expressions such as this go back to Goethe. He speaks of spiritual eyes in, for instance, the short essay 'A Few Remarks (Goethe's Scientific Writings)', edited by Rudolf Steiner, in *German National Literature* published by Joseph Kürschner, Vols. 114-117, Berlin and Stuttgart 1883-1897, reprinted Dornach 1975, CW 1a, p.107 or also in his autobiography *Dichtung und Wahrheit (Poetry and Truth)*, Part 3: 'I saw myself, albeit not with corporeal eyes but with those of the spirit, approaching me on horseback on the same road...' The aerial spirit Arial, in the first Scene of the first Act of *Faust*, Part 2 (line 4667 on) speaks of spiritual ears: 'Listen! Hear the hour nearing! Ringing out to spirit-hearing. Now the new day is appearing...'

23 Rudolf Steiner bases this example on Vincent Knauer (1828-1894); see his work *The Principal Problem of Philosophy in its Evolution and its Partial Resolution from Thales to Robert Hamerling*, Vienna/Leipzig 1892, Lecture 21: *Founts of Knowledge*, p136f.

24 Lecture of 24 February 1912 in Munich: 'Hidden Depths of Soul Life'—not published to date.

25 See previous note.

26 Lecture of 9 February 1912 in Vienna (contained in the volume *Esoteric Christianity*, CW 130); Rudolf Steiner speaks of this once again in the lecture of 27 August 1913 in Munich (contained in the volume *Secrets of the Threshold*, CW 147).

27 Helena Petrovna Blavatsky, 1831–1891, daughter of the Mecklenburg family of Hahn, who settled in Russia. Gifted from childhood with spiritual talents, but also very headstrong. In an act of rebellion she married Nikifor von Blavatsky, over thirty years her senior, from whom she immediately separated, however. Following long journeys across many continents, she encountered the Master known to her since her childhood visions as Mahatma M when she was in London in August 1851. At his behest she studied and trained herself in occult methods in preparation for working within an occult society. In 1873 she travelled to New York to combat and elucidate its overwhelming Spiritualism (or Spiritism). Here she founded the Theosophical Society in 1871 with Colonel Olcot, whose headquarters transferred in 1879 to India. In 1886 she left India and lived mainly in London until her death. Her most significant works are *Isis Unveiled—a Master Key to Ancient and Modern Mysteries, Sciences and Philosophies* (2 volumes, New York, 1877); *The Secret Doctrine—The Synthesis of Science, Religion and Philosophy* (2 volumes, London, 1888). Rudolf Steiner often speaks about H.P. Blavatsky, including in the lectures *The Occult Movement of the Nineteenth Century*, CW 254; in the lectures of 7 May 1906 in *Origins of Spiritual Science*, CW 96; on 28 March 1916 in *The Human Spirit*, CW 167; on 12 March 1916 in 'The Spiritual Background of the First World War', vol. 1 (not translated), CW 174B; and lectures of 9 and 16 December 1916 in *The Karma of Untruthfulness*, vol. 1, CW 173.

28 See page 531 on the Theosophical Society in Rudolf Steiner's report 'About Theosophical Work' in *Lucifer Gnosis*, CW 34: 'The fundamental tenets of the Theosophical Society are: 1: To form the core of a brotherly community, spread across *all of humanity*, without reference to race, religion, societal class, nationality or gender. 2: To promote the study of comparative religions, philosophies and sciences; 3: To carry out research into natural laws not accounted for by conventional science and into the forces slumbering in the human being.'

29 At the beginning of the lecture Rudolf Steiner spoke the following words of thanks: 'May I express my heartfelt thanks for the kind words of the General Secretary of the Swedish section, Group Captain Kinell, and may I in turn perhaps address words from my innermost soul to you, that I am happy, from the depths of my heart, that on the journey from Helsingfors [Helsinki] I am able to spend a few days with you in Stockholm, talking about issues and truths that so closely affect us. My heartfelt greeting is just as warmly felt as the loving words of the General Secretary.'

30 John 4.

31 Matthew 5-7; Luke 6: 20-49.

32 *The Education of the Child in Light of Spiritual Science*, 1907 in *Lucifer Gnosis*, CW 34, also available as a separate edition.

33 Sanskrit word which can be literally translated as 'all-working, all-creating'. In the *Rig Veda*, this denotes personified creative activity (X, 81-82). See also Rudolf Steiner's lectures of 24 June 1909 in *The Gospel of St. John in Relation to the Other Three Gospels*, CW 112; of 21 September 1909 in *The Gospel of Luke*, CW 114, as also that of 13 April 1912 in *The Spiritual Beings in the Heavenly Bodies*, CW 136. See also the article by Herman Berger, 'The Mythology of Vishvakarman', in the newsletter *The Goetheanum*, No. 42/1993.

34 *Shuddhodana*, sixth century BCE, Prince of Kapilavastu in Northern India, father of Gautama Buddha.

35 Matthew 24: 30; also i.a. Mark 13: 26; Luke 21: 27.

36 *The Spiritual Guidance of the Individual and Humanity*, (1911) CW 15.

37 Philippians 2: 8.

38 See the 11th part (V. 489-491) of Homer's *Odyssey*: 'I would rather serve as slave to another man, a man with no land and livelihood, than be a king over all the rotting corpses.' Transl. Sententiae Antiquae.

39 Chapter 1: Pythagoras: 'Herakleidos Ponticos writes to him [i.e. Pythagoras] with an expression he often repeated, that he had dwelt on Earth ages before as Aithalides and had been thought to be Hermes' son; […] Some time later, he appeared again on Earth as Euphorbos and had been wounded by Menelaos […] After Euphorbos died, his soul transmigrated into the body of Hermotimos, who in turn wanted to attest to this and to this end went (over) to the Branchides, where he entered the temple of Apollo and pointed to the shield, which Mene-

laos had hung there. Menelaos [...] had dedicated the shield to Apollo after leaving Troy.'

Also in Ovid's *Metamorphoses* does Pythagoras (Part 15, V. 160-164) tell of his incarnation as Euphorbos:

I am still conscious now that, at the time of the Trojan War,
I was Panthous' son, Euphorbos, to whose breast was fastened
the weighty spear of the second Atrides.
Not long since did I recognize it in Argos of the Abantes,
in Juno's temple, that very shield, which my left [arm] had borne.

40   See Acts of the Apostles 9: 2-9.

41   See i.a. *The Spiritual Guidance of the Individuality and Humanity* (1911), CW 15, and *Universe, Earth, Human Being*, CW 105.

42   Julian the Apostate: 331-363, actually Julian Flavius Claudius, Roman Caesar: though brought up to be a Christian, Julian turned to the ancient Mystery cults of former ages, the reason for his being named Apostate (renegade, turncoat). Aged 31 he was murdered on a campaign in Asia.

43   See the incisive elaboration by Rudolf Steiner in the lectures of 30 December 1910 in *Occult History*, CW 126, and of 16 September 1924 in *Karmic Relationships*, vol. 4, CW 238.

44   Tycho Brahe, 1546–1601: Danish astronomer, worked under King Rudolf III in Prague; on the basis of his numerous observations his pupil Kepler developed his famous laws. He himself developed the Tychonic system of the universe, which was a compromise between the Copernican and Ptolemaic systems.

45   Suleyman (Suleiman) II, 1495-1566, Turkish Sultan, besieged Vienna 1529, died 5 September 1566 while on a military campaign against Hungary.

46   On the occasion of an eclipse of the Moon on 28 October 1566, Tycho Brahe delivered a few Latin verses, in which he prophesied the death of Sultan Suleyman [the Magnificent]. Several weeks later, news of Suleyman's death arrived. In fact he had died on 5 September, before the eclipse of the Moon, cause for some to mock Tycho's prophetic powers. He defended himself, however, by going into Suleyman's horoscope in great detail, from which he had surmised his death.

47   Easter 1912, first appearance of the *Anthroposophical Soul Calendar*. It did not subsequently reappear in the form given it by Imme von Eckhardtstein. The new edition of 1925 is in the form by Rudolf Steiner in which it has since been published. The *Soul Calendar*, also published

as *Calendar of the Soul,* is contained in the volume *Truth-Wrought Words,* CW 40, also available as a separate volume.

48 'White Lotus Day': death day of H.P. Blavatsky on 8 May 1891; see also note 27.

49 Georg Wilhelm Friedrich Hegel, 1770-1831, German Idealist philosopher. See Rudolf Steiner's descriptions of him in the chapter 'Reactionary World Views' in *The Riddles of Philosophy* (1914), CW 18, and German Idealism in Hegel's way of thinking in *The Riddle of Man*, CW 20.

50 The poem 'Eleusis—to Hölderlin' was written in 1796. See also *Georg Wilhelm Friedrich Hegel's Life* as described by Karl Rosenkranz, supplement to Hegel's Works, Berlin 1844, p. 78ff. The version quoted is translated by C.T. Bryan.

51 *obol:* small ancient Greek coin of low denomination.

52 Max Müller, 1823-1900, one of the most famous orientalists of the nineteenth century, researcher into languages and religions and professor at Oxford University. Works include *History of Ancient Sanskrit Literature* (1859), *Lectures on the Science of Language* (1861); *Introduction to the Science of Religion* (1874), *The Sacred Books of the East* (1876).

53 Published in the words of A.P. Sinnett, *The Occult World*, 1881.

54 President and co-founder of the Theosophical Society, Henry Steel Olcott (1832-1907). See also his work *Old Diary Leaves*.

55 Socrates, 470–399 BCE, Greek philosopher, and his pupil Plato, 429–347 BCE; Gaius Julius Caesar, 100–44 BCE, Roman General and Caesar; Johann Wolfgang von Goethe, 1749–1832; Baruch Spinoza, 1632–1677, leading Dutch philosopher of Rationalism, mathematician and optician.

56 Johann Gottlieb Fichte, 1762–1814, Philosopher of German Idealism; initially at University of Jena, later in Berlin following dismissal on grounds of an article seemingly speaking against religion.

57 Raphael Santi, 1483–1520, see also lecture of 30 January 1913 in *Results of Spiritual Research*, CW 62; a chronological overview of Steiner's lectures on Raphael and his work is published in the pamphlet series of articles contributing to Steiner's Complete Works, Booklet 82, Dornach, Christmas 1983. For the series of incarnations mentioned here, Elijah—John the Baptist—Raphael—Novalis, see the address of 28 September 1924, as also supplementary remarks to this in *Karmic Relationships*, vol. 4, CW 238, as also the article by Hella Wiesberger, 'The Exhibition in 1965' in Contributions to Rudolf

Steiner's Collected Works, vol. 14, Michaelmas 1965, and the art insert with four portrait drawings of four personalities by William Scott Pyle in the above-mentioned contributions to the CW, vol. 43/44, Christmas 1973.

58   Michelangeo Buonarroti, 1475–1564, sculptor, painter, architect of the Italian Renaissance, polymath.

59   The prophet Elijah (Hebr. Yahweh is God), see primarily Kings 1: 17-21 and Kings 2: 1 & 2. Likewise in the New Testament, it is often spoken of Elijah, whose return is expected and is fulfilled in John the Baptist (Matthew 11: 10 and 14; Mark 9: 12f.; Luke 1: 16f. and 76).

60   *The School of Athens*: mural by Raphael in the Camera della Signatura in the Vatican. Cf. also Steiner's elaboration of this in the lecture of 5 May 1909 in *Rosicrucianism Renewed*, CW 284, of 30 January 1913 in *Results of Spiritual Research*, CW 62, and that of 1 November 1916 in *Art History as a Reflection of Inner Spiritual Impulses*, CW 292.

61   *The Sistine Madonna*: see Rudolf Steiner's remarks in the lectures of 4 August 1908 in *Universe, Earth, Human Being*, CW 105, and that of 2 September 1908 in *Egyptian Myths and Mysteries*; also of 30 January 1913 in *Results of Spiritual Research*, CW 62; further of 1 November 1916 in *Art History as a Reflection of Inner Spiritual Impulses*, CW 292.
      Goethe only remarked, regarding a secret visit to Dresden: 'The few days of my stay in Dresden were devoted solely to visiting the Art Gallery. The antiques were still in the pavilions of the Great Garden; I declined to visit them, as I did all the other Dresden treasures, being simply too full of the conviction that in the Art Gallery collections much must still be hidden from me. So I rather took on trust the value of the Italian masters instead of forming my own insights into them.' (*Poetry and Truth*, Part II, Book 8). Herman Grimm reflects the view of the times as follows: 'The Dresden authorities had put it about that the child on the arm of the Madonna appeared of mean nature and his expression sullen. It seemed the two angels at the bottom had been added by a student. It was even maintained that an understudy of Raphael had painted the Madonna or, worse still, it was not by Raphael at all. It is possible that Goethe was influenced by Gallery wardens, with whom he had become acquainted and, swept along with such opinions, did not have the strength to uphold what may have been his contradictory inner feelings'. 'Raphael's *Sistine Madonna* would have illumined him like a Sun; but he passes it by' (*The Life of Raphael*, Ch.

9, 5th edition, Stuttgart and Berlin 1913, p.284). However, Goethe did see it later, in 1813, as the reminiscences of Heinrich Freiherr von Hess recall, but which was possibly unknown to Herman Grimm and Rudolf Steiner (*Goethe's Conversations*, Zurich 1969, Vol. 2, p.827). Hess recounts: 'So I marvelled at the Madonna of St. Sixtus by Raphael—with which I was familiar from copper etchings and copies—under the world-encompassing gaze of the Child and the profound, virginal countenance and presence of the Mother of this divine child. Goethe reinforced my earlier sense with few words. Stepping up to the painting he said: "You see here—painted with the greatest master strokes in the world—child and God and mother and virgin simultaneously represented in divine transfiguration. This painting alone is a world, a replete artists' world, which—even had he painted nothing else—must have rendered its creator immortal!"'

62   Voltaire, 1694–1778, influential writer and philosopher of the Enlightenment, commentator on many political and artistic issues of the time and exerting much influence through his writings.

63   Novalis, 1772-1801, whose real name was Friedrich von Hardenberg. His works include *Heinrich von Ofterdingen, Hymns to the Night, Fragments*.

64   Matthew 25: 40.

65   See note 52.

66   Max Müller wrote: 'Once there was a man with a peculiar power to grunt exactly like a pig and he made a good deal of money by showing off his power of mimicry to the common people. In one village where he was giving an exhibition, a holy man passed by, who decided to teach a lesson to these credulous people. He advertised that he would show them a better performance, with much better grunting, free of cost. People flocked to him and, producing a real pig, he squeezed it to make it grunt. But the people said: "Is that all? We hear that every day, what's there to it?" And they all went away. The sage said: "Here is a splendid lesson. We seldom care for reality and always go in for imitation."' See *Scholar Extraordinary. The Life of Professor the Rt. Hon. Friedrich Max Müller, P.C.* by Nirad C. Chaudhuri, London 1974, p. 328f.; also lecture of 2 December 1909 in *Transforming the Soul*, Vol. 1, CW 58.

67   In order to disseminate this teaching, Annie Besant and Charles Leadbeater founded the Order of the Star of the East, a grouping within the Theosophical Society.

68   This painting by Raphael is in the National Gallery, London.

69   See note 61.

70   Imme von Eckhardtstein, 1871–1930, had been a member of the
      Theosophical Society since 1905, then of the Anthroposophical Soci-
      ety; since 1909 she had been responsible for costume production for
      the Mystery Dramas in Munich—in which she also appeared as an
      actor—and later in Dornach too; she drew the zodiac for the *Calendar
      of the Soul* 1912/13. Further details in the Newsletter *Goetheanum*, No.
      20 of 1930, in an obituary by Marie Steiner. Also in a short biograph-
      ical sketch in *On the History and Contents of the First Section of the Esoteric
      School from 1904 to 1914*, CW 264.

71   Master Eckhart, 1260–1327, Dominican and Mystic, taught in Paris,
      Strasbourg and Cologne; later accused of heresy. See: *Meister Eckhart,
      the German Works: 64 Homilies for the Liturgical Year. I; Meister Eckhart, The
      Essential Sermons, Commentaries, Treatises and Defence.*

72   Johannes Tauler, 1300–1361, mystic, preacher in Strasbourg. For more
      about him and his meeting with the 'Unknown Person from the High-
      lands' see the chapter 'Friendship with God' in Rudolf Steiner's *Mysti-
      cism at the Dawn of the Modern Age*, CW 7. Works: *Johannes Tauler's Sermons.*

73   Matthew 18: 20.

74   Matthew 25: 40.

75   *The Soul's Probation*, the second of Steiner's *Four Mystery Dramas* (1910-
      1913), CW 14.

76   Rudolf Steiner's severance from the Theosophical Society and the
      founding of the Anthroposophical Society took place at Christmas
      1912 in Cologne.

77   Matthew 2: 1-12.

78   Empress Eudocia, 400–460. Ingenious and reportedly beautiful daugh-
      ter of the Athenian Leontios, under the name of Eudocia, became the
      wife of Emperor Theodosius II and converted to Christianity in 421.
      She was banished from the court on grounds of slander and died in
      Jerusalem in 460. The description of the life of the martyr Cyprian in
      'Cyprian and Justina' is all that remains of her poetry.

79   Translator's note: With thanks to Brian P. Sowers, *In Her Own Words—
      Life and Poetry of Aelia Eudocia*, Center for Hellenistic Studies, Harvard
      University. Edited by C. Bryan.

80   Immediately before the lecture, Marie von Sivers, later Steiner, had
      recited Novalis' *Spiritual Songs.*

81   See lectures held in Berlin between 28 December 1912 and 1 January
      1913 in *The Bhagavad Gita and the Letters of Paul*, CW 142.

82   Spinoza taught—based on neo-Platonism and Descartes—a pantheistic

philosophy of necessity. He saw the liberation from the rule of affected-ness or emotion as an ethical ideal; human beings were to be led by clear insight into essential laws. Goethe expressed in his autobiography, *Poetry and Truth*, the effect on him of this world outlook as follows: 'This spirit, which had such an incisive effect on me, and who was to have such an influence on my entire way of thinking, was Spinoza. Having searched fruitlessly the world over for a means of educating my wondering being, I lit upon the *Ethics* of this man. Whatever I may have gleaned from this work, whatever I may also have read into it, I cannot quantify; suffice that here I found a tranquilliser of my passions and it seemed as though a wide and clear view across the sense and ethical worlds opened up. [...] The all-soothing peace of Spinoza contrasted with my all-excited striving, his mathematical methods were contrary to my poetic sensibilities and descriptive manners, and precisely this measured presentation, which one was not inclined to apply to ethical matters, made me into his fervent pupil, into his most decided admirer. Spirit and heart, intellect and senses sought me out with essential elective affinity and, through this, the most disparate beings were united.' (Part III, volume 14.) 'I surrendered to this lecture and believed, by looking into myself, never before to have viewed the world so clearly.' (Part IV, vol. 16.)

83   The sacred knowledge of the Indians, revealed by the holy men, the rishis; the oldest surviving writings of the Indian—and indeed of any Indo-European literature.

84   At Wieland's funeral, 23 January 1813, Goethe remarks to Johannes Daniel Falk (Falk and Goethe depicted as close personal friends in *Goethe's Conversations*, Zurich 1969, p771): '[...] I take the various classes and ranks as the ultimate constituent of all beings, likewise as the point of origin of all phenomena in nature, which I would like to call *Souls*, because from them emanates the ensoulment of the total-ity, or perhaps rather *Monads*—let us always remain with this term of Leibniz'! To express the simplicity of the simplest entity, I could hardly wish for a better term. Now, some of these Monads or points of ori-gin are, as experience demonstrates to us, so small, so negligible, that they are highly suited only to serving a single, subservient purpose and existence. Others, on the other hand, are quite strong and powerful. These latter tend to snatch into their circle of influence everything that approaches them and to transform it into something belonging to them, that is, into a body, into a plant, into an animal or, at a more elevated level, into a star. They continue to do this until the micro- or

macro-world—whose intention inhabits them spiritually—also manifests physically and externally. Only these latter would I like to call *souls*. It follows from this that there exist world-monads, world-souls, just as there are ant-monads, ant-souls and that both are—in respect of their origin, while not a total unity, then in their archetypal being—related to one another.'

85   Sankya philosophy: one of the six classic-orthodox Indian philosophical systems. See also Rudolf Steiner's exposition on Sankya philosophy in the lectures of 28, 29 and 30 December 1912, included in the volume *The Bhagavad Gita and the Letters of Paul*, CW 142; as also in the lecture of 16 September 1909 in *The Gospel of Luke*, CW 114.

86   See Johann Gottlieb Fichte's *The Vocation of Man*, Frankfurt and Leipzig 1800, where in the second book, *Outlines of the Doctrine of Knowledge*, he says: 'All reality transforms itself into a wonderful dream, without a life about which it dreams, and without a spirit, which dreams it; into a dream which, in a dream of itself, is of itself held together. The *beholding* or observation is the dream. *Thinking*—the source of all being and all reality, which I imagine of my being, of my strength and of my purpose—is the dream of that dream.'

87   On 5 October 1791 Novalis writes to his philosophy professor, Reinhold, in Jena (1758-1823): 'Schiller, who is greater than a million everyday people, who could wring from those ambition-free beings we call spirits the wish to become mortal, whose soul seems to have shaped nature with love, con amore, whose ethical majesty and beauty alone could rescue a world in which he lived from its deserved downfall...' Novalis' writings, 4th vol. *Letters and Diaries* (no. 21).

88   This poem is in the (paralipomenic) supplement to *Heinrich von Ofterdingen*; see Tieck's report on its planned continuation (Novalis' Writings, vol. 2, *Poetry*). The last line is, in Novalis' original, 'The whole inverted being hence'.)

Rudolf Steiner's Collected Works

T HE German Edition of Rudolf Steiner's Collected Works (the *Gesamtausgabe* [GA] published by Rudolf Steiner Verlag, Dornach, Switzerland) presently runs to 354 titles, organized either by type of work (written or spoken), chronology, audience (public or other), or subject (education, art, etc.). For ease of comparison, the Collected Works in English [CW] follows the German organization exactly. A complete listing of the CWs follows with literal translations of the German titles. Other than in the case of the books published in his lifetime, titles were rarely given by Rudolf Steiner himself, and were often provided by the editors of the German editions. The titles in English are not necessarily the same as the German; and, indeed, over the past 75 years have frequently been different, with the same book sometimes appearing under different titles.

For ease of identification and to avoid confusion, we suggest that readers looking for a title should do so by CW number. Because the work of creating the Collected Works of Rudolf Steiner is an ongoing process, with new titles being published every year, we have not indicated in this listing which books are presently available. To find out what titles in the Collected Works are currently in print, please check our website at www.rudolfsteinerpress.com (or www.steinerbooks.org for US readers).

Written Work

CW 1   Goethe: Natural-Scientific Writings, Introduction, with Footnotes and Explanations in the text by Rudolf Steiner

CW 2   Outlines of an Epistemology of the Goethean World View, with Special Consideration of Schiller

CW 3   Truth and Science

CW 4   The Philosophy of Freedom

CW 4a Documents to 'The Philosophy of Freedom'

CW 5   Friedrich Nietzsche, A Fighter against His Time

CW 6   Goethe's Worldview

CW 6a   Now in CW 30

CW 7   Mysticism at the Dawn of Modern Spiritual Life and Its Relationship with Modern Worldviews

CW 8   Christianity as Mystical Fact and the Mysteries of Antiquity

CW 9   Theosophy: An Introduction into Supersensible World Knowledge and Human Purpose

CW 10   How Does One Attain Knowledge of Higher Worlds?

CW 11   From the Akasha-Chronicle

CW 12   Levels of Higher Knowledge

CW 13   Occult Science in Outline

CW 14   Four Mystery Dramas

CW 15   The Spiritual Guidance of the Individual and Humanity

CW 16   A Way to Human Self-Knowledge: Eight Meditations

CW 17   The Threshold of the Spiritual World. Aphoristic Comments

CW 18   The Riddles of Philosophy in Their History, Presented as an Outline

CW 19   Contained in CW 24

CW 20   The Riddles of the Human Being: Articulated and Unarticulated in the Thinking, Views and Opinions of a Series of German and Austrian Personalities

CW 21   The Riddles of the Soul

CW 22   Goethe's Spiritual Nature and its Revelation in 'Faust' and through the 'Fairy Tale of the Snake and the Lily'

CW 23   The Central Points of the Social Question in the Necessities of Life in the Present and the Future

CW 24   Essays Concerning the Threefold Division of the Social Organism and the Period 1915-1921

CW 25   Cosmology, Religion and Philosophy

CW 26   Anthroposophical Leading Thoughts

CW 27   Fundamentals for Expansion of the Art of Healing according to Spiritual-Scientific Insights

CW28   The Course of My Life

CW 29   Collected Essays on Dramaturgy, 1889-1900

CW 30   Methodical Foundations of Anthroposophy: Collected Essays on Philosophy, Natural Science, Aesthetics and Psychology, 1884-1901

CW 31   Collected Essays on Culture and Current Events, 1887-1901

CW 32   Collected Essays on Literature, 1884-1902

CW 33   Biographies and Biographical Sketches, 1894-1905

CW 34   Lucifer-Gnosis: Foundational Essays on Anthroposophy and Reports from the Periodicals 'Lucifer' and 'Lucifer-Gnosis,' 1903-1908

CW 35   Philosophy and Anthroposophy: Collected Essays, 1904-1923

CW 36   The Goetheanum-Idea in the Middle of the Cultural Crisis of the Present: Collected Essays from the Periodical 'Das Goetheanum,' 1921-1925

CW 37   Now in CWs 260a and 251
CW 38   Letters, Vol. 1: 1881-1890
CW 39   Letters, Vol. 2: 1890-1925
CW 40   Truth-Wrought Words
CW 40a Sayings, Poems and Mantras; Supplementary Volume
CW 42   Now in CWs 264-266
CW 43   Stage Adaptations
CW 44   On the Four Mystery Dramas. Sketches, Fragments and Paralipomena on the Four Mystery Dramas
CW 45   Anthroposophy: A Fragment from the Year 1910

Public Lectures
CW 51   On Philosophy, History and Literature
CW 52   Spiritual Teachings Concerning the Soul and Observation of the World
CW 53   The Origin and Goal of the Human Being
CW 54   The Riddles of the World and Anthroposophy
CW 55   Knowledge of the Supersensible in Our Times and Its Meaning for Life Today
CW 56   Knowledge of the Soul and of the Spirit
CW 57   Where and How Does One Find the Spirit?
CW 58   The Metamorphoses of the Soul Life. Paths of Soul Experiences: Part One
CW 59   The Metamorphoses of the Soul Life. Paths of Soul Experiences: Part Two
CW 60   The Answers of Spiritual Science to the Biggest Questions of Existence
CW 61   Human History in the Light of Spiritual Research
CW 62   Results of Spiritual Research
CW 63   Spiritual Science as a Treasure for Life
CW 64   Out of Destiny-Burdened Times
CW 65   Out of Central European Spiritual Life
CW 66   Spirit and Matter, Life and Death
CW 67   The Eternal in the Human Soul. Immortality and Freedom
CW 68   Public lectures in various cities, 1906-1918
CW 69   Public lectures in various cities, 1906-1918
CW 70   Public lectures in various cities, 1906-1918
CW 71   Public lectures in various cities, 1906-1918
CW 72   Freedom—Immortality—Social Life
CW 73   The Supplementing of the Modern Sciences through Anthroposophy
CW 73a Specialized Fields of Knowledge and Anthroposophy
CW 74   The Philosophy of Thomas Aquinas
CW 75   Public lectures in various cities, 1906-1918
CW 76   The Fructifying Effect of Anthroposophy on Specialized Fields
CW 77a The Task of Anthroposophy in Relation to Science and Life: The Darmstadt College Course
CW 77b Art and Anthroposophy. The Goetheanum-Impulse

CW 78   Anthroposophy, Its Roots of Knowledge and Fruits for Life
CW 79   The Reality of the Higher Worlds
CW 80   Public lectures in various cities, 1922
CW 81   Renewal-Impulses for Culture and Science—Berlin College Course
CW 82   So that the Human Being Can Become a Complete Human Being
CW 83   Western and Eastern World-Contrast. Paths to Understanding It through Anthroposophy
CW 84   What Did the Goetheanum Intend and What Should Anthroposophy Do?

Lectures to the Members of the Anthroposophical Society
CW 88   Concerning the Astral World and Devachan
CW 89   Consciousness—Life—Form. Fundamental Principles of a Spiritual-Scientific Cosmology
CW 90   Participant Notes from the Lectures during the Years 1903-1905
CW 91   Participant Notes from the Lectures during the Years 1903-1905
CW 92   The Occult Truths of Ancient Myths and Sagas
CW 93   The Temple Legend and the Golden Legend
CW 93a   Fundamentals of Esotericism
CW 94   Cosmogony. Popular Occultism. The Gospel of John. The Theosophy in the Gospel of John
CW 95   At the Gates of Theosophy
CW 96   Origin-Impulses of Spiritual Science. Christian Esotericism in the Light of New Spirit-Knowledge
CW 97   The Christian Mystery
CW 98   Nature Beings and Spirit Beings—Their Effects in Our Visible World
CW 99   The Theosophy of the Rosicrucians
CW 100   Human Development and Christ-Knowledge
CW 101   Myths and Legends. Occult Signs and Symbols
CW 102   The Working into Human Beings by Spiritual Beings
CW 103   The Gospel of John
CW 104   The Apocalypse of John
CW 104a   From the Picture-Script of the Apocalypse of John
CW 105   Universe, Earth, the Human Being: Their Being and Development, as well as Their Reflection in the Connection between Egyptian Mythology and Modern Culture
CW 106   Egyptian Myths and Mysteries in Relation to the Active Spiritual Forces of the Present
CW 107   Spiritual-Scientific Knowledge of the Human Being
CW 108   Answering the Questions of Life and the World through Anthroposophy
CW 109   The Principle of Spiritual Economy in Connection with the Question of Reincarnation. An Aspect of the Spiritual Guidance of Humanity
CW 110   The Spiritual Hierarchies and Their Reflection in the Physical World. Zodiac, Planets and Cosmos

CW 111   Contained in CW 109

CW 112   The Gospel of John in Relation to the Three Other Gospels, Especially the Gospel of Luke

CW 113   The Orient in the Light of the Occident. The Children of Lucifer and the Brothers of Christ

CW 114   The Gospel of Luke

CW 115   Anthroposophy—Psychosophy—Pneumatosophy

CW 116   The Christ-Impulse and the Development of I-Consciousness

CW 117   The Deeper Secrets of the Development of Humanity in Light of the Gospels

CW 118   The Event of the Christ-Appearance in the Etheric World

CW 119   Macrocosm and Microcosm. The Large World and the Small World. Soul-Questions, Life-Questions, Spirit-Questions

CW 120   The Revelation of Karma

CW 121   The Mission of Individual Folk-Souls in Connection with Germanic-Nordic Mythology

CW 122   The Secrets of the Biblical Creation-Story. The Six-Day Work in the First Book of Moses

CW 123   The Gospel of Matthew

CW 124   Excursus in the Area of the Gospel of Mark

CW 125   Paths and Goals of the Spiritual Human Being. Life Questions in the Light of Spiritual Science

CW 126   Occult History. Esoteric Observations of the Karmic Relationships of Personalities and Events of World History

CW 127   The Mission of the New Spiritual Revelation. The Christ-Event as the Middle-Point of Earth Evolution

CW 128   An Occult Physiology

CW 129   Wonders of the World, Trials of the Soul, and Revelations of the Spirit

CW 130   Esoteric Christianity and the Spiritual Guidance of Humanity

CW 131   From Jesus to Christ

CW 132   Evolution from the View Point of the Truth

CW 133   The Earthly and the Cosmic Human Being

CW 134   The World of the Senses and the World of the Spirit

CW 135   Reincarnation and Karma and their Meaning for the Culture of the Present

CW 136   The Spiritual Beings in Celestial Bodies and the Realms of Nature

CW 137   The Human Being in the Light of Occultism, Theosophy and Philosophy

CW 138   On Initiation. On Eternity and the Passing Moment. On the Light of the Spirit and the Darkness of Life

CW 139   The Gospel of Mark

CW 140   Occult Investigation into the Life between Death and New Birth. The Living Interaction between Life and Death

CW 141   Life between Death and New Birth in Relationship to Cosmic Facts

CW 142   The Bhagavad Gita and the Letters of Paul
CW 143   Experiences of the Supersensible. Three Paths of the Soul to Christ
CW 144   The Mysteries of the East and of Christianity
CW 145   What Significance Does Occult Development of the Human Being Have for the Sheaths—Physical Body, Etheric Body, Astral Body, and Self?
CW 146   The Occult Foundations of the Bhagavad Gita
CW 147   The Secrets of the Threshold
CW 148   Out of Research in the Akasha: The Fifth Gospel
CW 149   Christ and the Spiritual World. Concerning the Search for the Holy Grail
CW 150   The World of the Spirit and Its Extension into Physical Existence; The Influence of the Dead in the World of the Living
CW 151   Human Thought and Cosmic Thought
CW 152   Preliminary Stages to the Mystery of Golgotha
CW 153   The Inner Being of the Human Being and Life Between Death and New Birth
CW 154   How Does One Gain an Understanding of the Spiritual World? The Flowing in of Spiritual Impulses from out of the World of the Deceased
CW 155   Christ and the Human Soul. Concerning the Meaning of Life. Theosophical Morality. Anthroposophy and Christianity
CW 156   Occult Reading and Occult Hearing
CW 157   Human Destinies and the Destiny of Peoples
CW 157a   The Formation of Destiny and the Life after Death
CW 158   The Connection Between the Human Being and the Elemental World. Kalevala—Olaf Åsteson—The Russian People—The World as the Result of the Influences of Equilibrium
CW 159   The Mystery of Death. The Nature and Significance of Middle Europe and the European Folk Spirits
CW 160   In CW 159
CW 161   Paths of Spiritual Knowledge and the Renewal of the Artistic Worldview
CW 162   Questions of Art and Life in Light of Spiritual Science
CW 163   Coincidence, Necessity and Providence. Imaginative Knowledge and the Processes after Death
CW 164   The Value of Thinking for a Knowledge That Satisfies the Human Being. The Relationship of Spiritual Science to Natural Science
CW 165   The Spiritual Unification of Humanity through the Christ-Impulse
CW 166   Necessity and Freedom in the Events of the World and in Human Action
CW 167   The Present and the Past in the Human Spirit
CW 168   The Connection between the Living and the Dead
CW 169   World-being and Selfhood
CW 170   The Riddle of the Human Being. The Spiritual Background of Human History. Cosmic and Human History, Vol. 1

CW 171   Inner Development-Impulses of Humanity. Goethe and the Crisis of the 19th Century. Cosmic and Human History, Vol. 2

CW 172   The Karma of the Vocation of the Human Being in Connection with Goethe's Life. Cosmic and Human History, Vol. 3

CW 173   Contemporary-Historical Considerations: The Karma of Untruthfulness, Part One. Cosmic and Human History, Vol. 4

CW 174   Contemporary-Historical Considerations: The Karma of Untruthfulness, Part Two. Cosmic and Human History, Vol. 5

CW 174a   Middle Europe between East and West. Cosmic and Human History, Vol. 6

CW 174b   The Spiritual Background of the First World War. Cosmic and Human History, Vol. 7

CW 175   Building Stones for an Understanding of the Mystery of Golgotha. Cosmic and Human Metamorphoses

CW 176   Truths of Evolution of the Individual and Humanity. The Karma of Materialism

CW 177   The Spiritual Background of the Outer World. The Fall of the Spirits of Darkness. Spiritual Beings and Their Effects, Vol. 1

CW 178   Individual Spiritual Beings and their Influence in the Soul of the Human Being. Spiritual Beings and their Effects, Vol. 2

CW 179   Spiritual Beings and Their Effects. Historical Necessity and Freedom. The Influences on Destiny from out of the World of the Dead. Spiritual Beings and Their Effects, Vol. 3

CW 180   Mystery Truths and Christmas Impulses. Ancient Myths and their Meaning. Spiritual Beings and Their Effects, Vol. 4

CW 181   Earthly Death and Cosmic Life. Anthroposophical Gifts for Life. Necessities of Consciousness for the Present and the Future.

CW 182   Death as Transformation of Life

CW 183   The Science of the Development of the Human Being

CW 184   The Polarity of Duration and Development in Human Life. The Cosmic Pre-History of Humanity

CW 185   Historical Symptomology

CW 185a   Historical-Developmental Foundations for Forming a Social Judgement

CW 186   The Fundamental Social Demands of Our Time—In Changed Situations

CW 187   How Can Humanity Find the Christ Again? The Threefold Shadow-Existence of our Time and the New Christ-Light

CW 188   Goetheanism, a Transformation-Impulse and Resurrection-Thought. Science of the Human Being and Science of Sociology

CW 189   The Social Question as a Question of Consciousness. The Spiritual Background of the Social Question, Vol. 1

CW 190   Impulses of the Past and the Future in Social Occurrences. The Spiritual Background of the Social Question, Vol. 2

CW 191　Social Understanding from Spiritual-Scientific Cognition. The Spiritual Background of the Social Question, Vol. 3

CW 192　Spiritual-Scientific Treatment of Social and Pedagogical Questions

CW 193　The Inner Aspect of the Social Riddle. Luciferic Past and Ahrimanic Future

CW 194　The Mission of Michael. The Revelation of the Actual Mysteries of the Human Being

CW 195　Cosmic New Year and the New Year Idea

CW 196　Spiritual and Social Transformations in the Development of Humanity

CW 197　Polarities in the Development of Humanity: West and East Material-ism and Mysticism Knowledge and Belief

CW 198　Healing Factors for the Social Organism

CW 199　Spiritual Science as Knowledge of the Foundational Impulses of Social Formation

CW 200　The New Spirituality and the Christ-Experience of the 20th Century

CW 201　The Correspondences Between Microcosm and Macrocosm. The Human Being—A Hieroglyph of the Universe. The Human Being in Relationship with the Cosmos: 1

CW 202　The Bridge between the World-Spirituality and the Physical Aspect of the Human Being. The Search for the New Isis, the Divine Sophia. The Human Being in Relationship with the Cosmos: 2

CW 203　The Responsibility of Human Beings for the Development of the World through their Spiritual Connection with the Planet Earth and the World of the Stars. The Human Being in Relationship with the Cosmos: 3

CW 204　Perspectives of the Development of Humanity. The Materialistic Knowledge-Impulse and the Task of Anthroposophy. The Human Being in Relationship with the Cosmos: 4

CW 205　Human Development, World-Soul, and World-Spirit. Part One: The Human Being as a Being of Body and Soul in Relationship to the World. The Human Being in Relationship with the Cosmos: 5

CW 206　Human Development, World-Soul, and World-Spirit. Part Two: The Human Being as a Spiritual Being in the Process of Historical Devel-opment. The Human Being in Relationship with the Cosmos: 6

CW 207　Anthroposophy as Cosmosophy. Part One: Characteristic Features of the Human Being in the Earthly and the Cosmic Realms. The Human Being in Relationship with the Cosmos: 7

CW 208　Anthroposophy as Cosmosophy. Part Two: The Forming of the Human Being as the Result of Cosmic Influence. The Human Being in Relationship with the Cosmos: 8

CW 209　Nordic and Central European Spiritual Impulses. The Festival of the Appearance of Christ. The Human Being in Relationship with the Cosmos: 9

CW 210   Old and New Methods of Initiation. Drama and Poetry in the Change of Consciousness in the Modern Age

CW 211   The Sun Mystery and the Mystery of Death and Resurrection. Exoteric and Esoteric Christianity

CW 212   Human Soul Life and Spiritual Striving in Connection with World and Earth Development

CW 213   Human Questions and World Answers

CW 214   The Mystery of the Trinity: The Human Being in Relationship with the Spiritual World in the Course of Time

CW 215   Philosophy, Cosmology, and Religion in Anthroposophy

CW 216   The Fundamental Impulses of the World-Historical Development of Humanity

CW 217   Spiritually Active Forces in the Coexistence of the Older and Younger Generations. Pedagogical Course for Youth

CW 217a Youth's Cognitive Task

CW 218   Spiritual Connections in the Forming of the Human Organism

CW 219   The Relationship of the World of the Stars to the Human Being, and of the Human Being to the World of the Stars. The Spiritual Communion of Humanity

CW 220   Living Knowledge of Nature. Intellectual Fall and Spiritual Redemption

CW 221   Earth-Knowing and Heaven-Insight

CW 222   The Imparting of Impulses to World-Historical Events through Spiritual Powers

CW 223   The Cycle of the Year as Breathing Process of the Earth and the Four Great Festival-Seasons. Anthroposophy and the Human Heart (*Gemüt*)

CW 224   The Human Soul and its Connection with Divine-Spiritual Individualities. The Internalization of the Festivals of the Year

CW 225   Three Perspectives of Anthroposophy. Cultural Phenomena observed from a Spiritual-Scientific Perspective

CW 226   Human Being, Human Destiny, and World Development

CW 227   Initiation-Knowledge

CW 228   Science of Initiation and Knowledge of the Stars. The Human Being in the Past, the Present, and the Future from the Viewpoint of the Development of Consciousness

CW 229   The Experiencing of the Course of the Year in Four Cosmic Imaginations

CW 230   The Human Being as Harmony of the Creative, Building, and Formative World-Word

CW 231   The Supersensible Human Being, Understood Anthroposophically

CW 232   The Forming of the Mysteries

CW 233   World History Illuminated by Anthroposophy and as the Foundation for Knowledge of the Human Spirit

CW 233a   Mystery Sites of the Middle Ages: Rosicrucianism and the Modern Initiation-Principle. The Festival of Easter as Part of the History of the Mysteries of Humanity

CW 234   Anthroposophy. A Summary after 21 Years

CW 235   Esoteric Observations of Karmic Relationships in 6 Volumes, Vol. 1

CW 236   Esoteric Observations of Karmic Relationships in 6 Volumes, Vol. 2

CW 237   Esoteric Observations of Karmic Relationships in 6 Volumes, Vol. 3: The Karmic Relationships of the Anthroposophical Movement

CW 238   Esoteric Observations of Karmic Relationships in 6 Volumes, Vol. 4: The Spiritual Life of the Present in Relationship to the Anthroposophical Movement

CW 239   Esoteric Observations of Karmic Relationships in 6 Volumes, Vol. 5

CW 240   Esoteric Observations of Karmic Relationships in 6 Volumes, Vol. 6

CW 243   The Consciousness of the Initiate

CW 245   Instructions for an Esoteric Schooling

CW 250   The Building-Up of the Anthroposophical Society. From the Beginning to the Outbreak of the First World War

CW 251   The History of the Goetheanum Building-Association

CW 252   Life in the Anthroposophical Society from the First World War to the Burning of the First Goetheanum

CW 253   The Problems of Living Together in the Anthroposophical Society. On the Dornach Crisis of 1915. With Highlights on Swedenborg's Clairvoyance, the Views of Freudian Psychoanalysts, and the Concept of Love in Relation to Mysticism

CW 254   The Occult Movement in the 19th Century and Its Relationship to World Culture. Significant Points from the Exoteric Cultural Life around the Middle of the 19th Century

CW 255   Rudolf Steiner during the First World War

CW 255a   Anthroposophy and the Reformation of Society. On the History of the Threefold Movement

CW 255b   Anthroposophy and Its Opponents, 1919–1921

CW 256   How Can the Anthroposophical Movement Be Financed?

CW 256a   Futurum, Inc. / International Laboratories, Inc.

CW 256b   The Coming Day, Inc.

CW 257   Anthroposophical Community-Building

CW 258   The History of and Conditions for the Anthroposophical Movement in Relationship to the Anthroposophical Society. A Stimulus to Self-Contemplation

CW 259   The Year of Destiny 1923 in the History of the Anthroposophical Society. From the Burning of the Goetheanum to the Christmas Conference

CW 260   The Christmas Conference for the Founding of the General Anthroposophical Society

CW 260a The Constitution of the General Anthroposophical Society and the School for Spiritual Science. The Rebuilding of the Goetheanum

CW 261 Our Dead. Addresses, Words of Remembrance, and Meditative Verses, 1906-1924

CW 262 Rudolf Steiner and Marie Steiner-von Sivers: Correspondence and Documents, 1901-1925

CW 263/1 Rudolf Steiner and Edith Maryon: Correspondence: Letters, Verses, Sketches, 1912-1924

CW 264 On the History and the Contents of the First Section of the Esoteric School from 1904 to 1914. Letters, Newsletters, Documents, Lectures

CW 265 On the History and from the Contents of the Ritual-Knowledge Section of the Esoteric School from 1904 to 1914. Documents, and Lectures from the Years 1906 to 1914, as well as on New Approaches to Ritual-Knowledge Work in the Years 1921–1924

CW 266/1 From the Contents of the Esoteric Lessons. Volume 1: 1904–1909. Notes from Memory of Participants. Meditation texts from the notes of Rudolf Steiner

CW 266/2 From the Contents of the Esoteric Lessons. Volume 2: 1910–1912. Notes from Memory of Participants

CW 266/3 From the Contents of the Esoteric Lessons. Volume 3: 1913, 1914 and 1920–1923. Notes from Memory of Participants. Meditation texts from the notes of Rudolf Steiner

CW 267 Soul-Exercises: Vol. 1: Exercises with Word and Image Meditations for the Methodological Development of Higher Powers of Knowledge, 1904–1924

CW 268 Soul-Exercises: Vol. 2: Mantric Verses, 1903–1925

CW 269 Ritual Texts for the Celebration of the Free Christian Religious Instruction. The Collected Verses for Teachers and Students of the Waldorf School

CW 270 Esoteric Instructions for the First Class of the School for Spiritual Science at the Goetheanum 1924, 4 Volumes

CW 271 Art and Knowledge of Art. Foundations of a New Aesthetic

CW 272 Spiritual-Scientific Commentary on Goethe's 'Faust' in Two Volumes. Vol. 1: Faust, the Striving Human Being

CW 273 Spiritual-Scientific Commentary on Goethe's 'Faust' in Two Volumes. Vol. 2: The Faust-Problem

CW 274 Addresses for the Christmas Plays from the Old Folk Traditions

CW 275 Art in the Light of Mystery-Wisdom

CW 276 The Artistic in Its Mission in the World. The Genius of Language. The World of Self-Revealing Radiant Appearances—Anthroposophy and Art. Anthroposophy and Poetry

CW 277 Eurythmy. The Revelation of the Speaking Soul

CW 277a The Origin and Development of Eurythmy

CW 278   Eurythmy as Visible Song
CW 279   Eurythmy as Visible Speech
CW 280   The Method and Nature of Speech Formation
CW 281   The Art of Recitation and Declamation
CW 282   Speech Formation and Dramatic Art
CW 283   The Nature of Things Musical and the Experience of Tone in the Human Being
CW 284/285 Images of Occult Seals and Pillars. The Munich Congress of Whitsun 1907 and Its Consequences
CW 286   Paths to a New Style of Architecture. 'And the Building Becomes Human'
CW 287   The Building at Dornach as a Symbol of Historical Becoming and an Artistic Transformation Impulse
CW 288   Style-Forms in the Living Organic
CW 289   The Building-Idea of the Goetheanum: Lectures with Slides from the Years 1920–1921
CW 290   The Building-Idea of the Goetheanum: Lectures with Slides from the Years 1920–1921
CW 291   The Nature of Colours
CW 291a   Knowledge of Colours. Supplementary Volume to 'The Nature of Colours'
CW 292   Art History as Image of Inner Spiritual Impulses
CW 293   General Knowledge of the Human Being as the Foundation of Pedagogy
CW 294   The Art of Education, Methodology and Didactics
CW 295   The Art of Education: Seminar Discussions and Lectures on Lesson Planning
CW 296   The Question of Education as a Social Question
CW 297   The Idea and Practice of the Waldorf School
CW 297a   Education for Life: Self-Education and the Practice of Pedagogy
CW 298   Rudolf Steiner in the Waldorf School
CW 299   Spiritual-Scientific Observations on Speech
CW 300a   Conferences with the Teachers of the Free Waldorf School in Stuttgart, 1919 to 1924, in 3 Volumes, Vol. 1
CW 300b   Conferences with the Teachers of the Free Waldorf School in Stuttgart, 1919 to 1924, in 3 Volumes, Vol. 2
CW 300c   Conferences with the Teachers of the Free Waldorf School in Stuttgart, 1919 to 1924, in 3 Volumes, Vol. 3
CW 301   The Renewal of Pedagogical-Didactical Art through Spiritual Science
CW 302   Knowledge of the Human Being and the Forming of Class Lessons
CW 302a   Education and Teaching from a Knowledge of the Human Being
CW 303   The Healthy Development of the Human Being
CW 304   Methods of Education and Teaching Based on Anthroposophy
CW 304a   Anthroposophical Knowledge of the Human Being and Pedagogy

CW 305   The Soul-Spiritual Foundational Forces of the Art of Education. Spiritual Values in Education and Social Life

CW 306   Pedagogical Praxis from the Viewpoint of a Spiritual-Scientific Knowledge of the Human Being. The Education of the Child and Young Human Beings

CW 307   The Spiritual Life of the Present and Education

CW 308   The Method of Teaching and the Life-Requirements for Teaching

CW 309   Anthroposophical Pedagogy and Its Prerequisites

CW 310   The Pedagogical Value of a Knowledge of the Human Being and the Cultural Value of Pedagogy

CW 311   The Art of Education from an Understanding of the Being of Humanity

CW 312   Spiritual Science and Medicine

CW 313   Spiritual-Scientific Viewpoints on Therapy

CW 314   Physiology and Therapy Based on Spiritual Science

CW 315   Curative Eurythmy

CW 316   Meditative Observations and Instructions for a Deepening of the Art of Healing

CW 317   The Curative Education Course

CW 318   The Working Together of Doctors and Pastors

CW 319   Anthroposophical Knowledge of the Human Being and Medicine

CW 320   Spiritual-Scientific Impulses for the Development of Physics 1: The First Natural-Scientific Course: Light, Colour, Tone, Mass, Electricity, Magnetism

CW 321   Spiritual-Scientific Impulses for the Development of Physics 2: The Second Natural-Scientific Course: Warmth at the Border of Positive and Negative Materiality

CW 322   The Borders of the Knowledge of Nature

CW 323   The Relationship of the various Natural-Scientific Fields to Astronomy

CW 324   Nature Observation, Mathematics, and Scientific Experimentation and Results from the Viewpoint of Anthroposophy

CW 324a   The Fourth Dimension in Mathematics and Reality

CW 325   Natural Science and the World-Historical Development of Humanity since Ancient Times

CW 326   The Moment of the Coming Into Being of Natural Science in World History and Its Development Since Then

CW 327   Spiritual-Scientific Foundations for Success in Farming. The Agricultural Course

CW 328   The Social Question

CW 329   The Liberation of the Human Being as the Foundation for a New Social Form

CW 330   The Renewal of the Social Organism

CW 331   Work-Council and Socialization

CW 332   The Alliance for Threefolding and the Total Reform of Society. The Council on Culture and the Liberation of the Spiritual Life

CW 332a   The Social Future
CW 333   Freedom of Thought and Social Forces
CW 334   From the Unified State to the Threefold Social Organism
CW 335   The Crisis of the Present and the Path to Healthy Thinking
CW 336   The Great Questions of the Times and Anthroposophical Spiritual Knowledge
CW 337a   Social Ideas, Social Reality, Social Practice, Vol. 1: Question-and-Answer Evenings and Study Evenings of the Alliance for the Threefold Social Organism in Stuttgart, 1919-1920
CW 337b   Social Ideas, Social Realities, Social Practice, Vol. 2: Discussion Evenings of the Swiss Alliance for the Threefold Social Organism
CW 338   How Does One Work on Behalf of the Impulse for the Threefold Social Organism?
CW 339   Anthroposophy, Threefold Social Organism, and the Art of Public Speaking
CW 340   The National-Economics Course. The Tasks of a New Science of Economics, Volume 1
CW 341   The National-Economics Seminar. The Tasks of a New Science of Economics, Volume 2
CW 342   Lectures and Courses on Christian Religious Work, Vol. 1: Anthroposophical Foundations for a Renewed Christian Religious Working
CW 343   Lectures and Courses on Christian Religious Work, Vol. 2: Spiritual Knowledge—Religious Feeling—Cultic Doing
CW 344   Lectures and Courses on Christian Religious Work, Vol. 3: Lectures at the Founding of the Christian Community
CW 345   Lectures and Courses on Christian Religious Work, Vol. 4: Concerning the Nature of the Working Word
CW 346   Lectures and Courses on Christian Religious Work, Vol. 5: The Apocalypse and the Work of the Priest
CW 347   The Knowledge of the Nature of the Human Being According to Body, Soul and Spirit. On Earlier Conditions of the Earth
CW 348   On Health and Illness. Foundations of a Spiritual-Scientific Doctrine of the Senses
CW 349   On the Life of the Human Being and of the Earth. On the Nature of Christianity
CW 350   Rhythms in the Cosmos and in the Human Being. How Does One Come To See the Spiritual World?
CW 351   The Human Being and the World. The Influence of the Spirit in Nature. On the Nature of Bees
CW 352   Nature and the Human Being Observed Spiritual-Scientifically
CW 353   The History of Humanity and the World-Views of the Folk Cultures
CW 354   The Creation of the World and the Human Being. Life on Earth and the Influence of the Stars

SIGNIFICANT EVENTS IN THE LIFE OF
RUDOLF STEINER

1829:	June 23: birth of Johann Steiner (1829–1910)—Rudolf Steiner's father—in Geras, Lower Austria.
1834:	May 8: birth of Franciska Blie (1834–1918)—Rudolf Steiner's mother—in Horn, Lower Austria. 'My father and mother were both children of the glorious Lower Austrian forest district north of the Danube.'
1860:	May 16: marriage of Johann Steiner and Franciska Blie.
1861:	February 25: birth of *Rudolf Joseph Lorenz Steiner* in Kraljevec, Croatia, near the border with Hungary, where Johann Steiner works as a telegrapher for the South Austria Railroad. Rudolf Steiner is baptized two days later, February 27, the date usually given as his birthday.
1862:	Summer: the family moves to Modling, Lower Austria.
1863:	The family moves to Pottschach, Lower Austria, near the Styrian border, where Johann Steiner becomes stationmaster. 'The view stretched to the mountains . . . majestic peaks in the distance and the sweet charm of nature in the immediate surroundings.'
1864:	November 15: birth of Rudolf Steiner's sister, Leopoldine (d. November 1, 1927). She will become a seamstress and live with her parents for the rest of her life.
1866:	July 28: birth of Rudolf Steiner's deaf-mute brother, Gustav (d. May 1, 1941).
1867:	Rudolf Steiner enters the village school. Following a disagreement between his father and the schoolmaster, whose wife falsely accused the boy of causing a commotion, Rudolf Steiner is taken out of school and taught at home.
1868:	A critical experience. Unknown to the family, an aunt dies in a distant town. Sitting in the station waiting room, Rudolf Steiner sees her 'form', which speaks to him, asking for help. 'Beginning with this

experience, a new soul life began in the boy, one in which not only the outer trees and mountains spoke to him, but also the worlds that lay behind them. From this moment on, the boy began to live with the spirits of nature . . .'

1869:   The family moves to the peaceful, rural village of Neudorfl, near Wiener Neustadt in present-day Austria. Rudolf Steiner attends the village school. Because of the 'unorthodoxy' of his writing and spelling, he has to do 'extra lessons'.

1870:   Through a book lent to him by his tutor, he discovers geometry: 'To grasp something purely in the spirit brought me inner happiness. I know that I first learned happiness through geometry.' The same tutor allows him to draw, while other students still struggle with their reading and writing. 'An artistic element' thus enters his education.

1871:   Though his parents are not religious, Rudolf Steiner becomes a 'church child', a favourite of the priest, who was 'an exceptional character'. 'Up to the age of ten or eleven, among those I came to know, he was far and away the most significant.' Among other things, he introduces Steiner to Copernican, heliocentric cosmology. As an altar boy, Rudolf Steiner serves at Masses, funerals, and Corpus Christi processions. At year's end, after an incident in which he escapes a thrashing, his father forbids him to go to church.

1872:   Rudolf Steiner transfers to grammar school in Wiener-Neustadt, a five-mile walk from home, which must be done in all weathers.

1873–75:   Through his teachers and on his own, Rudolf Steiner has many wonderful experiences with science and mathematics. Outside school, he teaches himself analytic geometry, trigonometry, differential equations, and calculus.

1876:   Rudolf Steiner begins tutoring other students. He learns bookbinding from his father. He also teaches himself stenography.

1877:   Rudolf Steiner discovers Kant's *Critique of Pure Reason,* which he reads and rereads. He also discovers and reads von Rotteck's *World History.*

1878:   He studies extensively in contemporary psychology and philosophy.

1879:   Rudolf Steiner graduates from high school with honours. His father is transferred to Inzersdorf, near Vienna. He uses his first visit to Vienna 'to purchase a great number of philosophy books'—Kant, Fichte, Schelling, and Hegel, as well as numerous histories of philosophy. His aim: to find a path from the 'I' to nature.

October
1879–1883:   Rudolf Steiner attends the Technical College in Vienna—to study mathematics, chemistry, physics, mineralogy, botany, zoology,

biology, geology, and mechanics—with a scholarship. He also attends lectures in history and literature, while avidly reading philosophy on his own. His two favourite professors are Karl Julius Schröer (German language and literature) and Edmund Reitlinger (physics). He also audits lectures by Robert Zimmermann on aesthetics and Franz Brentano on philosophy. During this year he begins his friendship with Moritz Zitter (1861–1921), who will help support him financially when he is in Berlin.

1880: Rudolf Steiner attends lectures on Schiller and Goethe by Karl Julius Schröer, who becomes his mentor. Also 'through a remarkable combination of circumstances', he meets Felix Koguzki, a 'herb gatherer' and healer, who could 'see deeply into the secrets of nature'. Rudolf Steiner will meet and study with this 'emissary of the Master' throughout his time in Vienna.

1881: January: '... I didn't sleep a wink. I was busy with philosophical problems until about 12:30 a.m. Then, finally, I threw myself down on my couch. All my striving during the previous year had been to research whether the following statement by Schelling was true or not: *Within everyone dwells a secret, marvellous capacity to draw back from the stream of time—out of the self clothed in all that comes to us from outside—into our innermost being and there, in the immutable form of the Eternal, to look into ourselves.* I believe, and I am still quite certain of it, that I discovered this capacity in myself; I had long had an inkling of it. Now the whole of idealist philosophy stood before me in modified form. What's a sleepless night compared to that!'
Rudolf Steiner begins communicating with leading thinkers of the day, who send him books in return, which he reads eagerly.

July: 'I am not one of those who dives into the day like an animal in human form. I pursue a quite specific goal, an idealistic aim—knowledge of the truth! This cannot be done offhandedly. It requires the greatest striving in the world, free of all egotism, and equally of all resignation.'

August: Steiner puts down on paper for the first time thoughts for a 'Philosophy of Freedom'. 'The striving for the absolute: this human yearning is freedom.' He also seeks to outline a 'peasant philosophy', describing what the worldview of a 'peasant'—one who lives close to the earth and the old ways—really is.

1881–1882: Felix Koguzki, the herb gatherer, reveals himself to be the envoy of another, higher initiatory personality, who instructs Rudolf Steiner to penetrate Fichte's philosophy and to master modern scientific thinking as a preparation for right entry into the spirit. This 'Master' also teaches him the double (evolutionary and involutionary) nature of time.

1882:   Through the offices of Karl Julius Schröer, Rudolf Steiner is asked by Joseph Kürschner to edit Goethe's scientific works for the *Deutschen National-Literatur* edition. He writes 'A Possible Critique of Atomistic Concepts' and sends it to Friedrich Theodor Vischer.

1883:   Rudolf Steiner completes his college studies and begins work on the Goethe project.

1884:   First volume of Goethe's *Scientific Writings* (CW 1) appears (March). He lectures on Goethe and Lessing, and Goethe's approach to science. In July, he enters the household of Ladislaus and Pauline Specht as tutor to the four Specht boys. He will live there until 1890. At this time, he meets Josef Breuer (1842–1925), the co-author with Sigmund Freud of *Studies in Hysteria,* who is the Specht family doctor.

1885:   While continuing to edit Goethe's writings, Rudolf Steiner reads deeply in contemporary philosophy (Eduard von Hartmann, Johannes Volkelt, and Richard Wahle, among others).

1886:   May: Rudolf Steiner sends Kürschner the manuscript of *Outlines of Goethe's Theory of Knowledge* (CW 2), which appears in October, and which he sends out widely. He also meets the poet Marie Eugenie Delle Grazie and writes 'Nature and Our Ideals' for her. He attends her salon, where he meets many priests, theologians, and philosophers, who will become his friends. Meanwhile, the director of the Goethe Archive in Weimar requests his collaboration with the *Sophien* edition of Goethe's works, particularly the writings on colour.

1887:   At the beginning of the year, Rudolf Steiner is very sick. As the year progresses and his health improves, he becomes increasingly 'a man of letters', lecturing, writing essays, and taking part in Austrian cultural life. In August–September, the second volume of Goethe's *Scientific Writings* appears.

1888:   January–July: Rudolf Steiner assumes editorship of the 'German Weekly' *(Deutsche Wochenschrift)*. He begins lecturing more intensively, giving, for example, a lecture titled 'Goethe as Father of a New Aesthetics'. He meets and becomes soul friends with Friedrich Eckstein (1861–1939), a vegetarian, philosopher of symbolism, alchemist, and musician, who will introduce him to various spiritual currents (including Theosophy) and with whom he will meditate and interpret esoteric and alchemical texts.

1889:   Rudolf Steiner first reads Nietzsche *(Beyond Good and Evil)*. He encounters Theosophy again and learns of Madame Blavatsky in the theosophical circle around Marie Lang (1858–1934). Here he also meets well-known figures of Austrian life, as well as esoteric figures like the occultist Franz Hartmann and Karl Leinigen-Billigen (translator of C.G. Harrison's *The Transcendental Universe*). During this period, Steiner first reads A.P. Sinnett's *Esoteric Buddhism* and Mabel Collins's *Light on the Path*. He also begins travelling, visiting Budapest, Weimar, and Berlin (where he meets philosopher Eduard von Hartmann).

1890:   Rudolf Steiner finishes Volume 3 of Goethe's scientific writings. He begins his doctoral dissertation, which will become *Truth and Science* (CW 3). He also meets the poet and feminist Rosa Mayreder (1858–1938), with whom he can exchange his most intimate thoughts. In September, Rudolf Steiner moves to Weimar to work in the Goethe-Schiller Archive.

1891:   Volume 3 of the Kürschner edition of Goethe appears. Meanwhile, Rudolf Steiner edits Goethe's studies in mineralogy and scientific writings for the *Sophien* edition. He meets Ludwig Laistner of the Cotta Publishing Company, who asks for a book on the basic question of metaphysics. From this will result, ultimately, *The Philosophy of Freedom* (CW 4), which will be published not by Cotta but by Emil Felber. In October, Rudolf Steiner takes the oral exam for a doctorate in philosophy, mathematics, and mechanics at Rostock University, receiving his doctorate on the twenty-sixth. In November, he gives his first lecture on Goethe's 'Fairy Tale' in Vienna.

1892:   Rudolf Steiner continues work at the Goethe-Schiller Archive and on his *Philosophy of Freedom. Truth and Science*, his doctoral dissertation, is published. Steiner undertakes to write Introductions to books on Schopenhauer and Jean Paul for Cotta. At year's end, he finds lodging with Anna Eunike, née Schulz (1853–1911), a widow with four daughters and a son. He also develops a friendship with Otto Erich Hartleben (1864–1905) with whom he shares literary interests.

1893:   Rudolf Steiner begins his habit of producing many reviews and articles. In March, he gives a lecture titled 'Hypnotism, with Reference to Spiritism'. In September, volume 4 of the Kürschner edition is completed. In November, *The Philosophy of Freedom* appears. This year, too, he meets John Henry Mackay (1864–1933), the anarchist, and Max Stirner, a scholar and biographer.

1894:   Rudolf Steiner meets Elisabeth Fürster Nietzsche, the philosopher's sister, and begins to read Nietzsche in earnest, beginning with the as yet unpublished *Antichrist*. He also meets Ernst Haeckel (1834–1919). In the fall, he begins to write *Nietzsche, A Fighter against His Time* (CW 5).

1895:   May, *Nietzsche, A Fighter against His Time* appears.

1896:   January 22: Rudolf Steiner sees Friedrich Nietzsche for the first and only time. Moves between the Nietzsche and the Goethe-Schiller

Archives, where he completes his work before year's end. He falls out with Elisabeth Förster Nietzsche, thus ending his association with the Nietzsche Archive.

1897: Rudolf Steiner finishes the manuscript of *Goethe's Worldview* (CW 6). He moves to Berlin with Anna Eunike and begins editorship of the *Magazin für Literatur*. From now on, Steiner will write countless reviews, literary and philosophical articles, and so on. He begins lecturing at the 'Free Literary Society'. In September, he attends the Zionist Congress in Basel. He sides with Dreyfus in the Dreyfus affair.

1898: Rudolf Steiner is very active as an editor in the political, artistic, and theatrical life of Berlin. He becomes friendly with John Henry Mackay and poet Ludwig Jacobowski (1868–1900). He joins Jacobowski's circle of writers, artists, and scientists—'The Coming Ones' (*Die Kommenden*)—and contributes lectures to the group until 1903. He also lectures at the 'League for College Pedagogy'. He writes an article for Goethe's sesquicentennial, 'Goethe's Secret Revelation', on the 'Fairy Tale of the Green Snake and the Beautiful Lily'.

1898–99: 'This was a trying time for my soul as I looked at Christianity. . . . I was able to progress only by contemplating, by means of spiritual perception, the evolution of Christianity. . . . Conscious knowledge of real Christianity began to dawn in me around the turn of the century. This seed continued to develop. My soul trial occurred shortly before the beginning of the twentieth century. It was decisive for my soul's development that I stood spiritually before the Mystery of Golgotha in a deep and solemn celebration of knowledge.'

1899: Rudolf Steiner begins teaching and giving lectures and lecture cycles at the Workers' College, founded by Wilhelm Liebknecht (1826–1900). He will continue to do so until 1904. Writes: *Literature and Spiritual Life in the Nineteenth Century; Individualism in Philosophy; Haeckel and His Opponents; Poetry in the Present;* and begins what will become (fifteen years later) *The Riddles of Philosophy* (CW 18). He also meets many artists and writers, including Käthe Kollwitz, Stefan Zweig, and Rainer Maria Rilke. On October 31, he marries Anna Eunike.

1900: 'I thought that the turn of the century must bring humanity a new light. It seemed to me that the separation of human thinking and willing from the spirit had peaked. A turn or reversal of direction in human evolution seemed to me a necessity.' Rudolf Steiner finishes *World and Life Views in the Nineteenth Century* (the second part of what will become *The Riddles of Philosophy*) and dedicates it to

Ernst Haeckel. It is published in March. He continues lecturing at *Die Kommenden,* whose leadership he assumes after the death of Jacobowski. Also, he gives the Gutenberg Jubilee lecture before 7,000 typesetters and printers. In September, Rudolf Steiner is invited by Count and Countess Brockdorff to lecture in the Theosophical Library. His first lecture is on Nietzsche. His second lecture is titled 'Goethe's Secret Revelation'. October 6, he begins a lecture cycle on the mystics that will become *Mystics after Modernism* (CW 7). November–December: 'Marie von Sivers appears in the audience. . . .' Also in November, Steiner gives his first lecture at the Giordano Bruno Bund (where he will continue to lecture until May, 1905). He speaks on Bruno and modern Rome, focusing on the importance of the philosophy of Thomas Aquinas as monism.

1901:   In continual financial straits, Rudolf Steiner's early friends Moritz Zitter and Rosa Mayreder help support him. In October, he begins the lecture cycle *Christianity as Mystical Fact* (CW 8) at the Theosophical Library. In November, he gives his first 'theosophical lecture' on Goethe's 'Fairy Tale' in Hamburg at the invitation of Wilhelm Hubbe-Schleiden. He also attends a gathering to celebrate the founding of the Theosophical Society at Count and Countess Brockdorff's. He gives a lecture cycle, 'From Buddha to Christ', for the circle of the *Kommenden.* November 17, Marie von Sivers asks Rudolf Steiner if Theosophy needs a Western–Christian spiritual movement (to complement Theosophy's Eastern emphasis). 'The question was posed. Now, following spiritual laws, I could begin to give an answer. . . .' In December, Rudolf Steiner writes his first article for a theosophical publication. At year's end, the Brockdorffs and possibly Wilhelm Hubbe-Schleiden ask Rudolf Steiner to join the Theosophical Society and undertake the leadership of the German section. Rudolf Steiner agrees, on the condition that Marie von Sivers (then in Italy) work with him.

1902:   Beginning in January, Rudolf Steiner attends the opening of the Workers' School in Spandau with Rosa Luxemburg (1870–1919). January 17, Rudolf Steiner joins the Theosophical Society. In April, he is asked to become general secretary of the German Section of the Theosophical Society, and works on preparations for its founding. In July, he visits London for a theosophical congress. He meets Bertram Keightly, G.R.S. Mead, A.P. Sinnett, and Annie Besant, among others. In September, *Christianity as Mystical Fact* appears. In October, Rudolf Steiner gives his first public lecture on Theosophy ('Monism and Theosophy') to about three hundred people at the Giordano Bruno Bund. On October 19–21, the

German Section of the Theosophical Society has its first meeting; Rudolf Steiner is the general secretary, and Annie Besant attends. Steiner lectures on practical karma studies. On October 23, Annie Besant inducts Rudolf Steiner into the Esoteric School of the Theosophical Society. On October 25, Steiner begins a weekly series of lectures: 'The Field of Theosophy'. During this year, Rudolf Steiner also first meets Ita Wegman (1876–1943), who will become his close collaborator in his final years.

1903:   Rudolf Steiner holds about 300 lectures and seminars. In May, the first issue of the periodical *Luzifer* appears. In June, Rudolf Steiner visits London for the first meeting of the Federation of the European Sections of the Theosophical Society, where he meets Colonel Olcott. He begins to write *Theosophy* (CW 9).

1904:   Rudolf Steiner continues lecturing at the Workers' College and elsewhere (about 90 lectures), while lecturing intensively all over Germany among theosophists (about 140 lectures). In February, he meets Carl Unger (1878–1929), who will become a member of the board of the Anthroposophical Society (1913). In March, he meets Michael Bauer (1871–1929), a Christian mystic, who will also be on the board. In May, *Theosophy* appears, with the dedication: 'To the spirit of Giordano Bruno'. Rudolf Steiner and Marie von Sivers visit London for meetings with Annie Besant. June: Rudolf Steiner and Marie von Sivers attend the meeting of the Federation of European Sections of the Theosophical Society in Amsterdam. In July, Steiner begins the articles in *Luzifer-Gnosis* that will become *How to Know Higher Worlds* (CW 10) and *Cosmic Memory* (CW 11). In September, Annie Besant visits Germany. In December, Steiner lectures on Freemasonry. He mentions the High Grade Masonry derived from John Yarker and represented by Theodore Reuss and Karl Kellner as a blank slate 'into which a good image could be placed'.

1905:   This year, Steiner ends his non-theosophical lecturing activity. Supported by Marie von Sivers, his theosophical lecturing—both in public and in the Theosophical Society—increases significantly: 'The German Theosophical Movement is of exceptional importance.' Steiner recommends reading, among others, Fichte, Jacob Boehme, and Angelus Silesius. He begins to introduce Christian themes into Theosophy. He also begins to work with doctors (Felix Peipers and Ludwig Noll). In July, he is in London for the Federation of European Sections, where he attends a lecture by Annie Besant: 'I have seldom seen Mrs Besant speak in so inward and heartfelt a manner... Through Mrs Besant I have found the way to H.P. Blavatsky.' September to October, he gives a course of 31 lectures for a small group of esoteric students. In October, the annual meeting of the German Section of the Theosophical Society, which still remains very small, takes place. Rudolf Steiner reports membership has risen from 121 to 377 members. In November, seeking to establish esoteric 'continuity', Rudolf Steiner and Marie von Sivers participate in a 'Memphis-Misraim' Masonic ceremony. They pay 45 marks for membership. 'Yesterday, you saw how little remains of former esoteric institutions.' 'We are dealing only with a "framework" ... for the present, nothing lies behind it. The occult powers have completely withdrawn.'

1906: Expansion of theosophical work. Rudolf Steiner gives about 245 lectures, only 44 of which take place in Berlin. Cycles are given in Paris, Leipzig, Stuttgart, and Munich. Esoteric work also intensifies. Rudolf Steiner begins writing *An Outline of Esoteric Science* (CW 13). In January, Rudolf Steiner receives permission (a patent) from the Great Orient of the Scottish A & A Thirty-Three Degree Rite of the Order of the Ancient Freemasons of the Memphis-Misraim Rite to direct a chapter under the name 'Mystica Aeterna.' This will become the 'Cognitive-Ritual Section' (also called 'Misraim Service') of the Esoteric School. (See: *Freemasonry and Ritual Work: The Misraim Service*, CW 265.) During this time, Steiner also meets Albert Schweitzer. In May, he is in Paris, where he visits Édouard Schuré. Many Russians attend his lectures (including Konstantin Balmont, Dimitri Mereszkovski, Zinaida Hippius, and Maximilian Woloshin). He attends the General Meeting of the European Federation of the Theosophical Society, at which Col Olcott is present for the last time. He spends the year's end in Venice and Rome, where he writes and works on his translation of H.P. Blavatsky's *Key to Theosophy*.

1907: Further expansion of the German Theosophical Movement according to the Rosicrucian directive to 'introduce spirit into the world'—in education, in social questions, in art, and in science. In February, Col Olcott dies in Adyar. Before he dies, Olcott indicates that 'the Masters' wish Annie Besant to succeed him: much politicking ensues. Rudolf Steiner supports Besant's candidacy. April–May: preparations for the Congress of the Federation of European Sections of the Theosophical Society—the great, watershed Whitsun 'Munich Congress,' attended by Annie Besant and others. Steiner decides to separate Eastern and Western (Christian–Rosicrucian) esoteric schools. He takes his esoteric school out of the Theosophical Society (Besant and Rudolf Steiner are 'in harmony' on this). Steiner makes his first lecture tours to Austria and

Hungary. That summer, he is in Italy. In September, he visits Édouard Schuré, who will write the Introduction to the French edition of *Christianity as Mystical Fact* in Barr, Alsace. Rudolf Steiner writes the autobiographical statement known as the 'Barr Document.' In *Luzifer-Gnosis*, 'The Education of the Child' appears.

1908:   The movement grows (membership: 1,150). Lecturing expands. Steiner makes his first extended lecture tour to Holland and Scandinavia, as well as visits to Naples and Sicily. Themes: St John's Gospel, the Apocalypse, Egypt, science, philosophy, and logic. *Luzifer-Gnosis* ceases publication. In Berlin, Marie von Sivers (with Johanna Mücke (1864–1949) forms the *Philosophisch-Theosophisch* (after 1915 *Philosophisch-Anthroposophisch) Verlag* to publish Steiner's work. Steiner gives lecture cycles titled *The Gospel of St John* (CW 103) and *The Apocalypse* (104).

1909:   *An Outline of Esoteric Science* appears. Lecturing and travel continues. Rudolf Steiner's spiritual research expands to include the polarity of Lucifer and Ahriman; the work of great individualities in history; the Maitreya Buddha and the Bodhisattvas; spiritual economy (CW 109); the work of the spiritual hierarchies in heaven and on earth (CW 110). He also deepens and intensifies his research into the Gospels, giving lectures on the Gospel of St Luke (CW 114) with the first mention of two Jesus children. Meets and becomes friends with Christian Morgenstern (1871–1914). In April, he lays the foundation stone for the Malsch model—the building that will lead to the first Goetheanum. In May, the International Congress of the Federation of European Sections of the Theosophical Society takes place in Budapest. Rudolf Steiner receives the Subba Row medal for *How to Know Higher Worlds*. During this time, Charles W. Leadbeater discovers Jiddu Krishnamurti (1895–1986) and proclaims him the future 'world teacher,' the bearer of the Maitreya Buddha and the 'reappearing Christ.' In October, Steiner delivers seminal lectures on 'anthroposophy,' which he will try, unsuccessfully, to rework over the next years into the unfinished work, *Anthroposophy (A Fragment)* (CW 45).

1910:   New themes: *The Reappearance of Christ in the Etheric* (CW 118); *The Fifth Gospel; The Mission of Folk Souls* (CW 121); *Occult History* (CW 126); the evolving development of etheric cognitive capacities. Rudolf Steiner continues his Gospel research with *The Gospel of St Matthew* (CW 123). In January, his father dies. In April, he takes a month-long trip to Italy, including Rome, Monte Cassino, and Sicily. He also visits Scandinavia again. July–August, he writes the first Mystery Drama, *The Portal of Initiation* (CW 14). In November, he gives 'psychosophy' lectures. In December, he submits 'On the

Psychological Foundations and Epistemological Framework of Theosophy' to the International Philosophical Congress in Bologna.

1911: The crisis in the Theosophical Society deepens. In January, 'The Order of the Rising Sun,' which will soon become 'The Order of the Star in the East,' is founded for the coming world teacher, Krishnamurti. At the same time, Marie von Sivers, Rudolf Steiner's co-worker, falls ill. Fewer lectures are given, but important new ground is broken. In Prague, in March, Steiner meets Franz Kafka (1883–1924) and Hugo Bergmann (1883–1975). In April, he delivers his paper to the Philosophical Congress. He writes the second Mystery Drama, *The Soul's Probation* (CW 14). Also, while Marie von Sivers is convalescing, Rudolf Steiner begins work on *Calendar 1912/1913*, which will contain the 'Calendar of the Soul' meditations. On March 19, Anna (Eunike) Steiner dies. In September, Rudolf Steiner visits Einsiedeln, birthplace of Paracelsus. In December, Friedrich Rittelmeyer, future founder of the Christian Community, meets Rudolf Steiner. The *Johannes-Bauverein*, the 'building committee,' which would lead to the first Goetheanum (first planned for Munich), is also founded, and a preliminary committee for the founding of an independent association is created that, in the following year, will become the Anthroposophical Society. Important lecture cycles include *Occult Physiology* (CW 128); *Wonders of the World* (CW 129); *From Jesus to Christ* (CW 131). Other themes: esoteric Christianity; Christian Rosenkreutz; the spiritual guidance of humanity; the sense world and the world of the spirit.

1912: Despite the ongoing, now increasing crisis in the Theosophical Society, much is accomplished: *Calendar 1912/1913* is published; eurythmy is created; both the third Mystery Drama, *The Guardian of the Threshold* (CW 14) and *A Way of Self-Knowledge* (CW 16) are written. New (or renewed) themes included life between death and rebirth and karma and reincarnation. Other lecture cycles: *Spiritual Beings in the Heavenly Bodies and in the Kingdoms of Nature* (CW 136); *The Human Being in the Light of Occultism, Theosophy, and Philosophy* (CW 137); *The Gospel of St Mark* (CW 139); and *The Bhagavad Gita and the Epistles of Paul* (CW 142). On May 8, Rudolf Steiner celebrates White Lotus Day, H.P. Blavatsky's death day, which he had faithfully observed for the past decade, for the last time. In August, Rudolf Steiner suggests the 'independent association' be called the 'Anthroposophical Society.' In September, the first eurythmy course takes place. In October, Rudolf Steiner declines recognition of a Theosophical Society lodge dedicated to the Star of the East and decides to expel all Theosophical Society members belonging to the order.

Also, with Marie von Sivers, he first visits Dornach, near Basel, Switzerland, and they stand on the hill where the Goetheanum will be built. In November, a Theosophical Society lodge is opened by direct mandate from Adyar (Annie Besant). In December, a meeting of the German section occurs at which it is decided that belonging to the Order of the Star of the East is incompatible with membership in the Theosophical Society. December 28: informal founding of the Anthroposophical Society in Berlin.

1913: Expulsion of the German section from the Theosophical Society. February 2–3: Foundation meeting of the Anthroposophical Society. Board members include: Marie von Sivers, Michael Bauer, and Carl Unger. September 20: Laying of the foundation stone for the *Johannes Bau* (Goetheanum) in Dornach. Building begins immediately. The fourth Mystery Drama, *The Soul's Awakening* (CW 14), is completed. Also: *The Threshold of the Spiritual World* (CW 147). Lecture cycles include: *The Bhagavad Gita and the Epistles of Paul* and *The Esoteric Meaning of the Bhagavad Gita* (CW 146), which the Russian philosopher Nikolai Berdyaev attends; *The Mysteries of the East and of Christianity* (CW 144); *The Effects of Esoteric Development* (CW 145); and *The Fifth Gospel* (CW 148). In May, Rudolf Steiner is in London and Paris, where anthroposophical work continues.

1914: Building continues on the *Johannes Bau* (Goetheanum) in Dornach, with artists and co-workers from seventeen nations. The general assembly of the Anthroposophical Society takes place. In May, Rudolf Steiner visits Paris, as well as Chartres Cathedral. June 28: assassination in Sarajevo ('Now the catastrophe has happened!'). August 1: War is declared. Rudolf Steiner returns to Germany from Dornach—he will travel back and forth. He writes the last chapter of *The Riddles of Philosophy*. Lecture cycles include: *Human and Cosmic Thought* (CW 151); *Inner Being of Humanity between Death and a New Birth* (CW 153); *Occult Reading and Occult Hearing* (CW 156). December 24: marriage of Rudolf Steiner and Marie von Sivers.

1915: Building continues. Life after death becomes a major theme, also art. Writes: *Thoughts during a Time of War* (CW 24). Lectures include: *The Secret of Death* (CW 159); *The Uniting of Humanity through the Christ Impulse* (CW 165).

1916: Rudolf Steiner begins work with Edith Maryon (1872–1924) on the sculpture 'The Representative of Humanity' ('The Group'—Christ, Lucifer, and Ahriman). He also works with the alchemist Alexander von Bernus on the quarterly *Das Reich*. He writes *The Riddle of Humanity* (CW 20). Lectures include: *Necessity and Freedom in World History and Human Action* (CW 166); *Past and Present in the*

Human Spirit (CW 167); *The Karma of Vocation* (CW 172); *The Karma of Untruthfulness* (CW 173).

1917: Russian Revolution. The U.S. enters the war. Building continues. Rudolf Steiner delineates the idea of the 'threefold nature of the human being' (in a public lecture March 15) and the 'threefold nature of the social organism' (hammered out in May–June with the help of Otto von Lerchenfeld and Ludwig Polzer-Hoditz in the form of two documents titled *Memoranda*, which were distributed in high places). August–September: Rudolf Steiner writes *The Riddles of the Soul* (CW 20). Also: commentary on 'The Chymical Wedding of Christian Rosenkreutz' for Alexander Bernus (Das *Reich*). Lectures include: *The Karma of Materialism* (CW 176); *The Spiritual Background of the Outer World: The Fall of the Spirits of Darkness* (CW 177).

1918: March 18: peace treaty of Brest-Litovsk—'Now everything will truly enter chaos! What is needed is cultural renewal.' June: Rudolf Steiner visits Karlstein (Grail) Castle outside Prague. Lecture cycle: *From Symptom to Reality in Modern History* (CW 185). In mid-November, Emil Molt, of the Waldorf-Astoria Cigarette Company, has the idea of founding a school for his workers' children.

1919: Focus on the threefold social organism: tireless travel, countless lectures, meetings, and publications. At the same time, a new public stage of Anthroposophy emerges as cultural renewal begins. The coming years will see initiatives in pedagogy, medicine, pharmacology, and agriculture. January 27: threefold meeting: 'We must first of all, with the money we have, found free schools that can bring people what they need.' February: first public eurythmy performance in Zurich. Also: 'Appeal to the German People' (CW 24), circulated March 6 as a newspaper insert. In April, *Towards Social Renewal* (CW 23) appears—'perhaps the most widely read of all books on politics appearing since the war'. Rudolf Steiner is asked to undertake the 'direction and leadership' of the school founded by the Waldorf-Astoria Company. Rudolf Steiner begins to talk about the 'renewal' of education. May 30: a building is selected and purchased for the future Waldorf School. August–September, Rudolf Steiner gives a lecture course for Waldorf teachers, *The Foundations of Human Experience (Study of Man)* (CW 293). September 7: Opening of the first Waldorf School. December (into January): first science course, the *Light Course* (CW 320).

1920: The Waldorf School flourishes. New threefold initiatives. Founding of limited companies *Der Kommende Tag* and *Futurum A.G.* to infuse spiritual values into the economic realm. Rudolf Steiner also focuses on the sciences. Lectures: *Introducing Anthroposophical*

Medicine (CW 312); *The Warmth Course* (CW 321); *The Boundaries of Natural Science* (CW 322); *The Redemption of Thinking* (CW 74). February: Johannes Werner Klein—later a co-founder of The Christian Community—asks Rudolf Steiner about the possibility of a 'religious renewal,' a 'Johannine church.' In March, Rudolf Steiner gives the first course for doctors and medical students. In April, a divinity student asks Rudolf Steiner a second time about the possibility of religious renewal. September 27–October 16: anthroposophical 'university course.' December: lectures titled *The Search for the New Isis* (CW 202).

1921:   Rudolf Steiner continues his intensive work on cultural renewal, including the uphill battle for the threefold social order. 'University' arts, scientific, theological, and medical courses include: *The Astronomy Course* (CW 323); *Observation, Mathematics, and Scientific Experiment* (CW 324); the *Second Medical Course* (CW 313); *Colour*. In June and September–October, Rudolf Steiner also gives the first two 'priests' courses' (CW 342 and 343). The 'youth movement' gains momentum. Magazines are founded: *Die Drei* (January), and—under the editorship of Albert Steffen (1884–1963)—the weekly, *Das Goetheanum* (August). In February–March, Rudolf Steiner takes his first trip outside Germany since the war (Holland). On April 7, Steiner receives a letter regarding 'religious renewal,' and May 22–23, he agrees to address the question in a practical way. In June, the Klinical-Therapeutic Institute opens in Arlesheim under the direction of Dr Ita Wegman. In August, the Chemical-Pharmaceutical Laboratory opens in Arlesheim (Oskar Schmiedel and Ita Wegman are directors). The Clinical Therapeutic Institute is inaugurated in Stuttgart (Dr Ludwig Noll is director); also the Research Laboratory in Dornach (Ehrenfried Pfeiffer and Gunther Wachsmuth are directors). In November–December, Rudolf Steiner visits Norway.

1922:   The first half of the year involves very active public lecturing (thousands attend); in the second half, Rudolf Steiner begins to withdraw and turn toward the Society—'The Society is asleep.' It is 'too weak' to do what is asked of it. The businesses—*Der Kommende Tag* and *Futurum A.G.*—fail. In January, with the help of an agent, Steiner undertakes a twelve-city German lecture tour, accompanied by eurythmy performances. In two weeks he speaks to more than 2,000 people. In April, he gives a 'university course' in The Hague. He also visits England. In June, he is in Vienna for the East–West Congress. In August–September, he is back in England for the Oxford Conference on Education. Returning to Dornach, he gives the lectures *Philosophy, Cosmology, and*

Religion (CW 215), and gives the third priests' course (CW 344). On September 16, The Christian Community is founded. In October–November, Steiner is in Holland and England. He also speaks to the youth: *The Youth Course* (CW 217). In December, Steiner gives lectures titled *The Origins of Natural Science* (CW 326), and *Humanity and the World of Stars: The Spiritual Communion of Humanity* (CW 219). December 31: Fire at the Goetheanum, which is destroyed.

1923:   Despite the fire, Rudolf Steiner continues his work unabated. A very hard year. Internal dispersion, dissension, and apathy abound. There is conflict—between old and new visions—within the Society. A wake-up call is needed, and Rudolf Steiner responds with renewed lecturing vitality. His focus: the spiritual context of human life; initiation science; the course of the year; and community building. As a foundation for an artistic school, he creates a series of pastel sketches. Lecture cycles: *The Anthroposophical Movement; Initiation Science* (CW 227) (in Wales at the Penmaenmawr Summer School); *The Four Seasons and the Archangels* (CW 229); *Harmony of the Creative Word* (CW 230); *The Supersensible Human* (CW 231), given in Holland for the founding of the Dutch Society. On November 10, in response to the failed Hitler-Ludendorff putsch in Munich, Steiner closes his Berlin residence and moves the *Philosophisch-Anthroposophisch Verlag* (Press) to Dornach. On December 9, Steiner begins the serialization of his *Autobiography: The Course of My Life* (CW 28) in *Das Goetheanum*. It will continue to appear weekly, without a break, until his death. Late December–early January: Rudolf Steiner re-founds the Anthroposophical Society (about 12,000 members internationally) and takes over its leadership. The new board members are: Marie Steiner, Ita Wegman, Albert Steffen, Elisabeth Vreede, and Gunther Wachsmuth. (See *The Christmas Meeting for the Founding of the General Anthroposophical Society*, CW 260.) Accompanying lectures: *Mystery Knowledge and Mystery Centres* (CW 232); *World History in the Light of Anthroposophy* (CW 233). December 25: the Foundation Stone is laid (in the hearts of members) in the form of the 'Foundation Stone Meditation.'

1924:   January 1: having founded the Anthroposophical Society and taken over its leadership, Rudolf Steiner has the task of 'reforming' it. The process begins with a weekly newssheet ('What's Happening in the Anthroposophical Society') in which Rudolf Steiner's 'Letters to Members' and 'Anthroposophical Leading Thoughts' appear (CW 26). The next step is the creation of a new esoteric class, the 'first class' of the 'University of Spiritual Science' (which was to have been followed, had Rudolf Steiner lived longer, by two more advanced classes). Then comes a new language for

Anthroposophy—practical, phenomenological, and direct; and Rudolf Steiner creates the model for the second Goetheanum. He begins the series of extensive 'karma' lectures (CW 235–40); and finally, responding to needs, he creates two new initiatives: biodynamic agriculture and curative education. After the middle of the year, rumours begin to circulate regarding Steiner's health. Lectures: January–February, *Anthroposophy* (CW 234); February: *Tone Eurythmy* (CW 278); June: *The Agriculture Course* (CW 327); June–July: *Speech Eurythmy* (CW 279); *Curative Education* (CW 317); August: (England, 'Second International Summer School'), *Initiation Consciousness: True and False Paths in Spiritual Investigation* (CW 243); September: *Pastoral Medicine* (CW 318). On September 26, for the first time, Rudolf Steiner cancels a lecture. On September 28, he gives his last lecture. On September 29, he withdraws to his studio in the carpenter's shop; now he is definitively ill. Cared for by Ita Wegman, he continues working, however, and writing the weekly installments of his *Autobiography* and *Letters to the Members/Leading Thoughts* (CW 26).

1925: Rudolf Steiner, while continuing to work, continues to weaken. He finishes *Extending Practical Medicine* (CW 27) with Ita Wegman. On March 30, around ten in the morning, Rudolf Steiner dies.

INDEX

A

Acts of the Apostles, 164
Ahriman/ahrimanic, 69, 177
    forces, 193
    powers, 192
Ahura Mazda, 104, 111
Ancient Greece, 46–47
Ancient Rome, 24, 195
Anthroposophical Society, 183,
    196, 198
anthroposophy, 1, 4–6, 8, 17, 44,
    93, 100, 102, 108–109, 112,
    120, 125, 165
    basis of, 109
    dissemination of, 11
    fundamental ethos of, 16
    purest, 166
astral body, 1, 6, 10–12, 14–16, 18,
    31, 36–38, 41, 43, 70, 128–129,
    153–154, 167–168, 193
    insufficient control of, 11
astral world, 21–22, 27, 168
Atlantis, 121, 163

B

Bible, 40, 62, 94, 112, 148, 154
Blavatsky, H.P., 137, 142–145, 159
Bodhisattva, 102–103, 106, 111–112,
    124, 146, 159, 161, 163

incarnations on Earth as,
    110–111
Buddha, 43, 102–103, 106,
    109–112, 124, 159, 161–163
    historical, 146
    life of, 112
    nature of, 125
Buddhism, 102, 110, 112, 125,
    146, 157–159, 162

C

Caesar, 135, 147
Christianity, 109–113, 122,
    124–125, 143, 146, 149,
    157, 161–163, 165, 187, 195
    anthroposophical, 166
    boundless mysteries of, 199
    denominational, 160
    esoteric, 160
    forerunner of, 163
    herald of, 164
    initiation truth of, 117
    inter-confessional, 148
Christian Justina, 186
Christ Jesus, 69, 93–94, 96, 105,
    111–112, 119, 121–122,
    124–127, 135, 148, 162, 178,
    181, 200–201
    assimilation of, 116–117
    being, 152

birth of, 195
Christian idea of, 147
child, 194, 196
cosmic, 185, 199
deeds of, 179–180
downwards, 118
enigma of, 92
etheric image of, 123
event, 186
force of, 106
forerunner of, 147–148
historical, 150
impetus, 95, 151, 177, 184
impulse, 111, 153, 161, 172
impulsion, 184
life of, 103
love of, 180
path to, 107, 110, 112
perception of, 27
principle, 104
spiritual return of, 81, 150–151
stimulus, 154, 164
supersensible, 122
union of, 113, 116
Christmas, 131, 168, 184,
　　195–197
Christ Spirit, 152–153, 185
conscience, 45–47, 51–52, 55–56
bad, 53, 57
human, 154
knowledge and, 50
moral imperative of, 155
pangs of, 21, 23, 46–47
sensitive, 54
stirring of, 46–47
consciousness, 21, 37, 43, 47, 58,
　　98–99, 102, 104–105, 114,
　　116, 128, 132, 167, 174, 190

clairvoyant, 44, 61, 160
daily, 62
dream, 49
factual, 67
human, 44, 81, 130–131
mundane, 91
naïve, 81
normal, 60–61, 66, 68–69,
　　79–80, 82–83, 91, 97,
　　130–131
ordinary, 62
primitive, 81
state of, 59, 64, 82, 85
threshold of, 36
upper, 62–63, 69, 86
wakeful, 49, 129
waking, 129
culture, 24–25, 69, 103, 163
of actual morality, 26
Eastern, 146
external, 24, 92
Greek, 26, 120
human, 105
oriental, 146
Persian, 104
spiritual, 146
western, 55, 147–148, 151
of will, 11
Cyprian, 186–188, 190

D

Devachan, 50, 57, 71, 73, 88
deeds in, 53
formless, 22
higher, 26
lower, 22
nature of, 78

realm of, 22–23, 71, 75–77
sense of, 76
world of, 72

E

Earth, 24, 30, 41, 45, 52, 55, 69,
    92, 104–106, 111, 114–116,
    128, 130, 132–135, 137, 146,
    150–151, 157, 159, 162, 164,
    167, 175, 177, 183, 192
  Buddha on, 110
  as Christ, 112, 118
  deed on, 179
  existence, 101
  humanity on, 153
  karma on, 121
  mission, 100, 117, 184
  physical, 152, 160
  religious faiths on, 109
  Soul of the, 152
  sphere of, 118–119
  spirits of, 129, 131, 153, 168,
    174
Earth Spirits, 129, 168
Easter, 136, 168–170
  festival of, 131
  mystery of, 166
  spiritual, 132
ego, 1, 11, 15, 18–19, 31, 63,
    99–101, 129, 172, 174–175,
    178, 180–181
  astral and, 167
  consciousness, 37, 98–100,
    105, 147
  folk, 163
  human, 97

Eightfold Path, 43
Elijah, 147–148, 150, 163–164,
    166, 199, 201
emotion/emotional, 22, 26, 87
  education, 26
  sensations, 23
  turbulence, 20–23
epoch, 25, 92, 153
  bygone, 108
  cultural, 26–27, 119
  Egypto-Chaldean, 132
  fifth post-Atlantean, 121, 132
  first post-Atlantean, 146
  fourth post-Atlantean, 103,
    120, 121
  human, 108
  Lemurian, 99
  third post-Atlantean, 132
Eschenbach, Wolfram von, 24
ether body, 1, 3–11, 16, 22,
    37–38, 40–41, 70, 84–86, 89,
    128, 153–154, 167, 193
etheric body, 1, 6–8, 18, 35–36,
    43, 52, 97, 128, 152
evolution, 74, 99, 102–103,
    107–108, 113, 118, 120, 122,
    154, 160–161, 178, 184–186,
    195–196

F

feeling, 18–23, 27, 46, 49, 52,
    67, 70, 78–80, 87, 89, 94, 98,
    101, 106, 109, 115, 119–120,
    124, 132, 135, 137–138, 146,
    197, 199–201
  of antipathy, 15

of awe, 153
of compassion, 154
of disgust, 85
habits of, 34
indistinct, 102
of love, 154, 184, 195
negative, 86
of occasion, 156
of power, 184
realm of, 85
right, 76–77
of rightness, 25
and sentiments, 159
symmetry of, 142
of sympathy, 83
undulations of, 25
of wonder, 153
Fichte, 147, 200

G

God, 32, 37–38, 50, 117–122,
　　124, 148, 164, 173, 176–178,
　　180, 194
creation of, 117
beneficial, 74
death of, 122
deed of, 179
divine, 161
pagan, 186
progressive, 160, 178
wisdom of, 191
Goethe, 147, 149, 165, 186,
　　199–200, 202
Good Friday, 148, 150, 166
Gospels, 93–96, 105, 107, 110,
　　116, 177–179

H

Harmony of Feeling, 142–143
Hebbel, 24–25
Holy Spirit, 43
human being, 3–4, 6, 8, 10–11,
　　15, 18–33, 35, 37–38, 40–44,
　　47–50, 55–59, 61, 70, 73–75,
　　77, 80, 84–86, 88–91, 96,
　　98–99, 101, 103–108, 110,
　　113–114, 116, 118–122, 124,
　　126–127, 129–132, 137, 142,
　　146, 149, 151–153, 159–160,
　　167–168, 172–173, 175–180,
　　185, 190, 196
constituent elements of, 97
healthy, 6
interfere, 115
nature of, 1
quality of, 72
sort of, 53
stratified structure of, 79
humanity, 27, 55–57, 92, 96,
　　100–101, 103–104, 106, 108,
　　113, 118, 121–124, 131–132,
　　141, 143, 145–149, 151,
　　153–155, 157, 160, 162, 166,
　　168, 171, 173, 175–178, 186,
　　191, 193–194, 199, 201
ancient wisdom of, 142
creators of, 118
earthly, 116
evolution of, 117
genuine progress of, 74
great ideal of, 183
pinnacles of, 184
humankind, 31, 74, 97, 106, 110,
　　112–117, 119, 121, 127,

130–131, 135, 137, 143, 146, 149, 160, 164, 167, 177, 179, 195, 197
  development of, 95
  essential being of, 3
  evolution of, 95
  future of, 181
  pinnacle of, 193
  threefold stream of, 201

I

I, 1, 18, 63, 99, 147, 172
  conscious, 38
  human, 97–98
  self-aware, 38
Imagination, 27, 61, 80–81, 83–85, 87–90
  visionary, 83
immorality, 26, 75
impulses of will, 18, 21–23, 26, 58, 79–80
inner soul life, 24
Inspiration, 80, 88
  darkened, 81
  primitive, 81
Intuition, 80

J

Jesus of Nazareth, 103, 105–106, 109, 111–113, 116–117, 121, 124, 151–153, 155, 161, 178, 199
John the Baptist, 124, 147–148, 150, 164, 166, 199

K

Kamaloka, 23, 50, 57, 70–71, 75, 88, 114
karma, 39–40, 67, 73, 87, 114, 121–122, 151, 156, 173, 197
  concept of, 39
  and reincarnation, 151, 178
  universal human, 57
knowledge, 48–56, 81, 88, 96, 108, 110, 131, 141, 145, 151, 153, 167, 172–173, 202
  anthroposophical, 92
  astrological, 132–133
  clairvoyant, 44
  external, 19, 94
  higher, 33–34, 39, 42–43
  imaginative, 61–62, 135
  path of, 31, 33–34, 38–39, 41
  philosophy and, 47
  real, 76, 111, 127
  spiritual-scientific, 6, 101, 148
  spiritual, 1, 7, 98, 125, 155, 157, 186
  true, 111
  true supra-sensory, 95
  truthful, 77

L

Law of Twelve Tables (*Leges Duodecim Tabularum*) 24
life body, 1, 4–5, 8–10, 154
Lord of Karma, 122
love, 112, 119, 122, 124, 146, 151, 172–173, 179, 191
  boundless, 194

compassion and, 154–155
deeds of, 173–176, 180–181
embodiment of, 192
goodness and, 185
impact of, 195, 197
impulse of, 178, 180, 197
mutual, 183
omnipotence of, 184
purity and, 28
sense-based, 175
sexuality and, 154
and simplicity, 190
substance of, 178
true, 174, 177, 201
universal human, 196
and warmth, 200
Lucifer/luciferic, 69, 113–114,
    117–119, 122, 160, 177–180
activities, 160
aspect, 113
beings, 30, 117
entities, 117
forces, 30, 100–102, 192
influence, 160, 177
outrage, 162
powers, 100–101, 191
principles, 118, 180
spirits, 118

M

Mary Magdalen, 62–63
Masters of Wisdom, 141, 143
Michelangelo, 147, 163
Middle Ages, 56, 148
Moon, 41, 51, 100, 104–105, 117,
    131–132, 134, 168–169, 175

morality, 29–31, 38, 74–75
actual, 26
age of, 27
exceptional, 35
incisive, 26
paradigm of, 33, 41
Müller, Max, 142, 158–159
Mystery of Golgotha, 42, 106, 111,
    113, 116, 118–124, 135, 144,
    147, 150–152, 160, 169–170,
    177–179, 185–186, 195

N

nature, 25, 30, 51, 54, 78, 98,
    119–120, 125, 155, 166–167,
    173, 175, 177–178
act of, 74
clairvoyant, 49
of evolution, 81
external, 132
forces of, 73, 192–193
fourfold, 1
historical, 94
human, 4, 28–29, 31, 55,
    99–101
inward, 56
laws of, 72, 74–76
moral, 38
mysteries of, 199
outer, 128–130, 132
physical, 64, 128–129, 131
physical-bodily, 18
realms of, 152
spirits, 117
spiritual, 23, 127
of things, 102

normal soul life, 23, 60, 80
Nostradamus, 19–20
Novalis, 151, 166, 198–203

O

occultism, 22, 66, 112, 174
  basic requirement of, 31
  western, 145
Osiris, 104, 106, 111, 119–121

P

Paracelsus, 20
physical body, 1, 4, 6–7, 16, 18,
    21, 37, 58–60, 80, 84, 87, 91,
    97, 102, 111–112, 125, 141,
    145–146, 151–154, 172, 193
physical plane, 33, 53, 73, 91,
    116, 118, 137, 161–162, 185,
    195
physical world, 22–23, 32–33,
    44, 48–50, 72, 74–76, 87–89,
    91, 120, 126–127, 143, 160
  creative, 90
  ordinary, 71
  qualities of, 117
Plato, 25, 147, 163

R

Raphael, 147–151, 163–166, 199,
    201
religions, 108–111, 113, 125,
    135, 163
  ancient, 32, 102

comparative, 142, 158–159
contemporary form of, 120
great founders of, 103, 112,
    122, 124, 161
holy, 102
old, 105

S

Schiller, 199, 201
self-knowledge, 61, 85, 87
Sistine Madonna, 149, 165
Socrates, 147, 163
soul
  attitude of, 107
  capacities, 34
  Christian, 186
  culture, 26
  of Elijah, 199
  group, 90, 117, 160, 180
  hidden depths of, 68–69, 79
  human, 3–4, 55, 82, 92–93,
    96, 103, 107, 122, 127, 131,
    136, 147, 149–150, 152–
    155, 164, 174–175, 191,
    193, 195, 199–201
  of John the Baptist, 199
  life, 23, 59–60, 67, 80, 84,
    172–173
  mood of, 42, 107, 150
  of Novalis, 200
  quality of, 28
  of Raphael, 199
  region, 50
  sensitive, 3
  strength of, 92
  temptress, 173

Soul Calendar, The, 135–136, 169
soul-spiritual beings, 37, 60
Spinoza, 147, 199–200
spirit, 21, 127, 131–132, 136,
    145, 152, 168, 173, 181,
    183, 185–186, 196–197,
    199–202
  luciferic, 118
  nature, 117, 168
spirit-king, 185
Spirit of Christ, 152
Spirits of the Earth, 129, 168,
    174
Spirits of the Sun, 104
Spirits of Truth, 73
spiritual beings, 73–74, 101, 129,
    134–136, 199
  divine, 117–118, 136
  higher, 132
  lower, 130
spiritual law, 72–75, 77
spiritual researcher, 17–18, 28
spiritual science, 1, 9, 11–12, 14,
    17, 21–23, 27–28, 39, 41, 48,
    50, 54–55, 57, 76, 79, 95–96,
    108, 130, 132, 134, 148–151,
    154–159, 162, 173–175, 182
  basis of, 112
  genuine, 107
spiritual worlds, 17, 21, 27, 28,
    38–45, 49, 51–53, 55, 57, 72,
    79, 81, 91, 94–95, 102–107,
    116–120, 123, 127–128,
    131–132, 135, 142, 144–145,
    148, 153–154, 167, 175,
    178–180, 196, 198
  existence of, 44

  knowledge of, 56
  natural and, 75
  potency of, 169
  purely, 50
  secret mysteries of, 108
St Luke's Gospel, 190–192, 194
St Paul, 118, 148, 164
subconscious, 61–63, 80, 82–91,
    174
  elements, 61
  human, 37, 85
  realities of, 82
Sun, 41, 47–48, 51, 71–72, 104,
    128, 130–134, 168–169,
    174–175

T

Ten Commandments, 31–32
Theosophical Society, 69, 77
theosophy, 77, 126, 130, 135,
    178, 190, 197
truth, 13, 24, 30, 68, 73–74,
    90, 93, 107, 109, 111, 118,
    124–125, 127, 129, 136, 145,
    153, 155, 174, 202
  core, 158, 162
  exceptional nuance of, 161
  and falsehood, 25, 72
  initiation, 117
  light of, 144
  occult, 115, 157
  purest, 141
  sacred, 110
  sense of, 146, 171
  unpleasant, 182

V

vision, 63–64, 68–69, 78, 81–85, 91, 103
  clairvoyant, 34–35, 71
  dim, 49
  external, 87
  intuitive, 151
  objective, 88
  power of, 33
  primal, 47
  purity and, 200
  spiritual, 185
  super-sensory, 35

W

White Lotus Day, 137
wisdom, 12, 131, 141, 175, 181, 184–185, 191, 194
  ancient Egyptian, 133
  celestial, 193
  Christian, 118
  cosmic, 193
  essential, 66
  heritage of, 135
  infinite, 176
  initiation, 109
  love of, 172–173, 179–180
  Masters of, 141, 143
  Mystery, 137
  omniscient, 194
  oriental, 142, 144
  and power, 177, 192, 195
  sacred, 96

A NOTE FROM RUDOLF STEINER PRESS

We are an independent publisher and registered charity (non-profit organisation) dedicated to making available the work of Rudolf Steiner in English translation. We care a great deal about the content of our books and have hundreds of titles available – as printed books, ebooks and in audio formats.

As a publisher devoted to anthroposophy…

- We continually commission translations of previously unpublished works by Rudolf Steiner and invest in re-translating, editing and improving our editions.

- We are committed to making anthroposophy available to all by publishing introductory books as well as contemporary research.

- Our new print editions and ebooks are carefully checked and proofread for accuracy, and converted into all formats for all platforms.

- Our translations are officially authorised by Rudolf Steiner's estate in Dornach, Switzerland, to whom we pay royalties on sales, thus assisting their critical work.

So, look out for Rudolf Steiner Press as a mark of quality and support us today by buying our books, or contact us should you wish to sponsor specific titles or to support the charity with a gift or legacy.

office@rudolfsteinerpress.com
Join our e-mailing list at www.rudolfsteinerpress.com

RUDOLF STEINER PRESS